CONFESSIONS
OF A
FORMER PROSECUTOR

ABANDONING VENGEANCE AND
EMBRACING TRUE JUSTICE

PRESTON SHIPP WITH ERIC WILSON

chalice
PRESS

Print: 9780827207530

EPUB: 9780827207547

EPDF: 9780827207554

ChalicePress.com

Printed in the United States of America

Endorsements for *Confessions of a Former Prosecutor*

In *Confessions of a Former Prosecutor*, Assistant Attorney General turned reform advocate Preston Shipp opens up his personal story of discovery and redemption working in criminal justice, discovering how unjust the system truly is, and who the bad guys actually are. Through deeply personal and compelling storytelling, Shipp lays bare and challenges the power dynamics of criminal justice, and offers an insider's perspective on the impact of punitive policies. *Confessions* acts as a personal confessional and sheds light on the human cost of a broken system, but it also offers tangible pathways toward meaningful reform. A must-read for policymakers, advocates, and anyone passionate about social justice, Shipp's book is a beacon of hope in the fight for a better tomorrow. Engaging, informative, and ultimately inspiring, this book is poised to spark crucial conversations and drive positive change in the pursuit of justice for all.

— Rabia Chaudry, attorney, advocate, and author of *Adnan's Story* and executive producer of the HBO documentary series *The Case Against Adnan Syed*

"I was in prison and you visited me," Jesus said. Preston Shipp has accepted the invitation and experienced the transforming power of Christ behind bars. I'm grateful for the ways he is bearing witness in these pages.

— Jonathan Wilson-Hartgrove, author of *Reconstructing the Gospel*

Preston Shipp preaches what he practices. His heartfelt work and life are inspiring and can help heal the deepest wounds this world suffers from. He believes in forgiveness and the miraculous work of love.

— Becca Stevens, founder and President of Thistle Farms.

Preston Shipp invites us to join him in his "ongoing conversion" journey—not as bystanders but as those who are open to challenge and change. Shipp's journey pushes us to abandon the "luxury of distance" and practice persistent proximity with those who are now or have been caged and criminalized. Through Preston's own story, we are prodded and inspired to reimagine justice and healing, redefine criminal legal systems and processes, and embody what Dr. King called "a radical revolution of values," a seismic shift in who and how we are, both individually and collectively.

— Janet Wolf, pastor and community organizer focusing on transformative justice.

If you prefer clichéd American conversion stories, you might look elsewhere. But if you're interested in an honest and unflinching chronicle of God's dogged and demanding work on a life, this is your book. For here Preston Shipp recounts a conversion that disrupted his well-engineered career path, called him to learn the new language of restorative justice, invited him to see and hear those whom society exiles and silences, and has inspired an often-unappreciated prophetic witness to our church and the world. Be prepared for this book to challenge your life and discipleship.

— Richard Goode, Professor of History at Lipscomb University and founder of the Lipscomb Initiative for Education (LIFE) Program

Table Of Contents

This book is made possible in part by
a generous donation from Edgar O. Coble
in memory of Reverend E. Oran and Allison Coble.

Foreword

By David Dark

One goes looking for the real ones. Let me explain.

The real ones are people who listen when you're talking to them, I mean actually listening, not pretending to listen as they're really mentally forming the words they're going to say once you stop talking. The real ones don't presume they know what you're going to say before you say it. They know—or they've come to know—that even beginning to know another person takes time and patience, slow talking *and* slow listening. They know that to love a person is to love a process. They know this about themselves.

Preston Shipp is a real one. In this volume, he gives us the profound gift of describing—with candor, courage, and conscience—his own process, chronicling the drama of the difficult and sometimes humiliating moral realizations that brought him to where he is today.

As is the case for many white male Christian Southerners in these United States (I speak as one myself), revolutionary moral movements across the country and around the globe have provided Preston a lot of incoming data to process. He's well acquainted with the defensiveness and the sense of white male grievance that's been capitalized on by pundits, politicians, and preachers his whole life long.

He's partaken of the heady mix of what Flannery O'Connor called the "Christ-haunted" and not remotely "Christ-centered" South, with ample doses of *The Dukes of Hazzard*, *Miami Vice*, and *Star Wars* thrown in. And, as you'll see, he makes the most of all of it. He takes it all personally, as real ones are prone to do, treasuring it and bringing it to bear, and then some, on the sometimes-unflattering data of his own life.

As a former criminal prosecutor, Preston methodically explains his passion and reasoning for making decisions that proved catastrophically costly for people over whom he exercised an inordinate power he later abjured. He reckons with his own complicity as "a cog in a broken wheel" and takes stock of what a euphemism like "a day at the office" really refers to in the calculus of our so-called justice system. He recalls his way of once relishing his suit and tie as if they were armor plating and his smooth speech, which he now sees as entirely too smooth. He serves as an eloquent and persuasive witness to his own experience as someone for whom certain career successes were abject moral failures, crushing real people, beautifully complex people with hopes and dreams and stories to tell about what they've been through.

He even compares his own addiction to feeling effective and successful as the crime-fighting good guy to the desperate material need and bodily craving of drug dealers and addicts whom he personally put away. He also recalls the perverse logic of his handy-dandy rationalization: "If I didn't do it, someone else would."

Preston is hellbent on carefully circling back through all of this as if his soul depends on it. By the time we reach the end of his text, we see that it does.

Because never circling back on the hurt we've administered is, as Preston shows, a form of hell that spreads like a contagion. Hurt people hurt people, as the saying has it. But Preston has a new one: "Healed people heal people."

And it's here that he takes us into the righteous space of beloved community. And most helpfully, Preston names names. If you've been drawn into the crew of people, caged and formerly caged, and been in relationship with those caged and formerly caged in Tennessee, you'll likely find some of them here. Tennessee-based singer-songwriter Julien Baker of boygenius says, "Punk teaches the same inversion of power as the Gospel. You learn the coolest thing about having a microphone is turning it away from your own mouth." Preston manages that coolest thing by sharing the microphone with a great cloud of loving and mostly living people you'll want to look up and possibly track down to enter the healing game he describes. The healing game that found *him*. The door to it is open right here in these pages.

What happened to Preston can happen to anyone. As he feelingly testifies, "Adversaries can become allies." And getting born again is an everyday do-over type of deal. In this, Preston functions among us as an everyday mystic practitioner with stories to tell. I intend nothing highfalutin or pious when I put it this way, but hear this: Preston chooses confession and contemplation over defensiveness and self-justification. He knows a mind that won't change is, in a deep sense, a goddamned mind.

This isn't to say God punishes or condemns anyone's mind. But, as Preston shows, the choice to *be* hard and to not yield or change course in the face of a moral realization—to not repent or confess—is a choice against wholeness and health and, if it helps to put it this way, salvation. It's a choice *against* grace, a choice to be a *dis*grace. An actual disgrace to oneself and to others. Preston decided he was disgracing himself by wielding the power of accusation (a power manifested in the lynching of Jesus of Nazareth) and made the necessary changes. He documents that process here for all to see and consider.

I could go on and on. I want to celebrate Preston's way of describing his first in-person meeting with men on Tennessee's death row as reminiscent of young Anakin Skywalker being examined by the Jedi Council. I want to talk about how Preston found *me* and how I was myself drawn into these circles and how one evening the two of us spent in a discernment session with our friends at Riverbend Maximum Security Institution felt like a visitation of the Holy Spirit. But ... this isn't the place for that.

This is the place for receiving the witness of Preston Shipp, a real one who, through the kindness of others, has journeyed his way toward becoming someone who's perfectly useless in the strategies of abusive people. He's a free and getting-set-free, healed and being-healed man. Heed the call for baseline moral seriousness he has heard and issues here. Hear his voice. Receive his witness.

— David Dark, Associate Professor of Religion and the
   Arts at Belmont University and author of *We Become
   What We Normalize*

[T]here must be a first step, a starting point from which a new approach to justice may begin. ... It is a step that the prophets, who see injustice clearly, provoke us to. ... This first step is confession.

— Randy Spivey, from the essay,
"Questioning Society's Criminal Justice
Narratives"[1]

---

[1] Randy Spivey, "Questioning Society's Criminal Justice Narratives" in *And the Criminals with Him: Essays in Honor of Will D. Campbell and All the Reconciled*, eds. Will D. Campbell and Richard C. Goode (Eugene, OR: Wipf and Stock, 2012), 187.

The Beginning

While I was studying political science at a conservative Christian college called Lipscomb University in Nashville, I obtained a summer internship in the local district attorney's office. There I watched prosecutors in action. They gave orders to police officers, negotiated with defense counsel, questioned witnesses, argued cases in court, and comforted victims and their families.

I was sold. This was the career for me, the fulfillment of a childhood fantasy of working in law enforcement, putting bad guys behind bars. This was right in line with my understanding of justice as punishment, reinforced by my understanding of how God punishes sin. I was confident this was God's will for my life.

I'll never forget the trial of an especially heinous case during the summer of my internship. A man had punished a young child by forcing her into scalding hot water, resulting in severe third-degree burns. I had never before been exposed to such callous brutality. What kind of cold-hearted monster could torture a child? It was the job of the prosecutor to see that such cruelty is punished harshly, not only to vindicate the victim but to ensure that no one else gets hurt.

During a break in the testimony, I overheard the young prosecutor ask the defense attorney, "How can you defend such a miserable dirtbag and still sleep at night?"

How, indeed, I wondered to myself. And why would anyone choose to align themselves with such a violent abuser?

I determined then and there which side I would stand on. I wanted to be the voice of justice for victims by doling out retribution to violent criminals who preyed on others. I would wear the white hat by serving as a prosecutor.

Going into my senior year of college, I became laser-focused on this goal. I took the law school admissions test, got a decent score, and in the fall of 1999, enrolled at the University of Tennessee College of Law. I signed up for any class I thought might be helpful to an aspiring prosecutor, including both sections of criminal law and procedure, evidence, and two sections of trial advocacy. I enrolled in a semester-long seminar on the death penalty. I even served as president of the Criminal Law Society.

I had never been so focused on a goal. I never forgot about that abused child. Every class got me closer to becoming a prosecutor who would pursue justice against anyone who broke the law and hurt others.

Law school tends to be an intense, rigorous experience, as Scott Turow recounts in *One L*, but I was pursuing my dream. Dreams don't come true unless you wake up and do the work. Every class I attended, every case I read, and every grade I earned got me closer to my goal.

After my second year of law school, I got a summer clerkship in the Knox County District Attorney General's office. Though I still had a year to go before graduating, I was sworn in as a special prosecutor to handle my own caseload.

I could hardly believe it. *I was doing it.*

I showed up each morning in a suit, just like those young prosecutors I so admired a few years before. I was mentored by a young assistant DA who was well-known for being tough as nails. She prepped me to be on my feet daily in the courtroom, making arguments, examining witnesses, consulting with law enforcement officers, negotiating plea agreements, and preparing witnesses to testify. Acting on her advice, in my spare time I studied the law, memorizing the statutory elements of various criminal offenses— such as theft, robbery, burglary, and assault—until I knew them like the back of my hand

My hard work was beginning to pay off. The career I had dreamed of was coming more clearly into focus.

Introduction

In 2004, just a stone's throw from where I grew up, worshiped, and went to school, a sixteen-year-old runaway was trapped in a nightmare I could never imagine. I grew up in a loving, stable family that attended church three times a week. She was a victim of sex trafficking. I knew nothing of violence, save an occasional scrap at school or a spanking at home. She had been raped at knifepoint. I was untouched by addiction. She was born into the chaos of drug and alcohol abuse, trauma, and neglect. Although we lived in the same city, our experiences could not have been more different. I knew nothing of her or her life. She was not part of my community. But one day, I would argue that she needed to spend the rest of her life in prison.

This is the job of a prosecutor, to make arguments to judges and juries about the fate of people you don't know. A day at the office can have permanent consequences for the defendants in the cases you're assigned. Prosecutors may argue that people they've never had an actual conversation with should spend a year, five years, ten, twenty, fifty years in prison. Then they go home, go to sleep, wake up, and make another argument about another person the next day. Often the only thing they know about these people is the worst thing they have ever done.

This was the world I lived in, the job I did ... and it made sense to me. Because I assumed that the people I made arguments against were bad and wrong, whereas I was good and right. The legal system in which I labored was the best system in the world. As a prosecutor, I promoted justice, so when I got up in the morning and went to sleep at night, I believed I was making the world a better place. I was going to have to learn from the very people I made arguments against that I did not even know what justice was, and that in order to make the world a better place, I would have to turn away from what I always wanted to be.

Life-Altering Decisions

This book describes my journey from serving as a successful career prosecutor in the Tennessee Attorney General's Office to becoming a friend and ally to people who are or have been incarcerated. I now advocate for sweeping criminal justice reform and an end to mass incarceration around the country. During this transition from an agent of retribution to an advocate for redemption, I have sojourned through deserts of doubt, mountains of regret, and swamps of my own prejudice. It has been a difficult road. In many ways, I feel I've gone from lost to found, but my reeducation is still ongoing and my journey far from over.

Others have written powerfully about the need for criminal justice reform and the critical need to protect the rights and dignity of those who are or have been incarcerated. I'm deeply indebted to authors like Michelle Alexander for her masterpiece, *The New Jim Crow*, and Bryan Stevenson for his bestseller, *Just Mercy*. They are both Black, trained defense attorneys, and uniquely qualified to teach with authority about America's original sin of racism and its ongoing impact on our system of laws, courts, and prisons.

Although I have been profoundly influenced by them, my experience is markedly different from theirs. First, I was a prosecutor. Unlike most other legal reformers, I didn't earn my stripes by fighting against an unjust, racist system. I was part of that system. From 2004 to 2008, I was a cog in a broken wheel that crushes individuals, families, and entire communities.

Second, I am a white man, and like most white men, my privilege has obscured my vision like a giant plank in my eye. I played a role, wittingly and unwittingly, in the systemic racism that fuels the machine. Once I started seeing more clearly, I watched disproportionate numbers of young men and women of color be fed through the gears, stripped of their personhood, and denied any true chance of bettering themselves or society.

Third, I am a product of white evangelicalism. I was raised in and trained to seek God's will in every aspect of my life. Although it took a while to feel it, there was a tension between my faith and my career. My job as a prosecutor to seek punishment often ran contrary to the teachings of Jesus, who offered forgiveness to and even identified himself with the very people I had aligned myself against. He opposed every unjust status quo—relentlessly, unapologetically—whereas I worked to maintain them. Why was I ever content to listen to sermons and sing songs about mercy and forgiveness and redemption on Sundays, then serve as an agent of vengeance the rest of the week?

Something had to give.

Part One

Retribution: Institutionalized Vengeance

Chapter 1

The Power of the Prosecutor

Taking on the bad guys was my childhood dream. Even as a boy in the 1980s, I had a strong sense of right and wrong, fair and unfair, and a desire to defend people who were mistreated or taken advantage of. This sense of justice was reinforced by my religious upbringing. My parents, Mike and Julia Shipp, raised me and my younger sister, Emily, in a conservative Christian denomination called the Church of Christ. We went to church three times a week—Sunday morning for worship and Sunday school classes, Sunday night for another worship service, and Wednesday night for a midweek gathering with more Bible classes and often a fellowship meal. I was active in the church youth group, which meant plenty of camps and retreats. Church was my place. Church people were my people.

Education was important to my parents, and they wanted to give Emily and me every opportunity to succeed. Therefore, they sacrificed in order to enroll us in private Christian schools. In addition to studying math, English, and history, we had daily Bible classes and weekly chapel services. I was a Bible Bowl champion.

The Bible is chock-full of stories of a vengeful God who punishes wrongdoers. There are more than 30 crimes in the Bible that carried the death penalty, including murder, adultery, striking or cursing one's parents, idolatry, violating the Sabbath rules, and blasphemy. Lest we think God got soft between the Old and New Testaments, there is a story in the Acts of the Apostles in which God strikes a couple dead for lying to the church about how much money they put in the collection plate. The Bible is where we get the phrase, "an eye for an eye, and a tooth for a tooth." Hours listening to sermons and sitting in Bible class confirmed that harsh retribution against people who break the law is indeed Biblical.

Many afternoons I came home from that Christian school on the Antioch side of Nashville and flipped on the TV for some law-and-order drama. My parents loved *Perry Mason, Matlock,* and other courtroom mysteries, but I craved a little more excitement. These were the days of *Magnum, P.I.* and *The A-Team.*

My absolute favorite of the 1980s crime shows was *Miami Vice.* What could possibly be cooler to an eight-year-old boy than cops in a black Ferrari chasing bad guys through the palm-tree-lined streets of Miami? I loved the flashy clothes, the MTV-inspired soundtrack, and the cigarette boats tearing through the foamy waves. For those who may not remember, Don Johnson and Philip Michael Thomas played a couple of tough undercover narcotics cops in south Florida. Beneath the pastel designer jackets they carried guns, always a breath away from a shootout with drug kingpins and smugglers. Like all heroes, they put their lives on the line to protect society.

How would it feel, I wondered, to work on the side of law and order, making society safer by putting criminals behind bars?

Ten years later, when I saw prosecutors at work, I got my answer.

After I married my college sweetheart, Sherisse Herring, attended law school, clerked for two years for a judge, and welcomed our first child, Lila Joy, to the world, I accepted a position as a prosecutor in the Tennessee Attorney General's Office.

This was nothing short of my dream job, the position I had coveted since seeing those prosecutors in action a few years earlier. I went to law school solely to become a prosecutor. Now I was seeing that dream come to fruition, confirmed on my new business cards: Preston Shipp: Assistant Attorney General. I wore this label proudly, convinced I was part of a justice system that protects law-abiding citizens. I thought of myself as one of the good guys. I believed prosecutors always wore the white hats. Sure, the machinery of American justice groaned and lurched along at times, bogged down by arcane wording and rules, but I was confident we were rumbling toward a better future for our children, one founded on law and order.

So early in my career, I had no idea that a case I was destined to work on would one day garner national attention; prompt tweets from Rihanna, Kim Kardashian, and Lebron James; and draw me into the spotlight while turning me inside out and threatening my very livelihood. I could not have anticipated my confidence ever turning into regret or my pride giving way to shame.

No, at this point in my life and career, there was no cause for anything but celebration. Sherisse and I were in a season of new beginnings, wrought with sleepless nights, joyous surprises, and toddler milestones. Lila Joy, true to her middle name, was a delight. My family and my career were just as I'd hoped they would be.

Although I knew the system was not perfect, (what system is?), it was the best system in the world, and my commitment to it was unwavering. I firmly believed in the process of constitutional rights, laws, and punishment designed to protect society, vindicate victims, and hold offenders accountable.

"You do the crime, you do the time" isn't just some pithy slogan; it's the criminal justice system in a nutshell.

Here there is not much room for the observation that a large percentage of violent offenders are themselves victims of violence. Tough-on-crime rhetoric seldom fails to acknowledge that, just as a disease cannot be cured by treating the symptoms, crime cannot be prevented without addressing the conditions in which it thrives. None of this factored into my mentality as a prosecutor, in which the easiest way to do the job is to keep things black and white.

I had much to learn—and to unlearn—and, as the great Vietnamese Buddhist teacher Thich Nhat Hanh said, "For things to reveal themselves, we need to be ready to abandon our views about them.[1]"

I was not there yet.

Actually, I wasn't even getting started.

The Most Powerful Actor in the System

Very early in my career I began to comprehend the true power wielded by prosecutors. As Michelle Alexander wrote, "It is the prosecutor, far more than any other criminal justice official, who holds the keys to the jailhouse door. ... The prosecutor is also free to

---

[1] Thich Nhat Hanh, *Being Peace* (Berkeley, CA: Parallax Press, 2009), 50.

file more charges against a defendant than can realistically be proven in court, so long as probable cause arguably exists—a practice known as overcharging.[2]"

I once prosecuted a case in which two young men got into a bar fight. Both had had way too much to drink. After a few quick, clumsy punches, the smaller of the two scurried out to the parking lot. The larger man stumbled after him. But the smaller guy had retrieved a tire iron from his truck to even the odds. At this point, the larger man grabbed a revolver from his waistband and fired a shot at the smaller man as he approached. The smaller man fell to the ground. He was ultimately taken to the hospital and treated for a gunshot wound to the leg. The cops who questioned the men and interviewed the available witnesses heard various, sometimes conflicted accounts of what happened. It was up to me, the prosecutor, to sort out who would be charged and with what crime.

Should they both be charged with aggravated assault, for example, as they both had used deadly weapons? Or only the one who actually got a chance to use his? Or should the man with the gun be charged with attempted murder? It was up to me, the prosecutor, to answer these critical questions.

I might decide that the man who fired the shot was acting in self-defense, as he only did so when the other man was approaching him with a tire iron. In that case, under Tennessee's stand-your-ground law, the man with the gun would have no duty to retreat before using deadly force. Therefore, no criminal charge against him would be warranted. What about the man who went and got the tire iron?

"He knocked out one of my teeth," the man had told the cops. But eyewitnesses said the fight was over when he left to get a weapon. Should he be charged?

I had to make these decisions; there is no appeal or further recourse.

Suppose I, having sole discretion over the charging decision, concluded that the man with the tire iron needed to be charged with aggravated assault, a felony punishable by several years in prison, because by arming himself with a weapon he caused a relatively harmless scuffle to escalate into a potentially deadly situation.

---

[2] Michelle Alexander, *The New Jim Crow: Mass Incarceration in the Age of Color Blindness* (New York: New Press, 2020), 102.

The power of the prosecutor does not end there.

Once the charge was brought, I, as prosecutor, had sole authority to decide whether to make a guilty plea offer and what it would be. Should I consider offering a lesser charge than felony aggravated assault?

"C'mon," the tire iron man's defense attorney argued, "look at the size of the other guy! He's like the Hulk! My client only went to get the tire iron to protect himself."

Maybe the defense attorney was right. Maybe I should cut the guy a break. He did get shot in the leg, after all. Maybe I should offer to let him plead guilty to misdemeanor assault and serve a year on probation if he would waive his right to a trial.

Such is the power of the prosecutor. He or she alone has the authority to put in motion the gears of the criminal legal system, directing the machine in a fateful direction before a judge or jury or even defense attorney ever becomes involved in the case. The impact of these initial decisions cannot be overstated. The power to decide whether to bring criminal charges, what charges to bring, and whether to make a guilty plea offer is the power to dramatically affect the trajectory of other people's lives.

Over forty years ago, Chief Justice Joe Henry of the Tennessee Supreme Court commented on the prosecutor's immense decision-making powers in *Pace v. State*, 566 S.W.2d 861, 867 (Tenn. 1978):

> He or she is answerable to no superior and has virtually unbridled discretion in determining whether to prosecute and for what offense. No court may interfere with his discretion to prosecute or not to prosecute, and in the formulation of this decision he or she is answerable to no one. In a very real sense this is the most powerful office in Tennessee today. Its responsibilities are awesome; the potential for abuse is frightening.

These words were particularly sobering to me in my role as prosecutor. I did not want to take lightly such a weighty responsibility. Once handed this amount of power, I wanted to wield it wisely—as an ethical lawyer, a husband and father, a man of sincere faith, and a public servant.

Stacked in My Favor

My first taste of power and success came during the summer after my second year of law school, when I got a clerkship with the county prosecutor's office. Despite the nerves and anxiety, I wore my suits and ties like armor for battle. I faced off with seasoned criminal defense lawyers, negotiated plea deals, and conducted scores of hearings. Of the cases I tried during these months, I lost only one. However, that win/loss ratio wasn't due to me being some kind of prosecutorial prodigy.

No, as the prosecutor, the deck was simply stacked in my favor.

In civil court, the parties square off on mostly equal terms. Mr. Jones's controversy with Mr. Smith is styled *Jones v. Smith*. In the world of criminal law, on the other hand, things are entirely different. The prosecutor, the most powerful actor in this drama, is not even a party to a criminal case, and neither is Mr. Jones, the actual victim who suffered the harm or loss. Instead, the theoretical "victim" in a criminal case is the entire state itself, whose laws were violated. Prosecutors are agents and representatives of the state, and have all of the state's resources at their disposal. The style of a criminal case, therefore, is *State of Tennessee v. Smith*. The power imbalance between the prosecutor and the defendant, reflected in the way the cases are styled, has enormous practical consequences.

Many defendants, unable to pay hefty lawyer fees, have only the aid of a public defender or one appointed by the court. Whereas prosecutors have at their immediate disposal the aid of an army of police investigators, the state crime laboratory, and experts in toxicology, ballistics, or forensics, for the defendant, any additional resources sought—such as independent testing of evidence, expert witnesses, or mental evaluations—must be requested by the defendant's lawyer in a motion and approved by the judge.

If the person charged with a crime cannot afford bail, consider the disparate impact of the passage of time on the defendant and the prosecutor. A delay of six months has little to no impact on the prosecutor, who simply moves on to other cases. For the defendant, on the other hand, a delay of six months means lost wages, separation from family, and the trauma of being incarcerated prior to a finding of guilt. Being incarcerated pretrial also creates a powerful incentive for defendants to accept a plea deal that releases them onto probation, even in cases when they may be innocent. Prosecutors can therefore leverage a defendant's desire to simply get out of jail to secure a guilty plea.

The disparity in power and resources between the defendant and the prosecutor simply cannot be overstated. Early in my career, I saw nothing wrong with this. Suited up as a prosecutor during that summer in Knoxville, I was certain the police officers and I were the white knights. We were the ones promoting justice and punishing the bad guys. Our motives were pure, our cause righteous. It would have been foolish not to use all the tools at our disposal.

Years later, my success as an Assistant Tennessee Attorney General was no less remarkable. I served as an appellate prosecutor, handling criminal appeals that flowed into our office from across the state of Tennessee. My job in case after case after case was to argue that the convictions and sentences people received were legally sound.

During my time as an appellate prosecutor, I wrote briefs in nearly three hundred cases, ranging from driving under the influence to first-degree murder. I loved the law, with all its nuances and intricacies. I made my arguments to the Court of Criminal Appeals, Tennessee Supreme Court, and federal courts, and they rarely decided against me.

Choices Come with Consequences

The first new leaves were blooming on the spring trees when a banker's box landed on my desk. Like many cases before it, it was full of court transcripts, pleadings, trial exhibits, and crime-scene photos. The defendant in the case was a sixteen-year-old runaway who had been tried as an adult; convicted of first-degree, premeditated murder; and sentenced to fifty-one years in prison. The young defendant had appealed the conviction and sentence, and the case had been assigned to me as the representative of the state.

The law is a tough business, and lawyers are trained to avoid emotion, as it could cloud our judgment and objectivity. The system makes frequent use of case numbers or simple labels like "defendant" to facilitate the distance lawyers are told to keep from the people whose fates they argue over. Therefore, this banker's box, despite it involving a child convicted of murder and sentenced to life in prison, was unremarkable to me. It was just another case, another brief I had to write.

I lifted the lid from the box and began spreading its contents on the large wooden desk in my office. Time to get to work.

My office was in the John Sevier State Office Building and overlooked James Robertson Parkway in downtown Nashville. On the other side of the building stood a statue of Sergeant Alvin York. Sergeant York is a state hero, one of the most decorated soldiers of World War I, and an embodiment of the spirit that has led to Tennessee being dubbed the Volunteer State.

From my corner office in this building over the previous few years, I had been trying to do my part as well, investing myself in work that mattered. I wasn't exactly arrogant, per se, but I did believe I was making a difference, which is all I ever wanted. I didn't want to just go to any old job, make money, and eventually retire. Anybody could go into finance or marketing. Any lawyer could draft a will or a contract. I wanted to do something that I felt was really significant. When a person is assaulted or robbed or killed, it is significant. How the person who is responsible for causing the harm will be held accountable and how the rights of the people who suffered the harm will be protected are matters of grave consequence. We look to prosecutors to help resolve these critical questions. This career would never be boring or inconsequential.

As an Assistant Attorney General, I served under the Tennessee Attorney General, the state's chief law-enforcement officer. The Attorney General represented the people of Tennessee in all kinds of matters of public interest, from enforcement of environmental laws and child-support actions to protecting consumers against predatory schemes and prosecuting antitrust violations. The Criminal Justice Division of the office handled statewide criminal prosecutions and appeals.

This is where I stepped in.

I considered myself a tough but fair man. When I began working on a case, I assumed the conviction and sentence were proper. After all, the American system of justice—with its constitutional rights, presumption of innocence, and requirement of proof beyond a reasonable doubt—is widely assumed to be the best in the world. However, should I find faults in any case, justice demanded that I concede error. I wasn't ignorant of some flaws in our legal system, particularly when it comes to how we treat at-risk youth.

The previous evening, I had read a bedtime story to my four- and one-year-old daughters, kissing Lila Joy on the cheek and swaddling Ruby Faith in her infant blanket. Sherisse and I adored them, just as my parents had adored me as a boy on this same side of town. But I knew not everyone was so fortunate.

Kids who didn't have the benefit of a stable family, who lived in poverty and were victims of abuse and trauma, are disproportionately represented in the prison system. Tragically, race also plays a significant role in which kids get swept up into the criminal legal system. In the case of the sixteen-year-old runaway who had been convicted of killing a man, all these factors were present.

By the time I was assigned the case, four years had passed since her initial arrest, two years since her conviction; she was now twenty years old. Average life expectancy for a female in the United States is seventy-nine years. Given that she would not even be eligible for review by the parole board until she had served fifty-one years, she would be sixty-seven before she even had the possibility of going free. This "life" sentence may as well have been a death sentence. By that time, my own daughters would be middle-aged women, hopefully with treasured memories of dances, college classes, honeymoons, new babies, and family vacations to the beach, the Grand Canyon, and Disney World.

It seemed so unfair, for someone so young to have already been doomed to life in prison. Even the toughest prosecutors hate to see teenagers make decisions that ruin the rest of their lives. The system I worked in could seem harsh at times. However, justice demanded that when people made choices that hurt others, they must be punished. The law is clear, actions have consequences

This girl, although she was very young, had taken a life, and she had a history of truancy, theft, and assault. Crime-scene photos revealed in graphic detail how the worst of her choices—to go with a man who was willing to pay her for sex—had resulted in the death of forty-three-year-old Johnny Allen. The murder occurred in the same part of town where I was raised, and despite questionable patterns in his personal life, Mr. Allen didn't deserve to die in a pool of his own blood. There was no bringing him back, and his friends and relatives were left to bear this grievous wound. They were victims looking to the state to bring about justice. It certainly wasn't always easy or pretty, but this is what I had signed up for when I determined to be a prosecutor.

I pulled the box closer and fished out the next set of documents.

Trials, Pleas, and Appeals

It wasn't within my purview to take issue with the findings of the trial judge and jury. I wasn't there to retry cases. Sorting out the truth of guilt and innocence had already been done when the conviction was secured. I wasn't paid to ask, in the case of the sixteen-year-old, why she had dropped out of school and moved in with a sex trafficker who got her hooked on drugs and made her have sex with men more than twice her age.

No, on appellate review, justice is all about adhering to the correct process.

Was she given a fair trial? Was evidence improperly admitted against her? Were her constitutional rights or any rules of procedure violated?

These are important questions. Despite everyone's best efforts, trial court practice can be a bit haphazard and frenetic. With the trial judge making rulings about the admissibility of evidence on the spot, there is an element in trial practice of flying by the seat of one's pants. To complicate matters further, jurors are not lawyers. They are not trained to decide complicated legal questions.

For these reasons, a convicted defendant has the right to appeal a conviction and sentence and have the case reviewed by a higher court. In addition to filing written briefs, they can request oral argument before the Court of Criminal Appeals or before the Tennessee Supreme Court.

Guilty pleas resolve the overwhelming majority of cases, so an appeal often marks the first time lawyers for the defendant and for the state really go toe-to-toe. Even after cases are decided by a jury, the appeal is a whole new ball game. Each party submits a detailed written brief applying legal precedent to the facts at hand. Both make nuanced arguments as to why the court should either deny relief by affirming the conviction and sentence or grant a new trial and send the case back to the lower court.

As we will see, the question of whether justice was done is largely a matter of whether all the procedural rules were followed. Therefore, the defense attorney typically argues on appeal that some rule violation by the cops, the prosecutors, or the judge merits reversal of the judgment. Perhaps a police officer took a statement without first advising the defendant of his or her constitutional rights, or searched the defendant's residence based on a warrant that listed a different address. Maybe the prosecutor made an improper inflammatory statement to the jury, or the judge increased the sentence based on an inappropriate aggravating factor.

A defendant may raise a host of errors in an attempt to gain relief from his or her conviction and sentence.

I loved appellate work. My typical day consisted of reading the opposing counsel's legal brief, studying the trial court transcript, and researching the legal issues presented. I spent a great deal of time reviewing relevant statutes and case law. I then drafted my own brief arguing the state's position that there were no errors— or, if there were errors, they did not affect the overall fairness of the trial.

This was not shoot-from-the-hip work. The ethics board and the Supreme Court had no patience for sloppy lawyering. Each brief I submitted to the courts needed to be carefully researched and crafted, temperate and refined.

Playing My Part

Most legal dramas and movies locate all the action in the trial courtroom. There, lawyers handle cases, cross-examine witnesses, make impassioned arguments to the jury, and showboat for the news cameras. They are the heroes of shows like *Law & Order* and movies like *A Few Good Men*, in which Tom Cruise skillfully breaks down Jack Nicholson on the witness stand by demanding, "I want the truth!"

Who can forget Matthew McConaughey in *A Time to Kill*, standing before an all-white Mississippi jury, pleading the case of a Black defendant who had murdered the two white men responsible for raping and torturing his little girl, asking them to close their eyes and imagine the crime from his point of view.

"Now," McConaughey urges, "imagine she's white."

In law school, I envisioned playing my part in such tense trial court scenes, jurors hanging on my every word; but real life wasn't the movies. My role as an appellate prosecutor was less dramatic and more academic. I didn't question many witnesses or negotiate with defense counsel. I spent a lot of time researching the law and crafting legal arguments to support the state's position.

Whereas trial lawyers are frequently in the courtroom, I averaged only two or three oral arguments a month. Still these court appearances were one of the best parts of my job, and I soon discovered I was in my element advocating the state's position. There were no jurors or witnesses present at an appellate argument. It was just the professionals, the defense attorney and the state's attorney arguing finer points of the law before a panel of judges.

For me, this was the legal profession at its best.

After the defense attorney finished his argument and went back to his seat at his table, it was my turn. This was the sweetest part of my job. All eyes were on me as I stood, buttoned my suit jacket, gathered my notes, and approached the podium.

I always began, "May it please the court, Preston Shipp, arguing on behalf of the state of Tennessee."

After I sailed through my presentation, the judges frequently peppered me with questions. They wanted to see how well I commanded the facts of the case and how knowledgeable I was about the law. If they tried to shoot holes in my argument, I had to defend my position—or potentially see all my work go to waste.

It was exciting as a young lawyer to match wits with opposing counsel, to prove myself before a group of judges, with the ultimate goal of vindicating society by punishing criminals. It was like a game of chess, as I saw it, and I loved to expose with surgical precision the weaknesses in the other side' case. If the case involved novel legal issues, it was even more gratifying to know the court's opinion would be published as legal authority that was binding on Tennessee courts going forward.

Of course, I was aware that the fate of real people was on the line, but lawyers are trained to maintain a professional distance from the people affected by their cases. Lawyers are advocates who represent the interests of their clients. My client was the state of Tennessee. I was always prepared, confident, and fully expected to win on behalf of the citizens who expected justice to be done.

The primitive roots of the adversarial system are found in the medieval practice of trial by battle, in which two parties or their representatives resolved a dispute through combat. The last man standing was declared the victor. Through competition, the truth was made manifest.

Today, although blood is no longer spilled, this adversarial nature is still evident in our criminal justice system. A local Nashville law firm even advertises itself as "gladiators in suits."

One side wins. The other loses.

The Art of Compartmentalization

Alone in my office near the state capitol, I studied the transcripts from the murder case involving the sixteen-year-old. Of course, the odds were stacked against her. Nationwide, over 80 percent of appeals are unsuccessful. For an appellate court to find reversible error is to admit there's been a breakdown somewhere in the process, and it's not often the wheels of justice grind to a halt and go into reverse. More than likely, she would be punished for the next fifty-one years.

My religious upbringing taught me all about forgiveness and redemption. I learned that God loves us like a good parent and is willing to forgive our sins and have a relationship with us. In the gospels, Jesus preached and modeled mercy, saying that he did not come to condemn the world but to save it. I learned to sing hymns like "Amazing Grace" that praised God for his willingness to pardon our sins. This was all foundational to my Christian faith.

Though I was a Christian, I worked as a prosecutor. Many of my colleagues were Christians as well. I did not perceive any conflict between those two worlds. My faith—the religious compartment—was grounded in forgiveness. I knew that we all have sinned and fallen short of God's glory, we are all in need of mercy and grace, and God makes redemption available to all. This does not negate the need for a system of laws and punishment. After all, the Bible also states that the law was made not for the righteous, but for lawbreakers. My job as a prosecutor went into this separate compartment, in which law, not grace or mercy, was controlling. I saw no contradiction in a belief in forgiveness and redemption at the spiritual level and punishing criminals at the worldly level.

Sitting at the computer in my office, trial transcripts and exhibits spread across my desk, I began crafting the state's response to the sixteen-year-old's appeal. Like all the defendants in my cases, I had never met her. I didn't know her story or background. If I had passed her in a hallway, I would not have even recognized her. Yet I was part of the brigade that would determine her fate for decades to come.

In my brief and later before the appellate judges, I argued persuasively that her appeal must be denied. In a callous disregard of human life, she had murdered and then robbed a man. In her own words, she had "executed" him. The evidence against her was sufficient to sustain the conviction for first-degree murder. There was no legal justification for wasting resources retrying the case. She had received due process in accord with her constitutional rights. Counsel had been appointed to her and argued her case, with a neutral judge presiding, and a jury of her peers had delivered its unanimous verdict. That verdict—guilty of first-degree, premeditated murder—mandated a life sentence, which in Tennessee was fifty-one years. Although she was only sixteen years old, she had committed the most heinous crime in the criminal code, and in the eyes of the law, she deserved every month, week, and day of those fifty-one years in prison.

This conclusion gave me no joy. Without question, it was a heartbreaking situation. As a prosecutor, however, I was simply a minister of the law. Therefore, I did not stop to think about my personal feelings about any of my cases. My job was to apply the law impartially to vindicate the victim, promote public safety, and ensure accountability for wrongdoing ... which I had done. I believed in the system and was confident that I was on the right side of justice. Tomorrow, I would move on to the next case. It would be many months before the Court of Criminal Appeals rendered its final decision. The legal system often moves at a glacial pace, grinding even time beneath its wheels.

After a couple of weeks of hard work, I finally put the finishing touches on my brief and filed it with the court. I shut down my computer and headed home, threading my truck through the heavy

Nashville traffic, past trees newly alive with vibrant spring foliage. The days were growing longer now. Our city's tallest structure, known locally as the Batman building, gleamed in the afternoon sun.

At home, I dropped onto the sofa with Sherisse after dinner to watch a new crime drama called *Breaking Bad*, in which the hero was anything but. Already, the heaviness of working on a murder case was fading from my thoughts.

I leaned my head back and took a deep breath. "The girls about ready for bed?"

"Lila and Ruby are waiting for their bedtime story."

A smile spread across my face. I gave Sherisse a kiss, then stood to attend to my fatherly duties.

The work of justice was not always black and white. Not every story had a happy ending. However, my goals of protecting the public from violence, holding people who caused harm accountable, and vindicating victims and their families were honorable. Society depends on people who are devoted to enforcing the law. This is what I had dreamed of doing since I was a kid. This was work that mattered. Now, as an Assistant Attorney General and appellate prosecutor, I had done my job faithfully, served my community, and fulfilled what I took to be my God-given tasks. Before long, I myself would hit the pillow, knowing I would sleep well.

Chapter 2

Lady Justice in All Her Glory
(Justice = Punishment)

Justice. The word pops up all the time in the legal profession. It is inscribed over the front door of the University of Tennessee College of Law in Knoxville: "Equal Justice Under Law."

Chiseled on the outside of the Davidson County Criminal Justice Building in downtown Nashville, it appears again: "The First Duty of Society Is Justice." You can see it on the cover of this book, along with our most common symbol of justice, a woman holding a set of balanced scales. In other depictions, Lady Justice wears a blindfold to reflect her impartiality and holds a sword to mete out vengeance. In America, "justice" is essentially a euphemism for punishment. When the scales are knocked out of balance by someone committing a crime, we bring the scales back into balance by punishing the person responsible.

My obligation as a prosecutor was to see to it that justice was done, which meant guilty people being harshly punished.

This is the way of thinking that I bought into. And why wouldn't I? It was almost exclusively how justice was portrayed on television, taught in universities, administered by courts, and given symbolic weight by black robes, pounding gavels, and immense granite columns.

If the first duty of society really is justice, we need to look deeper into what justice actually means.

I suspect something in all of us rises up at perceived injustice, particularly when innocent and vulnerable people have been harmed. The desire for vengeance is a strong, knee-jerk reaction, but it can lead us down a dark road. We do not address violence and lawbreaking with more violent lawbreaking. For these reasons, we don't leave it to individuals or heated mobs to administer justice. We need impartial judges, lawyers, and unbiased juries. We need a system of laws, not vigilantism.

While pursuing my law degree, I was taught to plug into the existing justice system like a factory worker trained to perform a task on an assembly line. I was not taught to think critically about what justice really is or what is required to produce a meaningful experience of justice. I had inherited an understanding of the word that was synonymous with punishment and retribution. Once I became an agent of retributive justice, I did just that. I used blame and pain to avenge not only the victims who suffered directly but also society, which suffered indirectly.

Justice = State-Sanctioned Revenge

As a society, we pay lip service to rehabilitation as a part of true justice; we even euphemistically refer to our system of prisons as a department of "correction." However, there is little question that punishment is our true goal. Anything less than a maximum sentence is viewed as being "soft on crime." When we speak of justice, what we have in mind is state-sanctioned revenge.

Michelle Alexander, graduate of Harvard Law School and Vanderbilt University, references how white people, on average, are more punitive than Black people, even though Black citizens are far more likely to be victims of crime. Rural white people, the least likely to suffer crime violence, are often the most punitive of all. This desire for retribution is also prevalent among religious communities, in which the values we allegedly learn in Sunday school—compassion, forgiveness, redemption, and second chances—are all too often absent from conversations about criminal justice.

For example, a few years ago, two eighteen-year-olds were arrested after breaking into a church building just around the corner from where I grew up. They didn't make off with much—$35, a cell phone, and some other small items. Nevertheless, the pastor of the church made it clear in a newspaper interview that even though he would pray for the trespassers, justice was his priority. Somehow,

I don't think he had in mind the prophet Amos's prayerful vision of a justice that flows like an unending stream and replacing empty worship services.

No, according to this pastor, prayer, by implication, was separate from, unrelated to, and insufficient to accomplish justice. A merciful God may handle eternal, spiritual matters, but more earthly concerns—such as kids breaking in and stealing a few things—were best addressed through the system of punishment, which is what we usually mean by justice being done.

A few years earlier, two employees of a convenience store were tragically killed during a robbery. After three suspects were arrested, the priest at the church the slain men attended told news reporters, "We are hoping for this, that the death penalty will be applied on all three ... even the juvenile person. ... If *justice* does not take revenge for these killings, this incident will be repeated once again. ... We need to be tough on these kinds of criminals" (emphasis added).

This priest expressed what many of us take for granted, and is the assumption on which the American criminal legal system is founded: that punishment is required to set things right. So impoverished is this common misunderstanding of justice that the priest believed the death penalty—the intentional killing of three more people, one of whom was a child and could not therefore be legally executed under the U.S. Constitution—would somehow produce "justice."

Two men had tragically died. A community was grieving. Most people would likely agree that, in order to reckon with the harm that was done, we must hold the people responsible accountable. According to this minister, however, accountability was not enough. He wanted blood. Three more killings needed to occur before his sense of "justice" would be satisfied. This is what is commonly known as the *myth of redemptive violence.*

This myth, that violence must be met with violence, is set forth in the Bible in Leviticus 24:

> If someone takes any human life, he must be put to death. ... If someone injures his neighbor, just as he has done, so shall it be done to him: fracture for fracture, eye for eye, tooth for tooth; just as he has injured a person, so shall it be inflicted on him.

"An eye for an eye" seems fair enough, and many people of faith use it as a guiding principle. But in so doing they ignore that it was directly contradicted by Jesus of Nazareth in the Sermon on the Mount; and, as Gandhi famously noted, it is a principle whose stubborn application will leave the whole world blind.

Perhaps if we can step outside of a cultural order that is so hellbent on vengeance and violence that a priest will advocate for executing children, we can muster the moral courage and imagination to embrace a broader, richer definition of justice, which can rightly be said is the first duty of society.

Author, activist, philosopher, and social critic Dr. Cornel West turned the conventional American understanding of justice on its head when he defined justice as what love looks like in public."

Justice looking like love? Is that the first duty of society? It certainly isn't how justice worked in the Tennessee Attorney General's office. And this wasn't the kind of justice I saw doled out to lawbreakers in movies and TV shows like *Miami Vice*.

Was there a way these two ideals could function together?

Isn't it love for victims of violence that causes us to punish wrongdoers? Isn't it love for public safety that leads us to incarcerate people who threaten it?

This may not be what Cornel West had in mind, but the apostle Paul himself wrote in Romans 13 that the government is God's minister, exists to punish evildoers, and does not bear the sword in vain. This is precisely what the American criminal justice system seeks to accomplish.

My First Lesson as a Clerk

When I was first starting out as a lawyer, it was unthinkable to me that I would ever be anything other than a career prosecutor. No, I was fully committed to seizing every opportunity to become a tough, effective advocate for the state. To that end, I began my legal career by clerking for two years for a judge on the Tennessee Court of Criminal Appeals. During my last year of law school, prior to passing the bar exam and becoming a licensed attorney, I worked as a research assistant for a professor who strongly encouraged me to seek a judicial clerkship before I began practicing.

"Preston," she said, "I believe it would be an invaluable experience for you. You'd benefit greatly from working for a judge and becoming acquainted with the judicial perspective before stepping into the role of advocate."

At first I resisted, my heart firmly set on achieving my dream career. Although being a prosecutor wouldn't involve speeding through the streets of Miami in a Ferrari, it would fulfill my earliest desires to be part of the law enforcement community, punishing criminals and putting things right.

One step at a time, I reminded myself. This professor knew what she was talking about. So, instead of applying for jobs in prosecutors' offices, I started interviewing with judges across the state. One day while I was not home, Sherisse received a call from Judge David H. Welles on the Court of Criminal Appeals. After introducing himself, he said, "I've called to offer Preston a job." Sherisse all but accepted on my behalf.

After graduation, Sherisse and I moved out of the little apartment in Knoxville that we had called home for three years. Clerking for Judge Welles meant we were returning home to Nashville, where we had both been raised.

As my law school professor predicted, clerking for Judge Welles gave me an invaluable introduction to the actual nuts and bolts of the criminal legal system. I'd studied theories in law school and learned to conduct preliminary hearings during my internship at the prosecutor's office in Knoxville, but I was now reading through court transcripts and drafting opinions for a judge. I felt like an apprentice learning a complex trade from an accomplished master.

Judge Welles was a busy man with a brilliant legal mind who had enjoyed a stellar career. He relied on me to read through the record of everything that had occurred in the lower court, research the law, and draft his legal opinions, which he then reviewed with a discerning eye. Although I had a lot of questions early on, I quickly settled into the role and became more confident as my understanding of criminal law and procedure grew. But every now and then I received a reminder that I still had a lot to learn.

One afternoon, Judge Welles called me into his chambers to discuss one of my draft opinions, which was not unusual. But this time

I could tell something was wrong. After quickly reviewing the facts of the case and legal issues raised, he directed my attention to one of the cases I had cited in support of his decision. What had I missed?

He peered at me over his glasses. "This case you cited, did you check to make sure it's still good law?"

I swallowed hard.

"Because it was overruled in a subsequent case."

I had dropped the ball. I was paid to research the law and reach the correct legal result, and I had gotten it flat wrong. If not for Judge Welles's attention to detail and keen knowledge of the law, I would have made him look bad by submitting an erroneous opinion in his name. This was a lesson I have carried with me ever since. When we claim to be about the work of justice, it is serious business. People's freedom and even their lives are literally at stake. There is no room for sloppy mistakes that may result in innocent people being punished or guilty people going free.

Lessons In Due Process

The most lasting lesson I learned while clerking for Judge Welles was that adhering to the correct process is of absolute and paramount importance. Most people are familiar with the phrase "due process" from the Fifth and Fourteenth Amendments to the U.S. Constitution, even if they don't know exactly what it means. Indeed, the Constitutional mandate that all citizens are entitled to a fair process before being denied their freedom is the very bedrock of our judicial system. Giving people the process to which they are due as a matter of Constitutional law is the main function of the criminal legal system. Every citizen accused of a crime is entitled to a fair process—without regard to wealth, race, education, and so on—before he or she can be denied life, liberty, or property. Because citizens are presumed innocent, proper procedural steps must be rigorously followed while moving them from their arrest to indictment to conviction to imprisonment.

Ensuring that all people receive a fair process does not, however, mean they are entitled to uniformity or even consistency of outcomes. Can two people accused of identical crimes receive very different sentences? Absolutely. It happens all the time. So long as the procedural steps are followed in each case, these discrepancies in outcome do not necessarily offend due process principles or our concept of justice. The legitimacy of the justice system is almost entirely a matter of adhering to the process and following all the rules, not the justness of the result. The significance of this distinction cannot be overstated.

As a clerk for Judge Welles, I didn't take long to notice the differences between arguments that were successful and arguments that failed on appeal. It all came down to effectively attacking the process.

Suppose I am convicted of a felony, such as stealing a television worth $500, and I'm sentenced to a year in prison. If I argue on appeal that a year in prison is simply excessive for stealing a television, that it's simply not fair or just, I will lose. The legislature has determined the sentence for this kind of felony, and the court's job is not to weigh the propriety or fairness of the legislature's decision. Taking issue with the actual outcome will not help me. To obtain relief, I need to show some problem with the process by which I was convicted, some violation of the rules. Perhaps the state was allowed to use hearsay testimony improperly during my trial or the prosecutor alluded to evidence the court had ruled inadmissible. Such procedural errors might entitle me to a new trial.

Or suppose, instead, that I am convicted for possession of marijuana. After being sentenced, I argue it is unfair to lock me up in Tennessee since marijuana is legal just across the state lines in Missouri and Virginia and no one was harmed by my actions. Again, I will lose, because Tennessee law states that possession of marijuana is a crime, regardless of whether anyone is hurt. That the outcome seems unfair or even nonsensical is irrelevant to the question of whether I can obtain relief from the verdict. Instead, I have to find a problem with the process according to which I was convicted. I might argue the marijuana was discovered by a police officer who stopped me without probable cause, a violation of my Fourth Amendment right against unreasonable searches and seizures. This might just get me off the hook.

Asserting that a sentence is unfairly long, that somebody else got less time, or that I should have been convicted of something less will not work.

The courts are not primarily concerned with what's fair. In this system, justice, we must remember, is defined in terms of process. If the process was followed and no rights were violated, the outcome will almost certainly not be disturbed.

I once worked on a case in which the body of a strangled woman was found in the trunk of a car in a junkyard. The cops interviewed all the junkyard employees, but they had no concrete leads ... no witnesses, no DNA samples, and no fingerprints. Although they were lacking hard evidence linking the crime to the responsible party, the lead homicide detective had a bad feeling about one of the employees. Therefore, the detective asked the man to come back to the police station under the guise of submitting another set of fingerprints. What the detective really wanted was another shot at questioning him.

When the employee arrived, the detective took him to an interrogation room in a secure part of the station. The detective lied to him, implying they knew he was guilty and that they had evidence he was guilty, but that disclosing the motive might result in a lighter sentence. Within a matter of a couple of minutes the man went to pieces. He confessed that he had picked up the woman for sex, but that afterward they got into a fight over how much money he owed her. Eventually things became violent, he wrapped his hands around her throat, strangled her, and left her body in the trunk of the car.

Based on this confession, the man was convicted of murder. There was just one problem. The detective did not advise the man of his Constitutional rights to remain silent and have a lawyer present during questioning, which is required before any in-custody interrogation by police. On appeal, the Tennessee Supreme Court agreed that this procedural rule was violated, and as a result, the murder conviction was reversed. The murderer went free.

Justice, you see, is defined in terms of process. Is it just for a man who admits to a cold-blooded killing to go free? Most of us would say no. But in our system, justice has little to do with the actual outcome of a case and everything to do with abiding by the process.

Is this the best way to think about justice? If "the first duty of society is justice," does it follow that the first duty of society is enforcing procedural rules? Is the outcome really irrelevant to the question of whether justice has been done? Is this what I went to law school for?

One Disturbing Phenomenon

Early in my career, I loved the prestige of being an Assistant Attorney General. I had a badge that allowed me to bypass security in state office buildings. I had a collection of suits, ties, and wingtip shoes to ensure that I always looked the part of a lawyer who meant business. When I had court, I grabbed my briefcase, strolled past the state capitol, and entered the limestone halls of the Tennessee Supreme Court Building. I breezed past the public gallery to the lawyers-only portion of the courtroom and took my seat at counsel's table. When it was my turn to address the court, the presiding judge would turn to me, say "General," and gesture for me to take the podium. I would rise from my seat, button my suit jacket, and make my argument, answering the judges' questions along the way.

When I didn't have court, I enjoyed sitting in my office and sifting through every detail of an appeal, researching the law, and crafting my argument. Every day I felt I was accomplishing justice for victims and making society safer. No case was insignificant.

But with each brief I wrote, I became increasingly aware of problems inherent in the system's emphasis of procedure over outcome.

I witnessed one disturbing phenomenon on a regular basis related to the system's elevation of process over outcome. When defendants filed appeals for relief from their convictions and sentences, they invariably attacked the process, knowing it was the only real avenue for relief. This emphasis on the procedure according to which they were convicted and sentenced caused them to see themselves as victims themselves—not of a crime but of an unfair process. It seemed to me this interfered with them accepting the consequences for their actions and again obscured the harm done to the actual victims. Even those whose wrongdoing was firmly established took issue with perceived violations of procedural rules because this was their only hope of having their sentences overturned. Perhaps they focused on a witness who wasn't allowed to testify, or a search warrant that contained inadvertent typographical errors, or a piece of evidence ruled irrelevant and inadmissible. Any perceived problem in the process took the focus off the harm suffered by the victim, which should have been centered.

This was only one way that the actual victim in a criminal case gets obscured and sidelined. Consider again the way a criminal case is styled: *State v. Jones.* Our system pits the person charged with a crime—the defendant—against the state. The state literally takes the place of the victim. The true victim is not a party to the case. His or her name is not in the case title. At best he or she is one of the state's witnesses. This legal abstraction of the state as the victim further blurs the identity of the real victim and the actual human impact of the time by suggesting the offense was actually committed against a faceless entity—the all-powerful, impersonal state.

When the legal system defines justice in purely procedural terms, it leads to all kinds of unintended consequences. It discourages accountability and the taking of responsibility by the guilty party, leading offenders to focus on perceived problems with the process instead of the actual harm they caused. If offenders perceive themselves as victims of an unfair process, it frustrates rehabilitation and sabotages potential reconciliation between them and the actual victims. "Justice as process" frustrates a true and meaningful experience of justice for both victims and offenders.

As these realizations took hold, I was becoming a little less idealistic about my role in the criminal legal system. However, many of my fellow prosecutors had worked in the system for years, even decades longer than I. I learned from these seasoned veterans that, although there is no perfect process for administering justice, we were still on the right side. After all, we were responsible for protecting victims and the public from people who inflicted harm.

Even so, it troubled me that the system sometimes seemed to value the process over an actual experience of justice.

It was about to get a lot worse.

The Myth of Deterrence

I was still thinking of justice almost exclusively in punitive terms. Guilty people needed to be punished for a host of reasons. In law school I'd learned numerous justifications for our system of laws and punishment.

First, deterrence is an unmistakable justification for punishing people who break the law. My old Jeep Wrangler isn't fast, but I would certainly be more likely to speed if not for fear of getting a ticket. Who doesn't love to roll down the windows, turn up the music, and put the pedal to the floor? It is the threat of likely consequences—a hefty fine, higher insurance premium, losing our license, the risk of an accident—that discourages us from breaking traffic laws.

We are taught early on to fear punishment, and advocates for harsher sentencing policies claim they will deter people from breaking the law.

This fails to account for the fact that violent crime is often committed in the heat of the moment, when people are not thinking rationally or weighing the possible consequences of their actions.

I once prosecuted a case in which a man shot and killed his best friend during a dispute over money that was owed for drugs. Both of the men had been abusing drugs and alcohol, and in an instant, a volatile situation became lethal. It is unlikely that either of the men contemplated the legal consequences of their actions in that moment.

Furthermore, the consequences of committing a crime may not be immediate. The gears of justice turn notoriously slowly in criminal cases. A person charged with a crime may wait years for a trial, then spend even longer going through appeals. In the case in which the man shot and killed his friend, almost three years passed between the crime and the denial of his appeal. Such distant consequences may not have much value for deterring crime.

We also know that poor people sometimes commit crimes simply to survive. I have lost count of the cases I prosecuted that involved writing a bad check for groceries at a discount store. With the criminalization of homelessness through laws prohibiting camping in public areas, we have essentially made some people's very existence illegal. Desperation tends to outweigh the threat of punishment.

Yet we act as though there is no problem we cannot punish our way out of. Our sentencing practices in the United States are much harsher than those in Europe, but our crime rates are higher in nearly every category, indicating that punitive policies—contrary to conventional American wisdom and the tough-on-crime rhetoric of some politicians—may offer little deterrent effect. Social activist Lee Griffith wrote, "In some US jurisdictions, the sentence for murder might be life in prison without parole or even execution, but for each year of the past three decades, US homicide rates have been between five and ten times greater than those in Europe.[1]"

The mistaken belief that harsh punishments deter crime is rooted in a misunderstanding about crime itself. We tend to wrongly assume that crime is a basic problem in society. But it is better understood as a symptom of deeper issues. Poverty, prior trauma and abuse, addiction, mental health issues, lack of access to meaningful educational and employment opportunities ... all of these are like the swamps that tend to breed crime. The man who killed his friend over drug money was unemployed, desperately poor, addicted to drugs and alcohol, and suffered from mental and physical disabilities. Harsh punishments that do not address these underlying issues will not effectively prevent crime, as we see year after year after year in our crime statistics.

What Makes for Safety?

I did not become an Assistant Attorney General to prosecute poor people for passing worthless checks for groceries. I wanted to protect innocent people from dangerous criminals, people who, if they were not neutralized, would victimize others. Humans have a fundamental need to feel safe and secure. Every time I argued for a particular sentence, I sought to safeguard the need we all have for safety. Protection of the public is one of the main purposes of government and a crucial component of any system of justice.

Our system of justice is predicated on the assumption that promoting public safety and punishing wrongdoers go hand in hand. When crime victims plead for justice to be done, we hear that as a demand for punishment of the guilty party. They look to the criminal justice system—and, specifically, to law enforcement and prosecutors—to carry this out. Every time the criminal courts hand down a stiff sentence, the media declares justice has won the day. Indeed, we want protection from the people we fear.

Prison, we like to think, makes us safer.

Prison, without a doubt, separates the wrongdoer from the victim, the victim's family, and free society. Before the offender can

---

[1] Lee Griffith, *God Is Subversive: Talking Peace in a Time of Empire* (Grand Rapids, MI: William B. Eerdmanns, 2011), 65.

return to regular life, he or she is expected to make an attitude and behavior adjustment: hence, the "Department of Correction."

But how much do these penitentiaries—places that allegedly cultivate penitence—really help bring about change? If crime is a symptom of deeper social issues like poverty, addiction, and mental illness, does separation from society do anything but compound the preexisting harm? We lump everyone together—violent and nonviolent, purposeful and negligent—assign them numbers, strip them of autonomy, and expect them to miraculously improve without guidance or hope. We put people in a violent place for years or even decades where they are dehumanized, stripped of their dignity, and may suffer physical, psychological, or sexual abuse, and expect them to magically emerge re-formed on the other side.

I once worked on the case of a man who, in a fit of rage, shot and killed a man he suspected had been sleeping with his wife. Because the defendant was in his own house at the time, the jury questioned whether he may have been acting in self-defense. Therefore, the jury convicted him of the lesser charge of voluntary manslaughter and sentenced him to eight years before he would be eligible for parole. As the man prepared for his parole hearing, he reached out to me and asked me to support his release. Because I didn't know anything about him or his efforts at rehabilitation, I declined but wished him well. He responded with a profanity-laced letter in which he threatened me and promised that God would damn me to hell.

I don't know what all issues this man may have been dealing with—mental health issues, substance abuse, or something else. Clearly, however, an extended period of incarceration in a maximum-security prison had not helped. He remained a danger to others and possibly to himself. I wondered what the Department of Correction had done to help correct him over the past eight years. And what harm might he cause if and when he was released?

I have seen some of our nation's prison cages and solitary confinement cells, and to our disgrace, our system of mass incarceration makes us less safe, not more.

Blind Justice

Deterrence and protection are indeed important, but how often does this punitive, process-based system fulfill those ends? In my role as a prosecutor, I wanted to believe the system produced justice, but my definition of it was shifting. Despite the ubiquity of the word "justice" in law schools, courtrooms, and the halls of power, I was having doubts that true justice was what we were promoting, or even seeking.

In many respects, justice seemed to be for sale in the American legal system; in the words of justice reform advocates, "If you've got the capital, you don't get the punishment." It's hard to ignore the ways that money and privilege impact the outcome of criminal cases. I saw firsthand the difference that a well-respected, highly paid private attorney could make. I prosecuted a simple assault case in which the young defendant's parents hired an expensive lawyer to represent him at the initial hearing. This particular lawyer typically charged a retainer fee of at least $15,000, and he specialized in federal, white-collar cases. The judge was clearly impressed at having such a notable attorney in his courtroom. Although there was ample evidence of guilt, the judge dismissed the case, finding there was not sufficient proof to send it on to the grand jury. My jaw fell open when the judge banged his gavel. I had no doubt that if the defendant had been a poor Black kid represented by a public defender, the judge would have bound the case over to the grand jury rather than dismiss the charge. It was the first time for me to see up close that for those with the money to retain expensive lawyers, especially when they have white skin and come from the right background, mercy and second chances are on the table. Lady Justice's blindfold notwithstanding, the system makes a big difference between people who do drugs in fraternity houses or suburban mansions and who do drugs in low-income housing projects.

That's not justice. Neither is thinking we can punish our way out of any social problem, such as poverty and homelessness, mental illness, and drug and alcohol addiction. And justice is certainly not sentencing children as young as twelve or thirteen to life in prison without the possibility of parole. Our addiction to punishment is not in accord with justice, but a betrayal of it.

I was starting to think that maybe justice shouldn't be blind after all, as though crime occurs in some kind of a vacuum. In order to right the balance of the scales in a meaningful way, Lady Justice needs to remove her blindfold and consider the entire human context in which a crime is committed. Only by correctly accounting for the many relevant factors can we begin to discern an outcome that will treat the underlying illnesses and not merely seek vengeance against the symptom. True justice will not show partiality based on money or skin color, but will take into account the many underlying factors that lead to a crime being committed.

Too often in my role as an appellate prosecutor, I was content leaving the blindfold in place. Lawyers are trained to trust the process. We are encouraged to not become emotionally invested in our cases. We do our jobs, conscientiously, diligently, and ethically. But we maintain a professional distance. This distance led me to make arguments about the fate of people I never got the chance to meet. This distance enabled the system to forever define a person by his or her worst moment. Is this how any of us would want to be treated? Yet, all too often I was willing to judge and condemn people when all I knew about them was the worst thing they'd ever done. What a dangerous position to allow myself to be in.

Chapter 3

An Education Behind Bars

While we were in college at Lipscomb University in the late 1990s, Sherisse and I both sang in the university choir, which is how we met. Many Sunday evenings during the school year, our chorus could be heard performing at local churches. There were always a few parents present, and the choir director would acknowledge them and have the students introduce them and say where they were from. When it was my turn, I would introduce my mom, but then casually mention that my dad wasn't present because he was "in prison."

Everyone familiar with my family knew the reason Dad was not there on Sunday nights was that he led his church's prison ministry.

From the time I was a small boy, I watched my Dad and Mom put their faith into action by serving people who were incarcerated. I was taught from a young age that God loves everyone, and that includes people who are in prison. But I also was taught that love doesn't negate the need for justice, which, as I've noted, almost always means harsh punishment. Therefore, despite my parents' example, I was convinced the people in prison deserved to be there. Good people, innocent people don't go to prison. Only years later would I discover how many folks end up behind bars because of mishandled evidence, pressured plea bargains, and inadequate representation.

"All too often," the American Bar Association has reported, "defendants plead guilty, even if they are innocent, without really understanding their legal rights. ... The fundamental right to a lawyer that most Americans assume applies to everyone accused of criminal conduct effectively does not exist in practice for countless people across the United States."[1]

Although I didn't yet comprehend all the injustices present in the criminal legal system, my parents' concern for people who were in prison showed me, that if nothing else, those people were loved by God and therefore had value. It was one of the greatest lessons of my childhood. Dad and Mom took the words of the Bible seriously when it states in Hebrews 13:3, "Continue to remember those in prison as if you were together with them in prison, and those who are mistreated as if you yourselves were suffering."

For many years, Dad headed out faithfully on Sunday afternoons to conduct worship services and share communion in local prisons. Mom was equally tireless, aiding these individuals as they were released. With money being tight for those reentering society, Dad and Mom helped them find jobs and housing, and bought food and diapers for their babies. Come Christmas time, Mom went gift-shopping for them so they would not do without.

After their release, various formerly incarcerated folks would come in and out of our lives: an older Black man nicknamed "Wolf," due to his long, white goatee; Bruce who, with his wife Patsy, did odd jobs around our house like painting and carpentry; and Clay and Rose, who, thanks to Mom and Dad, were able to live with their kids in a house owned by the church and joined us for Thanksgiving and Christmas celebrations.

There was never any hesitation, fear, or judgment from my parents, even as Mom was walking at night in an unfamiliar part of town to take diapers to Wolf and his wife for their new baby. People who had spent years in prison became family friends.

The Punishment Never Fully Ends

My parents knew that finding employment and housing are daunting hurdles for formerly incarcerated people. They did the crime and the time, to cite a familiar retributive phrase. In theory, they had paid their debt to society. Yet their punishment never really ends. For the rest of their lives, they are rendered "infamous" under the law,

---

[1] "ABA CJS Plea Bargaining Task Force," American Bar Association, accessed February 26, 2024, https://www.americanbar.org/groups/criminal_justice/committees/taskforces/plea_bargain_tf/.

which means labeled as convicted felons. On every employment and housing application, they must check "Yes" by the question, "Have you ever been convicted of a felony?" The next likely stop for that application? The trash can. In many states, people with criminal records are denied food stamps, educational opportunities, and other public benefits, while also forfeiting the right to vote. More than 19 million Americans are permanently disenfranchised as the result of a felony conviction.

How many business owners are prepared to hire someone who was recently released from prison?

How many property managers will rent to someone with a criminal record?

What if they are Christians? Will that make any difference?

It's easy to pay lip service to rehabilitation and second chances while keeping in place policies and practices that leave little room for a prosperous future.

In fact, it's not at all uncommon for these onerous burdens to drive people back to the very behaviors that first got them into trouble. Michelle Alexander has pointed out that we set returning citizens up to fail rather than succeed: "What is most remarkable about the hundreds of thousands of people who return from prison to their communities each year is not how many fail, but how many somehow manage to survive and stay out of prison against all odds."[2]

In the Shipp household, we saw many of these remarkable people with our own eyes. I learned from my parents' example that no one is beyond the hope of redemption.

From Wedding Bells to Razor Wire

Thankfully, Sherisse also believes in second chances and redemption.

During my college years, I was focused in equal parts on making good grades and having as much fun as possible. Serious romantic relationships were not a priority until I started dating Sherisse my senior year. Then it was a whirlwind.

Soon after graduation in 1999, we said our wedding vows before family and friends (I only recently learned that some of the people in attendance wrongly assumed and gossiped that Sherisse

---

[2] Alexander, *The New Jim Crow*, 176.

was pregnant) and shot off for a honeymoon in Fort Lauderdale. We hadn't been back more than twenty-four hours before we packed our meager belongings into a U-Haul van and headed east to Knoxville, where I would attend law school at the University of Tennessee. Those three years passed quickly, with many friends and memories made; then we returned home to Nashville for me to begin my clerkship with Judge Welles.

In the summer of 2002, Sherisse and I started attending a church in an affluent Nashville suburb that had a vibrant young marrieds group. Knowing from my Dad's experience how hard it can be to get people to volunteer for church ministries, when we placed membership, I decided to follow in his footsteps and serve in the prison ministry.

Only two other men were committed to this work, and I figured they could use the help. I was inspired by my parents, but I also knew from their experience that prison ministry doesn't rank high on most Christians' priority list. Despite Jesus' crystal-clear command in Matthew 25 to visit people who are in prison, precious few Christians would ever consider doing so. It turns out many Bible-believing Christians tend to believe only some parts, and it's usually the ones that keep them pretty comfortable. Even good, religious folk prefer to avoid people who are in prison.

Following my Dad's example, on the fourth Sunday night of every month, I drove an hour west of Nashville to the Turney Center Industrial Prison and Farm, a prison complex nestled in the rolling hills of rural Tennessee, to serve as a religious volunteer. Razor wire fencing contrasted with the tall green trees that lined the nearby winding Duck River as my colleagues and I arrived in the parking lot.

We led a traditional worship service, inviting the men who joined us to sing, pray, take the Lord's Supper, and talk with us about the Bible. Some guys came only once every few months, and I had to work at remembering their faces. Others attended faithfully every single month, and I got to know these fine gentlemen by name—Jerry, Johnny, Randall, and Hector; Fred, Joseph, Jacob, and Ray. Month after month we got to know each other, and they became friends.

However, it was challenging to develop relationships that go deep. Our visits were limited in frequency and duration, and we were outsiders, after all. There was no way for us to know what their daily lives were like. And traditional models of prison ministry often preponderate against really getting to know the men who are locked up. The unspoken assumption in these scenarios is that the religious volunteers possess something the folks on the inside need—specifically, Jesus and salvation.

Traditional prison ministry tends to operate as a one-way street, with the outsiders doing all the praying and preaching and singing and talking, while the insiders are expected to sit quietly and behave, like schoolchildren, opening their mouths only to softly sing along with familiar hymns.

For my part, this perceived gulf only widened when I accepted a position as an Assistant Attorney General.

Of course, I didn't tell the men at the Turney Center about my day job. It's not that I was in any way ashamed. No, I firmly believed that I was fulfilling God's will for my life by putting lawbreakers in prison. After all, according to Paul in Romans 13:1–4, "Let everyone be subject to the governing authorities. ... But if you do wrong, be afraid, for rulers do not bear the sword for no reason. They are God's servants, agents of wrath to bring punishment on the wrongdoer." Retribution was part of God's plan, and there was no prohibition in scripture of Christians serving as prosecutors, police officers, judges, guards, or wardens. Many people go to church on Sunday and then put on a badge or a black robe on Monday, much like I put on a suit and tie and went to the Attorney General's office. I believed in both grace for our sins and punishment for our crimes. However, I did not know whether the men at the prison would see it that way. Although I saw no conflict at the time, I did not want my career to be a stumbling block for them as we sang and prayed together. Therefore, I saw no reason to broadcast it.

Looking back, I can see that as long as I kept my faith, values, and morals in a separate compartment from other aspects of my life, such as my career, it was easy to not notice what should be obvious conflicts. I kept my monthly visits to the prison in one box—in which I sang and spoke to those in prison, as I had seen my Dad do my whole life. My job was in another box—in which I argued that people who committed crimes must be held accountable. Lawbreakers were required to pay a price. This is the moral justification for the criminal justice system. All of the agents of the system, from cops to prosecutors to judges, are encouraged to accept the system as morally justified on this basis.

My parents' example kept me from seeing people who were in prison as undeserving of my concern. They had modeled enough of the gospel for me to understand God's care for those in chains. However, I believed that the system worked and that the people who were in prison deserved to be there. I knew that everyone was capable of being renewed and restored, but this did not negate the need for punishment. I wouldn't be able to hold these competing beliefs in tension for long. Faith in mercy, forgiveness, and redemption—without corresponding works—is dead.

Unplugging from the God of Religion

Like so many people raised in church, I never seriously questioned the spiritual beliefs I inherited. I trusted that the doctrines that were handed to me by my parents, preachers, and Bible teachers were sound. At the heart of that system of beliefs about the nature of the universe was an all-powerful, all-knowing God who rewarded those who obeyed him and punished those who did not.

This sort of binary, black-and-white way of thinking is useful for establishing social cohesion. There are good people, and there are bad people. Our group is right and good, and other groups are wrong and bad. It also makes for effective prosecutors.

The us versus them mentality appeals to our tribalistic instincts and our desire for security. My group and I don't have to worry whether we're saved if we can point to people outside our group who are lost. If our group has cornered the market on orthodoxy, it's everyone else who's guilty of heresy. Of course, this self-serving, self-justifying approach ignores the fact that Jesus of Nazareth had a habit of casting the outsider, the bad guy, and the heretic as the heroes of his stories.

In my church experience, so much emphasis was placed on believing the right things that being a Christian was largely a matter of giving one's intellectual assent to a set of abstract doctrines about God, Jesus, the virgin birth, the significance of Jesus being executed, the nature of his resurrection, and so on. All this was largely to the exclusion of the possibility that being a Christian was about embodying a set of practices. There's a reason not many church-goers have ever obeyed Jesus' command to visit people in prison. If I believe all the right things about Jesus, maybe I don't really have to follow Jesus.

Although my experiences at the Turney Center Prison had led me into a season of questioning, I didn't unplug with a quick tug from the socket. It happened gradually, with the help of various friends and mentors.

Years earlier, my friend Hunter was one of the first to help me think in terms not merely of right beliefs (orthodoxy) but of right practices (orthopraxy). Acquaintances from our undergraduate days at Lipscomb, Hunter and I reconnected in Knoxville when we were both in graduate school at the University of Tennessee. I was in my early twenties, newly married, and quite certain that going to law school to become a prosecutor was God's will for my life. Everything fit tidily in my compartments of marriage, school, and career. I thought I had all the right answers.

Hunter, the son of missionaries to Brazil, wasn't studying religion, yet his Christian faith was unlike any I had seen. For Hunter, it seemed that being a Christian was not a part of his life, one compartment among several. It was the essence of who he aspired to be in all facets of his life. Like yeast, his faith worked its way into all the other boxes—his relationships, his career, what he spent his money on ... everything.

What, I wondered, made him so different?

Hunter believed pretty much exactly as I had been raised to about God, salvation, worship, and all the rest. But he also seemed to have a strong sense that it was not simply what we believe, but what we do, that defines us as Christians. Jesus expected us to do what he said, such as treat others as we'd want to be treated, embrace nonviolence, and love even our enemies. As I considered Hunter, I began to wonder what it would look like to seriously engage Jesus' most challenging teachings, and the degree to which all my beliefs and doctrines had any real impact on my daily life.

If I were in court, and I had to prove beyond a reasonable doubt that I was a Christian, what evidence could I introduce, other than where I happened to park myself for one hour on Sunday mornings?

After twenty-plus years of going to church and seventeen years of religious education, what practical difference did my Christian faith actually make?

When I considered myself and many of the people who pack the pews on Sundays, we seemed to be just as materialistic and greedy, judgmental and inhospitable, anxious and angry, self-righteous and hypocritical as a lot of non-Christians. Waking up to how little my Christian faith seemed to impact my daily life led to something of an identity crisis. This should be the most important thing, so surely it made some difference, something I did because of my faith that I wouldn't do otherwise. Somehow, I just couldn't think of anything. Desperate for any answer, I decided to do something I knew I wouldn't do if I weren't a Christian. I committed to daily Bible study. In the basement of the law school library, I would pull out my Bible and read a few passages. I thought that reading the Bible might be something I could point to that I did just because I was a Christian. It didn't dawn on me that, as helpful as study can be, it is almost exclusively a private affair. All my years of church attendance and religious education had done nothing to help me know how to externalize Christianity. The nagging questions about my faith not only persisted as I left law school and began my career, they multiplied.

Cloud of Witnesses

The church that Sherisse and I attended where I got involved in the prison ministry had a thriving young marrieds class. A man in his early thirties, who was both discerning and wise, led the class. His name was David Woodard. David reminded us,

> The early church was not an institution with payrolls and property holdings. What we call 'church' would have been unthinkable to the first Christians. It's time we shed our preconceived ideas about church and even the nature of the gospel. Remember, as we study the Book of Acts, we are witnessing the beginnings of a subversive, revolutionary community offering an alternative to the ways of empire.

I was hooked. I had never thought of church this way before. This was a Christian faith that would make a difference.

Like Hunter, David helped create the space for me to think about my faith in a new light. To quote Jedi Master Yoda, I was beginning to unlearn what I had learned. Another friend from the young marrieds class named Greg and I began meeting regularly for lunch. Over Cajun food, Irish pub fare, and barbecue, we discussed books by progressive Christian thinkers like Brian McLaren and Marcus Borg, who gave us new language and a fresh paradigm for engaging our faith. We were soon joined by our church's new minister of spiritual formation, Scott Owings.

Scott was a Texan who had recently moved back to the United States after serving as a missionary to the Czech Republic. Not quite fifteen years my senior and a little further down the path, he challenged my assumptions about what faith even was and assured me not to panic when I saw no path ahead of me. He introduced me to the contemplative writings of Henri J. M. Nouwen, Thomas Keating, Richard Rohr, and Thomas Merton.

I discovered the "new monastics"—Shane Claiborne and Jonathan Wilson-Hargrove—young activists who, in the spirit of people like Dorothy Day and Daniel Berrigan, sought to live out a gospel that is actually good news to the poor and a threat to the dehumanizing powers that oppress them. German theologian and anti-Nazi dissident Dietrich Bonhoeffer became a profound influence, particularly through his thoughts on radical discipleship when the larger church culture has lost its saltiness. Baptist preacher and Civil Rights leader Will Campbell became a role model as I sought to embody a faith with the ministry of reconciliation at the center.

These friends and authors became my cloud of witnesses, inspiring and accompanying me in my quest to learn what it means to be a Christian.

It was during this period of religious deconstruction that I began my career as an appellate prosecutor in the Tennessee Attorney General's office. The old wineskins that held the faith I inherited were cracking. My confidence in the American system of laws and punishment, on the other hand, had not yet been shaken. I was rejecting pat answers to complex theological questions, but still swallowing hook, line, and sinker the myth of redemptive violence that manifested itself in courtrooms across the nations. I was no longer a religious fundamentalist, but I was something of a legal fundamentalist. I had been seeking a more authentic practice of the Christian faith. To get there, I was going to need to scrutinize my career as an advocate for retribution in the same way that I had the religious teachings I had received.

These two strains of my life were about to converge.

An Alternate Approach to Prison Ministry

In April of 2006, I received an email from Dr. Richard Goode, my former advisor and history professor at Lipscomb. Richard was aware of my work at the Turney Center and wanted to discuss an idea he had for an alternate approach to prison ministry, one that was rooted in education.

When I was an undergrad, Richard was one of the professors whose classes I took as often as possible. His unconventional approach to teaching American history gave me permission to ask hard questions about issues I had largely taken for granted. In our study of Colonial America, we spent a semester asking, "Who were the first Americans?" The theme for another of his classes, which focused on the turn of the last century, was, "What is 'the American dream?'"

How could I not be interested in hearing his thoughts on prison ministry?

For a few years, Richard had been involved in a program at Vanderbilt Divinity School that offered graduate-level theology courses at nearby Riverbend Maximum Security Institution. It was spearheaded by a member of the Divinity School faculty named Harmon Wray, a restorative justice pioneer who had been a mentor to Richard, and Janet Wolf, a Methodist minister and community organizer.

On an unseasonably hot spring day, Richard and I sipped coffee at Portland Brew in Nashville's trendy 12 South district.

"Tell me what y'all do at Riverbend, Richard." I put a napkin under my cup. "How do you have a college class at a prison?"

"Well, it definitely has a different feel from a university campus," he answered. "Each week, seminary students travel to the prison, go through security, and have their class alongside the people at the prison."

I had never heard of anything like this before.

"Do the people at the prison do all the same work as the divinity students?"

"Yep. It's all the same. Same texts, same assignments, everything. And you should see the caliber of the work the inside students produce."

I leaned forward, intrigued. I had been doing traditional prison ministry at my church for about four years, and I had grown up watching my Dad do the same. Although what Richard described felt familiar, it also seemed deeper and more profound than what usually passes for ministry. Bringing two very different groups of people into the same space for rich conversation was novel and exciting. I wanted to hear more.

"That has to be so good for the insiders, to have that kind of academic opportunity."

"Absolutely," Richard agreed. "You know how it is in prison. The classes and programming leave a lot to be desired. For people in prison to be able to take graduate classes at a school like Vanderbilt is almost unheard of.

He paused before continuing: "The impact on the traditional students is just as profound. They come into the class with all of the usual preconceived ideas about what prisoners are like, and those get blown apart in the first hour."

Richard has always been a master at playing devil's advocate, and I think he recognized, in ways I didn't yet, the contradictions I was facing in my ministry and career. He peered at me through his glasses.

"Janet Wolf, who also teaches in the Vanderbilt Divinity program, asks why we settle for a prison ministry that does little more than make us chaplains of an unjust order. Have you ever thought about that, Preston?"

I had not, and my head was starting to spin.

"Think about it. In traditional prison ministry, we act as though we're taking Jesus to the people at the prison, but that's the exact opposite of what Jesus says in Matthew 25, right? He says that we go there to meet him. That kind of turns our notion of 'ministry' on its head, doesn't it?"

I felt like the ground was shifting under my feet. My mentor's words had unlocked something in me, and a door had opened just a crack.

I had never considered how limited the traditional approach to prison ministry is. I had been quite comfortable with the paradigm that we take Jesus into the prison, but Richard showed me that I had it backward. Richard was combining his career—university professor—with his Christian vocation to care for people who are in prison. There was no division. My own tendency to compartmentalize my life into separate boxes was immediately called into question. How would this change my work at the Turney Center, I wondered.

In a flash over coffee, I sensed that my religion was too small and my view of justice too narrow. For the first time I questioned whether I was in the right job.

"So how can I help?" I was eager to know.

Richard had a mischievous look in his eye. "I want to start a prison program at Lipscomb."

Clarence Jordan, founder of Koinonia Farm, where Black and white Christians in the Jim Crow South lived together, called his interfaith community "a demonstration plot for the kingdom of God." Richard believed that having Lipscomb University offer college classes at a local prison could serve as such a demonstration plot—a place to teach, share, experiment with ideas, and most importantly, form an alternative community in which the labels that tend to divide us don't count for as much. The Vanderbilt Divinity program was already thriving at the men's prison. Richard wanted to implement something similar at the undergraduate level at the Tennessee Prison for Women.

"The women at the prison will earn credits toward a college degree," Richard explained. "And the Lipscomb students will receive an education they won't soon forget."

"And how in the world will we get both TDOC and Lipscomb to cooperate?" I wanted to know.

"That," he conceded, "is no small task."

Institutions are ponderously slow to move and notoriously suspicious of new initiatives. I could scarcely imagine the red tape involved in the Tennessee Department of Correction getting convicted felons enrolled as college students, or admitting bright-eyed undergrads into a maximum-security prison. We believed, nevertheless, education was a proven way of reducing recidivism, and the prison would be wise to embrace it.

On Lipscomb University's end, there was the question of funding. Private colleges don't give away credit hours, particularly to prisoners with little to no money. Richard and I were convinced, however, that as a school that markets itself as "Christian," Lipscomb must take seriously the call to make its academics available to the "least of these," of whom Jesus speaks in Matthew 25.

We agreed it was worth the time we would invest trying to convince the DOC and Lipscomb to partner together.

Richard set down his coffee. "Before I go, may I suggest a good book?"

"It's been quite a while since you assigned me a text," I replied.

With that he handed me a copy of a thin paperback titled, *Changing Lenses*[3] by Howard Zehr, which would radically alter my views of crime, justice, and Christianity itself.

Far Too Easy to Label

Over the next few months, starting with *Changing Lenses*, I read everything I could get my hands on that critiqued our current criminal legal system, which focuses almost exclusively on punishment, and pointed toward something new, something more restorative and transformative. I was being exposed to a way of thinking about the system that I didn't learn in law school, or while clerking for a judge, or while serving as an appellate prosecutor. I had been trained to uncritically plug into a retributive, process-obsessed, adversarial system. Now I was learning to question the legitimacy of the very goals of that system.

I remember sitting in bed, going back and forth between highlighting passages and taking copious notes, feeling like I was

---

[3] Howard Zehr, *Changing Lenses: A New Focus for Crime and Justice* (Harrisonburg, VA: Herald Press, 1990).

being introduced to a whole new world. Many evenings, as Sherisse pulled dinner together, I read out loud to her poignant passages and eye-opening stats. She was as floored as I was. Zehr wrote:

> [J]ustice will not be served if we maintain our exclusive focus on the questions that drive our current justice systems: What laws have been broken? Who did it? What do they deserve? True justice requires, instead, that we ask questions such as these: Who has been hurt? What do they need? Whose obligations and responsibilities are these? Who has a stake in this situation? What is the process that can involve the stakeholders in finding a solution?[4]

> Retributive theory believes that pain will vindicate, but in practice that is often counterproductive for both victim and offender. Restorative justice theory, on the other hand, argues that what truly vindicates is acknowledgment of victims' harms and needs, combined with an active effort to encourage offenders to take responsibility, make right the wrongs, and address the causes of their behavior. By addressing this need for vindication in a positive way, restorative justice has the potential to affirm both victim and offender and to help them transform their lives.[5]

> Restorative justice expands the circle of stakeholders— those with a stake or standing in the event or the case—beyond just the government and the offender to include victims and community members also.[6]

I was a good lawyer. I knew how to play my role in the system. How had I never before questioned our overreliance on punishment? Why had I never stopped to ask why the needs of the parties—both the person who suffered harm and the person who caused it—are not centered? It is possible that a system that knows only how to punish isn't a just system at all?

---

[4] Howard Zehr, *The Little Book of Restorative Justice* (New York: Good Books, 2002), 63.

[5] Zehr, *The Little Book of Restorative Justice*, 59.

[6] Zehr, *The Little Book of Restorative Justice*, 13.

My parents had spent years ministering to people in prison and helping them get on their feet when they were released. Why did it seem I was doing just the opposite in my current position? I wasn't providing men and women with the hope or help they desperately needed. I was hammering them down, delivering the punishment our system deemed just—finishing one case and moving on to the next one.

In his book, *Rethinking Incarceration*, Dominique DuBois Gilliard, Director of Racial Righteousness and Reconciliation for the Evangelical Covenant Church, explained:

> Crime is never merely an individual breaking the law; it is always a communal transgression that fractures shalom. God's justice is restorative and reconciling as opposed to retributive and isolating. Our criminal justice system quarantines people who cause harm, which subsequently harms them through punitive measures and dehumanizing conditions. ... God's justice moves toward restoration, reintegration, and redemption. God's justice is inherently connected to healing the harmed, restoring what has been lost, and reconciling those who are estranged from God and community. God's heart and justice are inherently restorative.[7]

Reading Zehr and Gilliard, I felt like I had been punched in the gut. I had felt so good about the work I was doing and the role I played in the legal system, but all these books were showing me that I had failed to ask many important questions.

Having spent my whole life in church and religious schools, why had I never been taught or considered that the justice of God always seeks restoration? Why had I never contemplated that every case I worked on involved a person, made in the image of God? The system I labored in quickly reduced them all to labels: defendant, felon, prisoner, murderer, rapist, thief. These labels obscured the fact that we are all fearfully and wonderfully made, unique expressions of divine love. Systems thrive when people are reduced to labels. Even

---

[7] Dominique DuBois Gilliard, *Rethinking Incarceration: Advocating for Justice That Restores* (Downers Grove, IL: InterVarsity Press, 2018), 178–79.

well-intentioned academic and religious institutions have trouble resisting this dehumanizing tendency. When it comes to managing large numbers of people ("human resources," our institutions might call them), labels are convenient, and systems use them to attach value based on education, experience, and position—or the lack thereof.

As my friend David Dark, noted author and professor of religion at Belmont University, has written,

> When I label people, I no longer have to deal with them thoughtfully. I no longer have to feel overwhelmed by their complexity, the lives they live, the dreams they have. ... There's hardly any action quite so undemanding, so utterly unimaginative, as the affixing of a label. It's the costliest of mental shortcuts.[8]

Picture a doctor. A garbage collector. A university president. A street musician. The person who checks you out at the grocery store or takes your order in a drive-thru. The financial advisor who helps people plan for the future. Are there big differences in how you value them, based on the labels they wear?

When even benevolent institutions such as churches, hospitals, and schools traffic in labels as a handy tool for constituent management, it should come as no surprise that punitive legal authorities use dehumanizing language as a tool of control.

Of course, I wore a label as well. In my office in downtown Nashville, I was called Assistant Attorney General, which dictated my daily role. I was bound by my label to oppose those labeled as defendants. Other people were labeled judges, and they got to wear special black robes. Their label gave them the power to make important decisions that people who wear other labels can't make. And the people labeled victims, those most directly affected by the harmful conduct, had little or no say at all in how cases were resolved.

I was learning so much, but I didn't know what to do with it. My mind was reeling, and I wasn't finding stable ground. At least every week or two, I went for long walks in Radnor Lake State Park, a protected natural area just south of Nashville. As I walked in silence,

---

[8] David Dark, *Life's Too Short to Pretend You're Not Religious* (Westmont, IL: InterVarsity Press, 2016), 13.

I tried to sort out my thoughts. There was such conflict between everything I was learning about justice as healing and transformation and my daily job of being a prosecutor. I wasn't sure where it all fit.

As I walked by trees, rocks, and turtles, I thought about how nothing in nature has to wrestle with meaning, purpose, and vocation. Moss and owls and herons just need to be themselves. But what about me? What was I supposed to be doing? I thought I knew, back when I decided to go to law school and become a prosecutor. But all these new thoughts called all of my old plans into question.

Richard Goode's vision of education and beloved community within prison walls offered me a way to look beyond a punitive system that reduces everyone involved in the process to labels, and instead to contemplate a demonstration plot for transcending such labels with their inherent us versus them dichotomy.

But would the Tennessee Department of Correction (TDOC) and Lipscomb University even give us the opportunity?

LIFE Comes into Being

To Richard's and my own amazement, in a matter of months, both Lipscomb and the TDOC green-lighted the initiative. The first course would be offered in the spring of 2007, at the Tennessee Prison for Women. The inaugural cohort would consist of fifteen carefully selected residents at the prison, whose tuition was funded by private donations. They would be joined by fifteen traditional Lipscomb students, who understood they would be studying at a prison. What we had first dreamed of less than a year earlier at Portland Brew and spent months envisioning together was about to be an accredited college course.

The program was called the Lipscomb Initiative for Education, or simply the LIFE Program.

As we discussed how to begin the curriculum, Richard thought it made sense to start with a law class. After all, the legal process was responsible for the division of our class into inside students and outside students. Half the class knew nothing about the criminal legal system; the other half had been condemned by it. Therefore, Judicial Process would be the first course offered.

"If you would, Preston, I'd like you to teach it."

I was surprised by his offer. Would fifteen people who were incarcerated want to hear from a prosecutor? Richard seemed to think so. Who better to dig into the nuts and bolts of the system than somebody who works in it every day? And thanks to the many books I had devoured in the past year, I was ready to lead a discussion not just explaining the criminal legal system but critiquing it.

I was also excited by the idea of serving as a Lipscomb University professor. My maternal grandmother had served for many years as secretary of the Department of History and Political Science; my mother, sister, brother-in-law, aunt, uncle, cousin, and many friends had gone to Lipscomb; and Sherisse and I met and fell in love there. Although I had never taught before, I felt confident that, as a prosecutor who was finally thinking critically about whether the criminal justice system really produces true justice, I could help make the first ever LIFE class a success.

"You sure you're okay with this?" I asked Sherisse as we decided whether to accept Richard's offer.

Sherisse, who was pregnant with our second daughter, Ruby, smiled. "I taught at least 20 pre-kindergarteners in Knoxville. You think I can't handle things here at home one night a week? Listen, I believe God has put this in front of us. We have to walk through this door that has opened. You're going to love it."

"It'll be a lot of extra work on top of my regular work schedule."

"We got this." She zipped up two-year-old Lila's onesie and took my hand. "I'd rather have you investing in something you really believe in than moping around the house, frustrated and conflicted all the time."

I had tried to not let my vocational crisis affect my family, but Sherisse had known me too long. She was with me when I dreamed of being a prosecutor. She threw me a huge party when I graduated from law school. She was the one who answered the phone when Judge Welles offered me my first job. She knew what working for the Attorney General's Office once meant to me. She could see that where I had once been full of confidence, I was now filled with questions. She knew that I was trying to find sure footing.

"This is bigger than either of us understands right now," she assured me, "but it's leading somewhere. This is something we have to do."

She was confident, and I knew she was right. "All right. I'll tell Richard I'm in. And do you really think I mope?"

That First Awkward Class

Every Wednesday night from 5 to 9 p.m. for sixteen weeks, the prison visitation gallery in the Tennessee Prison for Women transformed into a college classroom. Fifteen Lipscomb students would make the drive to West Nashville each week to participate in a class with fifteen people serving lengthy prison terms. Two very different worlds collided.

While Lipscomb was explicitly Christian, and Richard envisioned the LIFE program as a Christian ministry, there was no test of faith or proselytizing. Our view was that something of God is within each person, and that as we got to know each other, we'd find that what we have in common far surpasses any possible differences.

Folks who are locked up are rarely asked to share their thoughts and opinions. It is one of the innumerable indignities they endure in prison, where every day is full of reminders that they are regarded as less than human. They are told when to get up, what to do, what to wear, what to eat, what to think. They are identified by number, clothed in outfits without form. Arbitrary searches and lack of privacy are regular parts of their existence.

When Richard and I arrived, cleared the security checkpoint, and entered the visitation gallery, we placed the metal desks in a circle to encourage open dialogue. We planned to address all students by their first names. We would provide them personal journals and textbooks, and instead of serving up pat answers during a long lecture, we'd cultivate dialogue through open-ended questions. The crimes of the women who joined us would not be known or up for discussion, unless they themselves volunteered that information.

It all sounded wonderful ... until that first awkward class.

While I was confident in my understanding of criminal law, I had never been responsible for leading an academic discussion, facilitating critical thinking, or even grading a paper. I had no idea how this would turn out. My chief worry was that the inside students would ignore every word out of my mouth once they learned I was a prosecutor, and the class might fail before it even began.

However, I soon discovered that each of the students, both inside and outside, had plenty of anxieties of their own.

Many of the inside students had not even graduated high school. To qualify for the LIFE Program, they had to earn their GED and pass an aptitude test. Nearly all of them were the first in their families to attend a college class, and for years they had been told they were worthless failures by abusive parents, spouses, and partners. Would they even be able to keep up with the traditional university students, for whom college classes were the norm? Furthermore, they didn't know how the traditional students would view them. Condemned by the criminal legal system and largely forgotten by society, they harbored feelings of insecurity and vulnerability. Would this be one more time when they were judged as lesser-than? Tiny flames of hope were lit by the offer of a free college education—prayers they prayed would not be extinguished..

As the outside students arrived at the prison, they also wrestled with fear. The fences, bars, and razor wire, the sheer dominating power of the institution, make an intimidating statement. These imposing walls exist not only to keep people who wear the label "prisoners" away from the rest of society, they block people on the outside from coming in to witness the ugly, dehumanizing work of state-sponsored, systemic vengeance. None of these college students had ever been to a prison or spoken to a person who was incarcerated, so they were nervous about meeting the inside students. One of our young scholars was so thoroughly shaken by the very appearance of the prison that he never even made it out of his car. He pulled right through the parking lot and headed straight back to the security and comfort of the Lipscomb campus. We'd have to catch up with him the following week, when he mustered the courage to come inside.

The outside students who made it into the prison passed through the security checkpoint. They were told to take off their belts and shoes and were ushered through a metal detector and patted down by a prison guard. For most of them, it was the first time being searched for contraband by a person wearing a badge. All they were allowed to bring in were their textbooks, a pen, driver's license, and car key. No purse, no cell phone, no money.

Unsettled by these initial impressions, they were then subjected to a 45-minute orientation video that played on the absolute worst stereotypes about people in prison. It cautioned against befriending inmates, as they were masters of deceit and manipulation and should never be trusted. Giving and receiving gifts was unacceptable. All physical contact, such as hugs, was prohibited between insiders and outsiders. Never give an inmate any personal contact information, the students were warned Never forget who the inmates are, what they have done, and what else they are capable of. The video went on to explain how outsiders should behave in the event of a hostage situation.

If these sheltered college kids weren't shaking in their boots upon arrival, they certainly were after this orientation. For all they knew, they were about to spend a semester sitting next to Hannibal Lecter.

Boy, did I have my work cut out for me.

While the Lipscomb kids were having their wits scared out of them, the fifteen inside students cautiously, quietly entered the visitation gallery all wearing the same blue prison-issued uniforms bearing the words, "Tennessee Department of Correction." They gratefully accepted their textbooks, Lipscomb University pens, and logoed folders and settled silently into their seats. One of them asked where their counterparts were so, because they had never seen it for themselves, I explained in detail the orientation video that was being shown to the outside students a few classrooms away. The inside students could not believe the dehumanizing caricature of people in prison, offensive to the point of being ridiculous.

Finally, the giant metal door slid open and in walked the fifteen wide-eyed outside students, looking like a group of frightened Urban Outfitters models. No one made eye contact or said a word. Some of the outside students looked like they expected to die there that night.

After everyone had settled into their seats, I took a deep breath. It was time to tell them who I was. "Hello, everybody," I began, hoping to sound confident. "My name is Preston Shipp, and I'm going to be leading our discussion. I work as a prosecutor in the Tennessee Attorney General's office." I tried not to wince as I said it.

I got a few surprised looks from the inside students, but nobody looked angry. In fact, they still seemed welcoming. Maybe they figured a prosecutor could help them learn about the criminal justice system as well as anybody. I was relieved that part was over and nobody had stormed out.

"I'm so excited to be here and am really looking forward to our conversations over the next few months," I said. "Now, before anyone passes out from nerves, let's all take a deep breath." If I expected even a snicker, I did not get it. "A whole lot of work has been done over the past year just to get us all together in this room, so let's just take a second to be thankful for the opportunity to be here this evening."

Still no response.

"Okay, maybe it would help if we go around the circle," I suggested, "and share what we are nervous about, what we're excited about, and what we hope to get out of this experience."

Nobody wanted to go first, and I felt like the walls were starting to close in like the trash compactor in *Star Wars*. The silence threatened to crush us. Had Richard Goode been too hasty in asking me to lead the class? He sat there, looking perfectly calm and content while I squirmed. My visions of intellectually stimulating conversation, thought-provoking questions, and energetic debate were fading. The success of this entire experiment required open dialogue, so if I couldn't get anyone to talk, we were sunk before we got started.

"Come on. Anybody. What are you anticipating? What's on your mind?"

"Well, I'll just say it," said a young woman in TDOC garb. Glancing around the circle, she said, "I'm afraid one of these Lipscomb kids is about to take me hostage."

The room erupted in laughter, thank God. A well-timed joke made a quick punchline of all the ways the system tries to dehumanize and demonize people who are incarcerated; to create fear and suspicion around them, as if they were monsters; to even make them question their own gifts, potential for good, and ability to succeed. It was exposed as bullshit. Our tendency to scapegoat the other was unmasked and the tension broken. We were already well on our way.

Incarceration Is Big Business

After we went around the circle to introduce ourselves and draft a class covenant—a set of principles that would guide our academic community—our class discussion that first week centered around the question I had been wrestling mightily with over the past year: What do we mean when we use the word "justice."

What does justice look like? If a person violates the law, what should be the consequences? Once a crime is committed, how is justice served? Does the state have the right to deliver punishment? Were current processes fair and ethical?

Most of the LIFE students, both insiders and outsiders, parroted the familiar refrain that justice is tantamount to punishment. Until the guilty are punished, justice is not served. The inside students were more mindful, of course, that the punishment should fit the crime and that excessive punishment is too often imposed. Everyone agreed, however, that justice for lawbreakers equaled punishment. When I asked about the relationship between justice and mercy, there was general agreement that they are essentially opposites.

"Is that right?" I asked. "So, in John, chapter 8, when the religious leaders bring to Jesus a woman caught in the act of adultery, and they ask Jesus whether she should be subject to the death penalty, justice would have been her receiving punishment?"

A few heads nodded.

"But instead," I asked, "Jesus showed her mercy, the opposite of justice?"

More heads nodded.

"So, this was an act of injustice on the part of Jesus?"

No response.

"And when the prophet longs for justice to roll down like mighty waters, he's talking about the death penalty?"

Confused looks.

We had a lot of ground to cover.

As we studied and discussed the judicial process, my own thoughts about the criminal legal system continued to evolve as a result of our class discussions. For example, never before had I contemplated the system's sheer size, reach, and overwhelming impact for real people, families, and communities. Over the past fifty years, unprecedented numbers of Americans have been swept up into the largest system of mass punishment in the history of the world. When I was born, in 1977, fewer than half a million people were held in federal and state prisons. Today, that number has climbed to almost two million. Another five million are on probation or parole, meaning 1 in every 31 U.S. adult residents is under the supervision of the American corrections system.[9]

In what sense can such a society meaningfully be called "the land of the free?"

Although the United States comprises around 5 percent of the global population, we currently incarcerate almost 25 percent of its prisoners. That is, one out of every four prisoners on Earth is caged in an American prison. We have the highest incarceration rate in the world—surpassing even China and Russia.

Where have we gone wrong?

Violent crime rates have actually trended downward over the past several decades. Despite the media's relentless focus on sensational crimes, our prisons aren't packed with violent perpetrators. Instead, they are filled with men, women, and youth caught up in the disastrous war on drugs.

Beginning in the 1980s under President Reagan, politicians and law enforcement agencies shifted their focus to preventing narcotics use. Instead of promoting drug rehabilitation and counseling services to break cycles of addiction, they focused on mass arrests of illicit drug users. Conviction rates soared, but the flow of illegal drugs into the country only grew. In the words of Glenn Frey's song, "Smuggler's Blues" (which was incidentally also the title of an episode of *Miami Vice*), "They say they're going to stop it, but it doesn't go away. They move it through Miami, sell it in L.A." It was exceptional to see a drug kingpin successfully prosecuted. It was the low-hanging fruit of street-level dealers and users who, thanks to stiff "three strikes, you're out" sentencing laws, went to prison for life, often for possession of insignificant amounts of marijuana.

Studies have repeatedly shown that people of all races use illegal drugs at approximately the same rate, but police departments center their interdiction on low-income, minority neighborhoods. And why not? Over and over, I have seen poor Black kids represented by public

---

[9] "Mass Incarceration Trends," The Sentencing Project, accessed February 26, 2024, https://www.sentencingproject.org/reports/mass-incarceration-trends/.

defenders plead guilty to drug charges before there's hardly been an opportunity to investigate the case, and white kids with well-off parents and high-priced lawyers who drag the case out until the prosecutor finally dismisses the charge. At every stage of the judicial process, Black people face tougher consequences than white people: They are more likely to be arrested for the same conduct; once arrested, they are more likely to be formally charged; once charged, they are more likely to be convicted; and once convicted, they are more likely to receive a sentence involving incarceration.[10]

As a result of this war on drugs, which is disproportionately a war against people of color, incarceration is big business. The U.S. annually spends approximately 80 billion dollars on the correctional system, shifting vital funds from education and health to keeping prisoners under lock and key.[11] Given that 800,000 people who are incarcerated serve as workers who contribute another $11 billion in goods and services, while earning only a few cents an hour, and it becomes clear why warehousing such a large segment of the American population is vital to the economy.[12]

Each year, private companies such as Core Civic (formerly Corrections Corporation of America) promote and profit from the lucrative prison-industrial complex. From 1990 to 2005, a new prison opened every ten days in this country. Privately owned prison companies secure government contracts to construct and staff prisons, complete with guarantees from the state that the beds in their facilities will be filled with inmates. The companies then hire professional lobbyists to encourage lawmakers to pass crime bills with extreme sentences, putting more people in prison cells for longer periods of time, thereby maximizing their profits. Each

---

[10] "An Unjust Burden: The Disparate Treatment of Black Americans in the Criminal Justice System," Vera, accessed February 26, 2024, https://www.vera.org/downloads/publications/for-the-record-unjust-burden-racial-disparities.pdf.

[11] "The Hidden Cost of Incarceration," The Marshall Project, accessed February 26, 2024, https://www.themarshallproject.org/2019/12/17/the-hidden-cost-of-incarceration.

[12] "US prison workers produce $11bn worth of goods and services a year for pittance," *The Guardian*, accessed February 26, 2024, https://www.theguardian.com/us-news/2022/jun/15/us-prison-workers-low-wages-exploited.

person warehoused in a private prison represents tens of thousands of dollars in the pockets of shareholders.[13]

As Harmon Wray noted in *And the Criminals with Him*, "There are now so many politically powerful, corporate economic interests which profit from incarceration, that they drive and often determine criminal justice practice."[14]

This corrupt arrangement is so dysfunctional that my friend Rahim Buford noted, while reflecting on his 26-year incarceration, he was worth more to the Tennessee economy when he was locked up than when he was finally released.

These jaw-dropping but often obscured facts were staggering to the LIFE class.

From the Mouths of Broken People

My own justice paradigm was shifting like seismic plates. I had seven years of college education and a career as a state prosecutor, yet I had so much more to learn, much of it from the students in that room, who I quickly recognized as the true experts on the devastating effects of mass incarceration on individuals, families, and communities.

I heard about how a teenager was pressured to plead guilty and accept a life without parole sentence not because she was guilty but to save the life of her friend, whom the prosecutor was threatening with the death penalty. I heard from more than one woman about the pain of being condemned as a murderer when all they were trying to do was protect themselves and their children from an abusive partner. Hearing these stories from the women in my class impacted me in profound ways that reading court records never had.

---

[13] "Private Companies Producing with US Prison Labor In 2020: Prison Labor In The US, Part II," Corporate Accountability Lab, accessed February 26, 2024, https://corpaccountabilitylab.org/calblog/2020/8/5/private-companies-producing-with-us-prison-labor-in-2020-prison-labor-in-the-us-part-ii.

[14] Harmon Wray, "Punitive Justice v. Restorative Justice: A Meditation on the Spirit of Punishment and the Spirit of Healing" in *And the Criminals with Him: Essays in Honor of Will D. Campbell and All the Reconciled*, eds. Will D. Campbell and Richard C. Goode (Eugene, OR: Wipf and Stock, 2012), 217.

Telling the truth can be hard. Listening to and receiving the truth, especially when it subverts our preconceptions of how the world works, can be even more challenging. As the inside students grew in confidence and trust, they shared how the trauma of incarceration only compounded the trauma in the circumstances surrounding their crimes. Almost all of them had stories of poverty, addiction, and abusive relationships.

"Not to be rude or anything," said one of the traditional college students, "but is it really abuse that leads to criminal behavior? Not everybody who commits a crime has been abused."

"Show of hands," an insider fired back. "How many of us have been physically or sexually abused?"

Every inside student's hand went up.

One woman, whom I'll call Paula, later described how she and her paramour conspired to kill her violent husband. Paula pled guilty to murder and was sentenced to a minimum of twenty-five years in prison. Her children hated her for what she had done, and she went for years without hearing from them or her grandchildren.

A young woman I'll call Nicki, who had fled her violently abusive and deeply dysfunctional home, was convicted of murder and sentenced to life without the possibility of parole ... even though she hadn't fired the gun. She was with the wrong people in the wrong place at the wrong time, and her life would never be the same.

A third woman, Carolyn, was trapped in a cycle of abuse. When her husband tired of beating her, he abused her child, both physically and sexually. Carolyn was terrified of the man. Despite often pleading with him to stop his behavior, she knew contacting the police would only enrage him. It might even make things worse. When at last others reported the abuse in the home, the authorities charged and convicted Carolyn of being an accessory to the abuse of her child.

We heard story after story of lives ruined, hopes dashed, futures destroyed.

"They aren't excuses," someone stated. "Just the truth of where we come from."

The outside students and I listened quietly. The gravity and significance of the stories, and the trust these women were placing in us by sharing them, made silence the only appropriate response. All too often, the media offers only sensationalized, 30-second sound bytes with the worst details of a crime, which creates in our minds the image of inhuman monsters. Even the transcripts of trials that I reviewed every day, often consisting of hundreds upon hundreds of pages, did not paint a full picture. Juries don't hear about generational trauma; the impact of prior victimization, which can aggravate mental health issues; the hopelessness and despair of living in crushing poverty; and the ways people develop addictions when they self-medicate to numb themselves to the pain of these vicious cycles.

In the face of such corruption, suffering, and injustice, how did these young women keep going, keep hoping, keep investing themselves in a future they might not be able to see? How were they able to succeed in college while they were held captive by this broken system? They were separated from their families, unable to regularly participate in their children's education, celebrations, milestones, or to provide emotional and financial support.

Could this academic community serve as a demonstration plot not just of bringing together people from different worlds, not just of upholding the dignity of all people without regard to what they may have done, but of the healing that can take place when we name and confess the injustices we have allowed to persist?

These women taught us by sharing the heartbreaking details of their lives that there are many more factors that true justice should account for, many more questions that a truly just system would ask than solely what law was broken, who is responsible, and what will the punishment be?

Early in the semester, one of the women wouldn't speak up in class. She was meek, barely able to make eye contact. As weeks passed, she gradually started to emerge from the shadows. She began to make a few thoughtful comments. Finally, through tears she shared with us the sexual abuse she had suffered since she was a child. After class, she received hugs and affirmation from everyone in the class. She looked as though she had laid down a heavy burden. She found that speaking her truth did not bring shame or judgment, but freedom. She became increasingly confident, trusting that she had insightful thoughts that would benefit the whole class.

Every crime has a human context. None occurs in a vacuum. Yet juries rarely hear all the details that must be taken into account in order to discern a way to begin making right what has gone wrong.

It was beginning to seem to me that this was what justice should be about. The first duty of society involves a holistic understanding of the context in which crimes are committed, which will enable us to heal the people who were impacted.

I thought of my two young daughters, Lila Joy and Ruby Faith, so precious and beautiful. It hurt me to even imagine them going through the things these women had endured. Who was I to assume a position that had me passing judgment on others? After all, each and every one of us needs grace. As the great Baptist preacher, prison abolitionist, and Civil Rights leader Will Campbell put it when he was challenged by a friend to offer a concise summary of the gospel, "We're all bastards, but God loves us anyway."

The two groups in our class, the women who lived at the prison and the well-to-do college students, began to value and befriend one another. No hostages were taken—by either side—and the categories of good and bad, us and them, were being obliterated.

We were learning together in our demonstration plot that, despite all evidence to the contrary, we are all very much the same. We all possess the potential to move beyond our worst moment and achieve great good.

More Than We Bargained For

The fifteen inside students in that first class were full of surprises. Not only were they kind, compassionate, welcoming, and hospitable—even to a prosecutor—they were also all brilliant. Although many hadn't been to school in years, or to college ever, they recognized this opportunity from Lipscomb and made the most of it. Diligent and conscientious in their studies, they more than proved themselves up to the task by consistently outperforming the traditional students.

As time went by, the inside students blossomed. They told stories that made us all laugh out loud, stories that made us cry, and stories that made us reevaluate the assumptions and prejudices on which our old justice paradigms rested. Each person was uniquely gifted in ways that our system of mass incarceration never accounted for.

One student named Sarah Bryant, who had been locked up since she was sixteen years old, was a profoundly talented poet. Her words had a depth and richness that inspired everyone with whom she shared them. One of the LIFE volunteers had a connection to Nikki Giovanni, one of the most prominent, brilliant African American poets to emerge from the Black Arts and Black Power Movements that were influenced by the Civil Rights Movement, and shared Sarah's poetry with her. Ms. Giovanni was impressed. So much so that she traveled to the Tennessee Prison for Women to surprise Sarah and read their poetry together. For Sarah, it was a dream come true.

It wasn't just the women in the classes who were leaning into a future they might not otherwise have thought possible. Every Wednesday night the LIFE class was monitored by a prison guard. One female guard sensed that there was more happening here than in the typical prison program. She listened to class discussions. She bought a copy of one of the textbooks. Eventually, she mustered enough courage to shyly approach Richard Goode and ask if there might be a place for her in the program.

"Is there room for me? Could I belong?"

These are some of the most persistent questions that we carry with us in a society built on competition, exclusion, and other-ing.

As Franciscan sister Nancy Schreck shows us, these are questions to which the gospel speaks:

> The starting place is Jesus' vision of and commitment to the inclusive love of God that welcomes all to the one table and creates a worldview that critiques any kind of exclusion. ... True community creates an aversion to the roots of violence which define another person as "other," that is, as outside the circle of care. ... Jesus always found those who had been pushed outside the circle of care and invited them back into the community. ... [N]o one is outside the circle of well-being.[15]

Of course there was room for this guard. I could attest that there is always room for one more in the beloved community, even for one who was once antagonistic to the community.

[15] Nancy Schreck, "The Faithful Nonviolence of Jesus," in *From Violence to Wholeness*, eds. Ken Butigan and Patricia Bruno (Las Vegas, NV: Pace e Bene Franciscan Nonviolence Center, 1999), 54–55.

Beloved Community is an acknowledgment that the only way for a peace to ever be sustainable, the only way that our people can always be safe, is if all people are free [including the] people who work in the very systems that are destroying our communities.[16]

Therefore, to our cohort of fifteen traditional college undergrads and fifteen inmates, we added one prison guard who had the audacity to ask whether the good news the LIFE Program offered was also available to her. After completing several LIFE classes, she left her position as a guard and started her own company baking gourmet cupcakes.

Together, we were learning to believe the good news that beloved community is possible.

Caught Off Guard

As profoundly as the LIFE Program impacted the women and even a few of the guards, in many ways it was the outsiders, the traditional students and instructors, who were challenged the most.

Dr. Paul Prill was another of my old college professors and mentors. He taught speech and communications classes, and as a former hippie, his anti-establishment views and radical approach to Christian discipleship set him apart among the very conservative university faculty. I loved Dr. Prill because he taught me when I was a very young man to be willing to question allegiances that I might otherwise deem to be beyond scrutiny. Sherisse loved Dr. Prill as well, so it made perfect sense for him to perform our wedding ceremony. Knowing gospel when he saw it, he also volunteered to teach in the LIFE Program.

One night Dr. Prill and I bumped into each other at a concert, and he told me to sit next to him for a minute. Without any hint or preview as to what he wanted to discuss, he said, "How do you do it every week?"

"What's that?" I asked.

"Leave the prison."

I was quiet, inviting him to say more.

---

[16] Kazu Haga, *Healing Resistance: A Radically Different Response to Harm* (Berkeley, CA: Parallax Press, 2020), 106–08.

"How do we go out there, week after week, have class, connect with these incredible people, encountering their brilliance, and then just walk away and go home and go to bed? How do we leave them there, locked away in cells, all their gifts and potential just being wasted? How do we live out here knowing they are living in there?"

Dr. Prill had been caught off guard by the beauty he found in the people who live behind prison walls and the tragedy of knowing they do not deserve to be despised and forgotten.

I didn't know how to answer Dr. Prill then. Now I'm close to fifteen years removed from that conversation, and his question is still with me. In some ways, it has been a defining question for my life ever since. I think if I could go back in time, I'd tell him that we don't just go on living our lives out here. We don't just walk away and go home and go to bed and wait for the next time to visit. Proximity to people who are incarcerated should change us and the way we live. We start taking the prison home with us. We find ways to be more connected to our friends who are locked up, such as by exchanging letters and calls. We read books by people who have been incarcerated to better understand the impact prison has on individuals, their families, and their communities. When we have the opportunity to speak on their behalf, such as when they come up for parole review, we advocate for them. And we invite others to join us.

One Wednesday night I invited a family friend who served as a criminal court judge to join us as a guest lecturer on the topic of sentencing. All the students were grateful and excited to get to meet and talk with an actual judge. For most of them, the only interaction they had ever had with a judge was to stand in disgrace while one labeled, condemned, and discarded them based on their worst moment. This interaction was going to be a lot different.

It started when the judge said that he tried to treat all the "criminals" who enter his courtroom with respect.

"Excuse me, your honor," said one of the inside students as she raised her hand to register her objection. "Every person in your courtroom who is charged with an offense is entitled to a presumption of innocence. They shouldn't be regarded as a 'criminal' until the prosecution has proven their guilt beyond a reasonable doubt."

The judge was taken aback.

"You're exactly right," he conceded. "They shouldn't be called criminals if they haven't yet been proven guilty. I was too quick to apply that label."

Another of the inside students challenged the fairness of the process by which people are crowded into prisons. The judge replied that first-time offenders are seldom sent to prison. Only after less restrictive measures have been tried and failed does a person end up serving serious time.

"Show of hands," the insider demanded. "How many in this class were first-time offenders?"

The majority of the inside students raised their hands.

Again, the judge's mouth fell open.

Our legal expert was getting an education. I knew the feeling.

Feeling empowered, one of the women asked him how often he visited prisons to see for himself what things were like in the place he sent people to allegedly pay their debt to society. He was forced to admit this was his first time stepping foot in a prison in quite a few years.

"Don't you think it would be a good idea to do so more often?"

He nodded. "Yes, it would."

After class, the judge and I passed through the checkpoint on our way out to the parking lot. The last remnants of daylight were slipping away. I wondered about his thoughts after the reception he had received. When I had invited him to join us, I hadn't intended to lead him into such a minefield.

"Those are some remarkable women in there," the judge told me. "They certainly gave me more than I bargained for."

"You and me both," I said. "Believe it or not, they started off shy a few weeks ago."

"Well, they've found their voices now, haven't they?"

The judge wanted to know what we had been studying. I gave him a copy of Howard Zehr's *Changing Lenses*, which was my trusty companion on this journey. As a preview, I told him that real justice demands that we ask better questions than how we punish people who break laws. Justice is about healing, not hurting. He thanked me and promised to read it.

Inspired, the judge did the unexpected. He invested passionately in an alternative restorative-justice-based court, which offered drug offenders an intensive two-year addiction recovery program—including treatment, counseling, and job training—in lieu of traditional punitive sentences. The recovery court program aims to help folks get back on their feet, not push them further down. Colloquially known as drug court, the program has been a resounding success, with approximately 70 percent of its graduates remaining arrest-free.

The judge liked our demonstration plot and decided to start one of his own.

Tearing Down a Mighty Big Wall

Our Judicial Process course, I quickly realized, was like a picture frame that gave structure and context to a work of art. The frame, although important, is never the focus. The art—the real point of the class—was forging relationships across the boundaries, both physical and social, that prison creates. We could easily have been studying literature or history or anything else. The subject matter was not the primary concern. The real work, the *telos*, was gathering outside students and inside students in the same space. Richard's goal all along was to use academics to promote reconciliation and community. As we studied Judicial Process, we were learning that the distinctions and divisions between us were largely artificial and capable of being healed and transcended. In the words of another instructor in the program, "It's not what you know, it's who you know it with."

The relationships formed during these Wednesday night meetings were more important than the coursework. Although the two groups of students occupied vastly different worlds—separated by literal walls, fencing, and razor wire—these distinctions and divisions were now recognized as artificial.

During break times, we chatted and laughed together, found out that we watched the same TV shows and listened to the same music. We all faced fears, harbored insecurities, and carried deep love for our families. We had dreams for our futures. We were the same.

Unjust systems thrive when we believe there is a legitimate chasm between people often deemed "normal" and those the system has institutionalized and excluded. The good news is that we are invited to stand in that gap. This is the vision of beloved community. Dividing walls, stereotypes, fear ... they can all fall.

Through the LIFE Program, Richard Goode used academics to create a place where the dividing lines no longer meant so much, and he was pleased to see the seeds he had sown beginning to bear fruit. He was tearing down a mighty big wall.

As the years have passed, some of the outside students have gone on to get law degrees and are now practicing criminal defense attorneys. Many of the inside students, having earned an associate's or bachelor's degree, have proven they deserve a second chance and have been released.

I think I have learned more than anyone, and I wonder if that was Richard's goal all along in asking me to teach. My 2006 meeting over coffee with Richard was the point at which my faith and my career first collided. I had been seeking a more authentic practice of the Christian faith. To get there, I was going to need to scrutinize my career as an advocate for retribution in the same way as I had the religious teachings I had received. Until this point, I had firmly believed in the system and thought that because it was inherently just, so was I. Now its glaring faults and inconsistencies, as well as the inadequacy of our definition of justice, were in focus. After making friends with the women in our class, I saw the system as a broken assembly line, and I came to regret the work I was called upon to do as an agent of retribution. By inviting me out to coffee to discuss his dream of the LIFE Program, Richard had opened the door to the next challenging phase of my journey.

How was I going to write another brief? How could I continue to labor in a system I no longer believed in, making arguments about the fate of people I didn't know, supporting the machine that discriminates against people of color from the point of arrest through sentencing, and that destroys people's lives under the rubric of "Correction?"

At every step, I felt I was betraying my new friends. Not only that, I was betraying the best ideals of my faith—mercy, forgiveness, redemption, and second chances. I no longer wanted to go to work at the Attorney General's Office. I didn't want to write any more briefs or make any more arguments. There was a whole world out there where justice focused on healing harm and reconciling relationships, but I was stuck in a world in which these are alien concepts.

Why, after all I knew about Jesus of Nazareth, would I cast the first stone?

Knowing that Jesus identified himself with prisoners and was tried and condemned as a criminal, why would I align myself against people who were of special concern to him?

Why did I ever dream of working in a system that goes out of its way to rob people of their dignity and personhood, a system that knows only how to punish, never heal, a system that was crushing people who I had come to regard as members of my community?

Every day I felt more and more like an imposter. I no longer believed in the work I once dreamed of doing. Meetings with my colleagues were increasingly uncomfortable, as I no longer shared their common faith in a system of retribution, but I didn't dare share any of this with them. They still believed they were wearing the white hats, but I had experienced something they never had—friendship with people who were in prison.

Standing in our kitchen, Sherisse and I talked about the conflict I was feeling.

"Maybe I should go work for the public defender's office," I said.

"Would it make you any happier?" she asked.

I didn't know.

"Instead of complaining so much I might feel like I was part of the solution."

As she got Lila Joy, our now three-year-old, and our brand-new baby girl Ruby Faith ready for bed, these issues weighed on her as much as they did me. This was our life, and she saw I needed a change. But what could be done? We had two little girls, bills to pay, and all I knew how to be was a criminal prosecutor. Now didn't seem like the time for any life-altering decisions.

Ironically, this nondecision, and a case I would work on the next year, would alter my life forever.

Part Two

Restoration:
Right Relationship

Chapter 4

Compassion Through Proximity

The end of the Judicial Process class marked the conclusion of one of the most meaningful periods of my life. By any measure, it was a great success. Yet it left me in a crisis of faith and career. I dragged myself into the Tennessee Attorney General's Office every day for the next year, wondering what on earth I was doing, how I had managed to get my career so wrong. Everything I thought I wanted to be and do was being turned upside down. Whereas before I believed I was seeing to it that justice was done, now I saw myself as an obstacle to it, my written briefs and oral arguments choking any possibility of true justice being done.

I was a worker on an assembly line that I had discovered was producing unsafe cars. I was expected to carry out my limited part of the process without ever asking about the integrity of the final product. A year earlier I was certain I had nothing to apologize for, as I trusted the process. "It's the best system in the world," we like to think. Now, having learned so much from the LIFE class, the readings and conversations, I realized I was part of a massive, faceless, unjust system for which no single actor feels responsible. I didn't know what I could do to bring about even modest change. If I tried to object by claiming the outcome of a case was unfair or a convicted person needed rehabilitative programming instead of prison time, the case would simply be reassigned to another attorney who would argue that the outcome of the case was proper. I was only responsible for tightening one small bolt on the assembly line, and if I didn't do it, someone else would.

The compassion that had been cultivated through my recent proximity to people who were incarcerated now altered everything. My involvement in church prison ministry and the LIFE Program put me in regular contact with people who were caged, and the parameters of my sense of concern and even kinship had expanded to include them.

They were not the monsters that the media often portrays them as. Quite the opposite.

I contemplated all that I had learned in the Judicial Process class, which was for me a Damascus Road moment, to invoke the life-changing experience of the apostle Paul set forth in Acts, chapter 9. Like Paul, I felt a force beyond my understanding had knocked me on my ass and demanded "Why are you persecuting me?" Like Paul after his conversion experience, I felt a pull to spend a few days away, being quiet, seeking to refocus.

For years I had talked with my dear friend Jeff McInturff about visiting a monastery in rural Kentucky for a silent retreat. Jeff was one of my best friends at church, and we had known each other since college. We were both at a point in our lives where we felt the need to dig deeper into our faith, so we agreed to spend a weekend at a beautiful Trappist monastery called the Abbey of Gethsemani about three hours from Nashville.

The monks at Gethsemani pray the Psalms together seven times a day, beginning at 3:15 in the morning. I slowly learned the cadence and rhythm of their unison chants, and I reflected on the truth that all of us are in need of grace. The women at the prison had extended grace to me by welcoming me, a prosecutor, into their community and trusting that I was more than the label I wore. How many times had I needed a second chance? And a third? And a fourth? All the way "up to seventy times seven."

As I walked deep in the woods that encircled the monastery, I contemplated the significance of mercy and forgiveness. The prodigal son in Luke 15 returned home in shame to beg his father for a second chance, but when his father saw him a long way off, he didn't even let the young man finish making his request. He interrupted his apology with hugs and kisses and lavished him with a second chance beyond anything the son could ever have asked for or imagined.

While I meditated on the many statues situated around the monastery grounds, I was reminded of the woman caught in adultery in John 8, who was legally subject to the death penalty. Jesus, however, sent all her accusers away so that he could give her a second chance, free from condemnation and violence.

My time at the monastery reinforced in my mind and heart that divine justice, according to Jesus of Nazareth, centers around second chances, redemption, and transformation. This is the kingdom and economy of God, which we are told is like a treasure hidden in a field, waiting to be found and enjoyed.

I saw no way I could continue laboring in a field that could not and would not produce good fruit. How could I go back to my job as a prosecutor?

On the other hand, I was in no position to walk away from my livelihood. Like Paul, I asked, "Lord, what do you want me to do?"

I left the monastery with strong convictions but no easy answers. The tension increased as my views of the gospel and justice evolved and expanded. Every case I handled stretched me further toward my breaking point. I remember one case in particular in which a man sold less than .5 grams of cocaine to a confidential police informant just inside a school zone. He hurt no one. But based on his criminal history, which consisted of a handful of convictions for drug possession and property crimes, and the location of the transaction, he received a sentence of 12 years in prison. Twelve long years for selling a tiny amount of a substance that was once included in Coca-Cola.

I had charted this path for myself from my boyhood days watching *Miami Vice*, when I thought putting drug dealers and other lawbreakers in prison would be so rewarding. Now it was my career, and my family depended on it. I had a significant amount of student loan debt as well. What was I to do when my chosen career was in conflict with my moral convictions? Was I supposed to walk away from my career, or betray my understanding of justice?

I felt a bit like the Gospel character Nicodemus, the religious leader who in John 3 who comes to speak with Jesus under cover of night. Nicodemus recognized good news when he saw it, and in Jesus he discerned God at work. Jesus, however, discerned that Nicodemus, accomplished and respected, might be holding on a little too tightly to things that would keep him from really experiencing the life Jesus offered.

"To see the kingdom of God, you must be born again," Jesus told him.

"How can someone be born when they are old? He can't enter his mother's womb a second time!" Nicodemus replied.

Sometimes we read this story and think Nicodemus was thick-headed and missed Jesus' metaphor completely. But I don't think so. Because I know a little bit of how Nicodemus may have been feeling in that moment when he got Jesus' point.

"It's too late, Jesus. I've invested in my education and training. I've worked hard for my career and accomplishments. My family depends on me. I can't start over now. You should have told me this when I was still in college. I could have declared a different major or not gone to law school. I'm sorry, but I can't do what you're telling me to do any more than I could literally be born again of my mother. It's just not possible."

Jesus, however, is relentless.

"The wind blows wherever it pleases," he replied to Nicodemus. "You hear it, but you don't know where it's coming from or where it's going. That's how it is with people who are born of the Spirit."

Like Nicodemus, I didn't know where this was going, but I finally did what I felt I was being called to do. In November of 2008, I walked into my deputy's office and quit my job as an Assistant Attorney General.

The Board of Professional Responsibility

Abandoning my career as a prosecutor was a difficult step to take. Sherisse and I had both devoted so much time, energy, and money for me to succeed in this career I had dreamed of, and now I was walking away from it. It was hard to not feel like a failure. My best laid plans had gone awry. Many of my former colleagues in the Attorney General's Office, who remembered how enthusiastic I had once been as a bright-eyed, up-and-coming prosecutor, seemed to think I was crazy. I suspected that a few family members and friends might have agreed.

At this point, however, it just seemed so clear to Sherisse and me that we were being called to something more, even if we couldn't see what.

With Sherisse pregnant with our third child, a boy we would name Levi, and plenty of bills to pay, I was grateful when a friend who was familiar with my situation let me know that the Tennessee Board of Professional Responsibility, which operates as an agency of the Tennessee Supreme Court, was looking to hire a lawyer to investigate allegations of unethical conduct by practicing attorneys. I dusted off my resume, went for an interview, and gladly accepted the position of Disciplinary Counsel.

On my first day, I was directed to a filing cabinet that contained about 200 pending ethics complaints against lawyers that I was responsible for investigating. If a complaint reflected a violation of the Rules of Professional Conduct, the ethics rules governing the legal profession, I could recommend professional sanctions ranging from private admonition to public censure to suspension or disbarment from the practice of law. Although I believed in holding lawyers accountable for the harm their unethical conduct caused to their clients and the legal profession, I still wondered if this was the right place for me. More than anything, I wanted to make a difference by bringing about change in the criminal legal system, change that would benefit the many people in prison I had come to regard as dear friends. That wasn't going to happen working in the field of legal ethics.

Sherisse and I agreed that I had to leave my career as a prosecutor, and I was very thankful to have found a new position that would meet my family's financial needs. My heart, however, was still in the world of criminal law. I had learned so much about our urgent needs for criminal justice reform, a shift in how we regard imprisoned people, and a new vision of justice that seeks healing, transformation, and reconciliation. I wanted to share what I had learned and be an effective catalyst for change. But how? I was desperate to make a difference for good in an attempt to counter the harm I had caused, but I didn't know where I could fit. I still felt lost.

The Only Condition of Happiness

When it comes to having spiritual experiences, Sherisse is far more sensitive than I. From the time she was a young girl, she has sensed in almost tangible ways the presence of God and even loved ones who have passed on. She is open to divine promptings that I don't really understand but neither do I question.

One brisk winter morning before sunrise, I had an experience of my own that was unlike anything that has happened before or since. As I lay in bed in that thin space between sleep and waking, a voice was in my mind, but it was not my voice. It was not audible; I didn't hear anything. It was not one of my usual thoughts or ideas, but it was not external to me. It was like a message had been implanted deep in my consciousness. The voice set in my brain four simple directives like pillars:

Wait.

Keep doing what you're doing.

It won't be long.

It will be clear as day.

All of a sudden, I was awake and fully aware that I had just received something very important. I didn't know what this experience was or where these words had come from, and lest people start to think I was coming unglued, I decided against telling anyone. Sherisse of all people would have understood, but for now I kept it to myself.

Nothing magical happened. There were no dramatic physical changes. My stress level didn't drop suddenly through the floor. My breath didn't flow more freely and, to my knowledge, my blood pressure didn't lower. I continued to get up every morning and spend my days investigating ethics complaints. My attitude and outlook, however, changed dramatically.

These four phrases gave me confidence and peace as I learned to trust that I was being carried by a current not of my making. I no longer felt like I had to figure out what I was being called to do and the steps I needed to take to get there. The current would take me where I needed to go. And most importantly, I had the profound sense that I was not going to have to do anything on my own.

Another Shot at LIFE (Keep Doing What You're Doing)

With the assurance I was on the right road, I worked diligently for the Board of Professional Responsibility, and I kept visiting the Turney

Center Prison through our church's prison ministry. My relationships with the men there grew deeper along with my understanding of the power of proximity. I tried to do away with the one-way street approach and incorporated open dialogue. As Richard Goode suggested, I no longer saw myself as taking Jesus into the prison, but going there to meet him.

Keep doing what you're doing. There were no other clear directions or landmarks. I had to simply trust the current.

All my old markers of success that were gain to me—education, career, titles, prestige—were becoming less and less important. I had to learn to let them go. I thought I had known God's will for my life, the direction I needed to take, and I blazed a trail and achieved my dream. Then I discovered I had gotten it all wrong. All there was left for me to do was wait.

Keep doing what I was doing.

Trust that it wouldn't be long and that it would be as clear as day when it was time for something new.

In January of 2009, Richard Goode again invited me to teach Judicial Process at the Tennessee Prison for Women to a new cohort of inside students. The LIFE Program was thriving, and the first cohort of students had completed six semesters of college classes. Their success had motivated other women to seek admission to the program.

I jumped at the chance. I was eager to say yes to any opportunity the current brought my way to seek and promote a justice that is transformative. I was so excited to finally be free to throw myself into every chance to make a positive difference because for so long I had only been compounding harm. I wanted this new phase in my life to matter. I reminded myself that as long as I waited and kept doing what I was doing, it would all be clear as day.

This time around, I did not feel so conflicted as when I taught my first course. When I introduced myself to the new students at the beginning of our first class, I was relieved to be able to say that I had served for years as a prosecutor but had left that position based largely on my experience with the first LIFE cohort. This is not to say my conscience was clean. I had made arguments in hundreds of cases, and people whose names I could not recall would be living with the consequences for years or even decades. I suspected that I would spend the rest of my life trying to atone for the ways that I had served as an agent of retribution against people I didn't even know. However, at least I had written my last brief and made my final argument. I was trying to turn the page and begin a new chapter. What better way to start than with another LIFE class? I anticipated another great academic experience during which we would think critically about the true meaning of justice, call the legitimacy of the adversarial system into question, explore the failings of a punitive and process-driven approach, and imagine creative and restorative alternatives that bring healing to both victim and offender.

Angels and Devils

One of the first opportunities I took to "say yes" to events that allowed me to share my experience as a prosecutor who had a conversion experience was when I presented at a small juvenile justice conference with Piper Kerman, author of the immensely successful *Orange Is the New Black*.

Piper is from the Boston area and spent thirteen months in a federal correctional facility for money-laundering. Since her release in 2005, she has written and spoken passionately about the crises of overincarceration of women in the United States. Nationally, the female prison population has rocketed over the past three decades. According to the ACLU, over 60 percent of these women have minor children and less than 20 percent are behind bars for violent conduct[1].

This was my first time meeting and listening to Piper. I'd left my position in the Tennessee Attorney General's Office and become an advocate for change, so many of the conference attendees did not know anything about my history as a prosecutor. Some, like Piper, had been incarcerated in the past or had loved ones behind bars and welcomed me as an ally.

Piper's presentation was on how to communicate effectively as an advocate with different audiences. She drew three circles on the

---

[1] "The First Step Act Is a Small Step for Incarcerated Women," American Civil Liberties Union, accessed February 22, 2023, https://www.aclu.org/news/prisoners-rights/first-step-act-small-step-incarcerated-women.

dry-erase board and wrote "Angels," "Devils," and "Neutral" above them. "Let's list the angels in our movement," Piper said. "These are the heroes, the people we can count on to support reform. These are our allies and friends."

"Family."

"Defense attorneys."

"The ACLU."

"That reporter at *The Nation*; she had my back."

Piper jotted down the answers in the Angels circle as they were called out. "Now what about the devils?" she asked. "Who are the people we are never going to convince to stand with us, the people we shouldn't even waste time trying to talk to?"

"Prosecutors," someone said, which was followed by groans of agreement.

That caused me to shift uncomfortably in my seat as I scanned the people in the room. I had certainly never thought of myself as a devil. I found the characterization pretty disturbing. All throughout my career, I had been trying to do the right thing as I understood it, but these people saw me as an enemy. How would they receive anything I had to say? I felt I had been reduced to a label, albeit one that I chose for myself, by people who did not yet know me.

Very much like I used to do to the people whose cases I worked on.

Regardless of how the crowd might react, I decided they deserved the truth. Full disclosure was my best option here.

Piper Kerman ended her session, and after a short break, it was my turn to address the small room of attendees.

I rose and began my session, "Unlikely Allies," by introducing myself and pointing to the "Devils" circle that was still on the board. "To tell you the truth, you may think I belong in this circle because I used to be a prosecutor."

There were audible gasps. I imagined they must be wondering why in the world was a prosecutor invited to be a speaker here? Folded arms and narrowed eyes dared me to go on. Tough crowd. I felt uneasy in that moment, even though I'd already faced the toughest crowd of all inside the women's prison.

My best strategy was to explain how justice is viewed from within the system. The more I could help this group understand where I had come from, how I had conceived of justice, what my priorities had been as a prosecutor, the better our chances of accomplishing great things together.

It's unusual for prosecutors and criminal justice reform advocates to come together in a spirit of cooperation instead of antagonism. However, if advocates understand the perspective of prosecutors, they may be able to persuade them to support reforms after all. I knew from experience that prosecutors are not devils. They care about victims and public safety, which are legitimate concerns. If we appeal to those values, we can show that many of the people who cause harm are themselves victims in need of our support, and that excessive sentences that do not address underlying problems make us less safe, not more.

"I'm relatively new to the work of criminal justice reform," I explained. "For years, I was a law-and-order, lock-'em-up-and-throw-away-the-key guy. But I changed my mind. And if change is possible for me, it's possible for others, and we can grow this movement for true justice."

Eleven years later, I'm still saying the same thing.

As Piper Kerman, the other presenters, and I addressed the conference attendees that day, I knew many listening could provide their own countless examples of our courts and prisons failing to meet the basic requirements of human decency. The justice system is often anything but a system that promotes true justice, leaving victims with unhealed trauma, unattended grief, and unanswered questions, and offenders feeling like victims themselves of an unfair, complex process that addresses only a symptom and not the deeper illnesses that produce crime.

"Being a prosecutor was my dream career," I told the crowd. "I thought I was doing exactly what I was supposed to be doing. I thought I was in the 'Angel' circle, even as I had a hand in locking up hundreds of people I did not know. The conversion in how I think about justice, the criminal legal system, and people who are incarcerated didn't happen overnight. So please don't give up on the people you may think of as your opponents. Adversaries can become allies."

After I concluded, the attendees of the conference were so gracious to me. They thanked me for being open to changing my mind and for being willing to share my story with them. They said it gave them hope that other people who were antagonistic to reform might also come around. I thanked them as well for being willing to welcome this "devil" who was trying to be an "angel." I had no idea the role they would later play in my life.

The Indignities Put upon People

The second cohort of LIFE students did not disappoint. Like their predecessors, they grew in confidence each week. Like all 2 million people warehoused in America's jails and prisons, they had been judged, condemned, labeled, and discarded. Yet they discovered they had profound value, dignity, insight, and ability. Their voices truly mattered. They made no excuses for the mistakes they had made or the harm they had caused. But they were not throwaway people, unfit to live in regular society. They were sweet and beautiful, with huge hearts and so much love to give.

Once again, they scored higher than the traditional college students on quizzes and papers.

A couple of the inside students immediately stood out, and they often sat next to each other. The more I got to know them, the more heartbroken I became at the injustices committed against them by family members, religious groups, law enforcement, and the courts.

Ashlee Sellars was funny and thoughtful. She was a leader whose words carried weight with both inside and outside students. I later learned she came from a background of severe abuse. When she fought back and called the cops on her abuser, they essentially took no action. Ashlee learned that she was very much on her own.

A few months later, Ashlee waited in a car while her friend burglarized a home. When the friend returned, he blurted out that he had killed the person who was inside. Ashlee didn't know what to do, but she didn't go to the police. Eventually they were both arrested, and at seventeen years old, she was threatened by the prosecutor with a sentence of life without the possibility of parole. With no family support, poor legal representation, and no knowledge of the judicial process, Ashlee pled guilty and received 25 years in prison.

She told us that she hated missing out on 25 years of memories with her sister and nieces and nephews. But for her, the hardest part of being locked up for so long at such a young age was the routine injustice, "the indignity that is put upon people and not being able to say or do anything about it."

Punishment Over Promise

Cyntoia Brown was equally intense, with wide dark eyes. At twenty-one, she was one of the brightest students in the class. She was a voracious reader, and her interests ranged from religion, philosophy, and psychology to history and cooking. For someone with this much excitement about education, our college program was a lifeline.

Cyntoia had an edge to her. Like her friend Ashlee, she felt betrayed by the system and distrusted authority figures. She was fiery and outspoken.

The first time one of our outside students mentioned God, Cyntoia's hand shot up. "Excuse me, but not everybody believes that. Some people think that ain't true." She glanced around, challenging the others to disagree with her.

As the weeks went by, and she found the LIFE Program to be a safe place for her, Cyntoia softened a bit. She continued to make our discussions more lively with keen intellect, quick wit, and strong opinions.

Although we didn't often discuss people's crimes in class, I knew there were several students who were serving life sentences for murder. Since Tennessee changed its sentencing scheme in 1995 as part of the draconian tough-on-crime era, a life sentence meant no opportunity for parole until after the person had served 51 years in prison, more than doubling the pre-1995 term of 25 years.

The General Assembly didn't analyze whether such a dramatic increase in the penalty benefited public safety, or whether it justified a corresponding, drastic increase in the cost associated with incarcerating a person for over half a century. If they had, they would have learned that such extreme prison sentences tend to make communities less safe, not more.

They might have been surprised to learn that people who commit crimes of violence routinely enjoy lower rates of recidivism upon release than people who commit nonviolence crimes. Violent crimes, such as murder, are typically committed by young people, and tend to be the product of a perfect storm of prior trauma, mental health issues, and a high-pressure, incendiary event that will never again occur. Youth who act violently are, like all kids, still developing in their ability to appreciate the consequences of their conduct, control their emotional impulses, and make rational decisions. As the frontal lobe of our brains becomes fully developed, we stop making the kinds of bone-headed decisions for which high school and college kids are notorious. As a result, young people, even those who commit harm, have profound potential to experience positive transformation. Those with life sentences often become model prisoners, quite capable of successfully reentering their communities upon release.

Ashlee, Cyntoia, and others in our class were clear examples of the dramatic change young people can experience as they invest in their own rehabilitation, through initiatives such as the LIFE Program. It was an honor and a joy to see them grow in confidence, to begin to realize their immense value and dignity, to claim their voices, and to lean into their futures.

The prosecutor in Cyntoia's case, however, wanted to ensure that she had no hope of a redeemed future. The way the prosecutor spoke about her and the way the media portrayed her only added to the significant trauma she had already endured at such a young age. By focusing only on imposing extreme punishment, the system had neglected the amazing promise that she had to transcend her worst moment and find creative ways to serve others.

Our inside students all believed the legal system had fallen short of achieving true justice in their cases, and our discussions and readings gave them the vocabulary to express their frustrations. We essentially spent a semester naming the myriad ways that the criminal legal system fails to produce justice and affirming that, while people must be held accountable for the harm they cause, institutionalized vengeance is no substitute for the healing and restoration that real justice seeks to bring about. Cyntoia was especially enthusiastic when it came to critiquing the current American justice system in order to envision something better.

One Wednesday night, I invited a victims' rights advocate to be our guest speaker. This speaker was very committed to harsh sentences as a form of vindication for the victims of violent crime. I imagine that for her, justice, punishment, and vengeance were basically synonyms. Like Cyntoia, she was not shy in her convictions, and she flatly told our inside students they were right where they belonged—behind bars, paying for their crimes.

Cyntoia was ready for a fight. "You know, the people who cause harm have almost always been victimized themselves. Why do you stop caring about them once they decide enough is enough?"

The victim's rights advocate seemed surprised by Cyntoia's keen insight, but not the least bit intimidated. It seemed like we could be a few breaths away from a shouting match.

"I know we may not all see eye to eye," I interjected. "But let's remember our class covenant to treat one another with respect as we learn together. Our goal is to hear all sides and create dialogue, not necessarily agree on every issue in one sitting."

The situation simmered down, but Cyntoia had a fire in her belly. She knew that the system was failing to produce healing for both victims and offenders.

She was both.

Easy Prey

Cyntoia had been locked up since she was sixteen years old, but her tragic story began before she was even born. Her mother was an addict who drank as much as a fifth of liquor a day throughout her pregnancy. As a result, Cyntoia suffered from fetal alcohol syndrome, which causes permanent mental, emotional, neurological, and behavioral issues. Cyntoia's health and well-being were sacrificed in utero to her mother's addiction.

As a small, helpless girl, Cyntoia's family continued to fail her. She was only two years old when her mother left her at a drug house so she could go elsewhere with friends to get high. Eventually another woman, recognizing that Cyntoia was all but abandoned, adopted her and attempted to provide her with a stable, loving home. Like many children who are victims of generational trauma, Cyntoia continued to struggle with her relationships, even with people who tried to help her. Although she was very bright, she had trouble in school.

As a young teenager, Cyntoia followed in her mother's footsteps by self-medicating her deep pain with drugs and alcohol. Despite her sharp mind, she dropped out of school, ran away from home, and ended up in a juvenile detention facility after living on the streets of Nashville.

Upon her release, she had nowhere to go—no family, no friends, no support, no home. She was easy prey for a child sex trafficker, and it wasn't long before a predator found and seduced her and convinced her she was his girlfriend. She lived with him in a cheap motel room, where they drank and did cocaine. She existed in a drug- and alcohol-induced haze as he abused her emotionally, physically, and sexually, and allowed others to do so as well.

At only sixteen, Cyntoia was a victim of sex trafficking—modern-day slavery. She was sacrificed again to the violence and perversion of sexual predators and the greed of a trafficker, who used the money she made to buy drugs and alcohol and pay for his motel room.

Cyntoia never seriously considered leaving. Like most traffickers, her supposed boyfriend threatened to find and kill her and her loved ones if she ever tried to escape. She had existed in a culture of violence from the time she was conceived, and violence now defined her only relationship.

One hot August afternoon, Cyntoia's trafficker sent her out onto the streets to make money. For protection, he gave her a small revolver to keep in her purse. She walked from the motel where they were staying to a nearby Sonic Drive-Thru. There a man well over twice her age offered to buy her dinner and intimated that he was interested in more.

He took Cyntoia to his house, where he showed her his gun collection and bragged about being an excellent marksman. Strung out on drugs and shaken from having been repeatedly assaulted over the past two weeks, Cyntoia was afraid of him. She believed he was going to hurt her. Eventually they ended up in the man's bed, but Cyntoia was convinced he was going to rape or even kill her. While his back was turned, she retrieved the pistol from her purse and shot him in the back of the head.

After stealing some money and a few of the weapons—she knew better than to return to the trafficker empty-handed—she fled the scene in the man's truck, used his cell phone to call 911, and went back to the motel room. The next day, the police arrived at motel and arrested Cyntoia for first-degree murder.

A Suitable Scapegoat

Cyntoia was a victim many times over long before she resorted to violence herself. At sixteen years old, she had been living in a hell that few of us can even imagine. Yet when the prosecutor, judge, and jurors looked at her, all they saw was a villain, a monster deserving of no compassion.

They didn't blame the mother who had victimized Cyntoia before she was born, the predator who enslaved her, or the lecherous degenerate who was willing to pay to have sex with a vulnerable child.

Cyntoia was condemned not just for the harm she caused but for all the evil she had endured since before she was born. In the Bible, a scapegoat was an animal on which all the sins of the community were symbolically placed before it was driven into the wilderness. In the same way, Cyntoia was banished from the society that failed her. She was like a mirror reflecting our society's worst untreated diseases: alcoholism and drug addiction, child abuse, untreated mental illness, failed educational and juvenile justice systems, rape, and modern-day slavery in the form of sex trafficking. However, when we—the prosecutors, jury members, judges, the whole alleged "justice" system—looked at her, we did not confess or repent for the ways we have let so many children slip through the cracks. Instead, we blamed her. We laid all the guilt and condemnation on a sixteen-year-old child and damned her to fifty-one years in a cage. It constituted a complete failure to imagine a better future, to trust in people's ability to change, to be faithful to the value of redemption.

By the time she enrolled in the LIFE Program, Cyntoia had already been in prison for five long years. Forty-six to go. While she was still a child, Cyntoia was thrown away as worthless, damned to spend the next half-century of her life attempting to atone for what she had done, which was only an extension of what had been done to her. She was sacrificed a final time to our retributive society's desire for vengeance.

True Justice Is ...

Rather than regard Ashlee Sellars or Cyntoia Brown as people in need of help, support, and community, the criminal legal system did further injury to them. It failed to see their crimes as symptoms of a sick society and made no attempt at healing them from years of poverty, addiction, and suffering at the hands of others. In fact, it compounded the harm by locking them in cages and cells where they would endure more of the same evils. The system lied and said they were the problem, had no regard for their potential to make positive change, and condemned them to suffer for many more decades.

If Lady Justice were tried as a neglectful, abusive parent, she would be found guilty. She should forfeit her deadly sword and be stripped of her self-righteous blindfold and be forced to see the terrible harm she is doing to millions of people like Ashlee and Cyntoia.

When the scales finally fell from my eyes, I was able to look at the inside students and see how profoundly gifted they were, how much they had to offer, not only within the context of the LIFE Program but outside prison walls. Over their years of incarceration, they had grown and matured and invested heavily in their own rehabilitation. Each of them had vast potential to do good and help others. They, like so many people hidden behind razor wire fencing and concrete, just needed an opportunity to prove it to someone.

I knew Cyntoia was a changed person. We exchanged books, shared jokes, and had side conversations about what she wanted to do with her life. She wanted to put her experience to work in service of others by helping at-risk youth avoid the tragic turns her life had taken. She was applying herself in the LIFE classes, as well as in other rehabilitative programs. Although she was serving a sentence of fifty-one years, she was nurturing hope that one day she would get a second chance.

After class, I was always tired. I had worked all day at the Board of Professional Responsibility, fought rush-hour traffic all the way across town, gone through the process of entering the prison, and led a three-hour discussion. I always looked forward to going home, hugging Sherisse, and hearing about Lila and Ruby's day. My friends, however, didn't get to go home after class. Although they had spent years in rehabilitative programming and shown themselves fully capable of succeeding on the outside, they didn't get to hug their families and relax on the couch. Every night, they went back to a cold cell, to guards barking orders and hundreds of rules and policies designed to strip them of their sense of dignity and humanity. I would wake up in my bed. They would awaken to another day of institutional slavery. The filthy, rotten system had not punished them enough yet.

There's a lot of talk about correction and rehabilitation, but where the rubber hits the road, it's a system that knows only how to punish. It has no regard for the great potential my amazing friends have to heal and transform into something wholesome and altogether different from their traumatic pasts.

The cases of people like Cyntoia made clear to me that the system's real goal is singular—vengeance. It exists to inflict suffering. That is not the first duty of society.

My friend Andrew Krinks—an educator, author, and social activist—has written, "true justice makes things right by remembering that all human beings are beloved by God."[2] True justice does not ignore human potential or violate human dignity. True justice does not treat abused children as hopeless and disposable. True justice does not compound trauma.

Our system of mass incarceration has not yet met a problem it can't make worse. It betrays our best values of compassion, healing, forgiveness, redemption, and second chances. It hurts instead of helps. Our society is neglecting its first duty.

Proximity Makes All the Difference

By late April of 2009, Sherisse had given birth to our son Levi, and the LIFE Program was approaching the end of another amazing semester. Becoming friends with people who were incarcerated was having a deeply transformative effect on me. Bryan Stevenson said it best: "Proximity to the condemned and incarcerated made the question of each person's humanity more urgent and meaningful, including my

---

[2] Andrew Krinks, "Why It Pays to Imprison: Unmasking the Prison-Industrial Complex," in *And the Criminals with Him: Essays in Honor of Will D. Campbell and All the Reconciled*, eds. Will D. Campbell and Richard C. Goode (Eugene, OR: Wipf and Stock, 2012), 217.

own."[3] I had come to realize that our system of laws and punishment fails to address the common underlying conditions that eventually manifest as criminal behavior, conditions that were present in the case of almost every inside student in the LIFE Program. Before, I had naively viewed crime as the problem and arrogantly assumed punishment was the solution.

This was too limited a view, too shortsighted a lens.

Proximity to an issue causes our vision to expand and our understanding to deepen. Proximity tears down walls. Proximity promotes empathy, compassion, and care.

My friendship with people like Ashlee Sellars, Cyntoia Brown, and others, who had endured years, even decades of separation from their families and community, helped me begin to understand that crime is not the result of one bad decision made by one bad person acting in a moral vacuum. No, the commission of a crime, particularly a violent crime, is at the bottom of a downward spiral, in which poverty and prior victimization swirl about with substance abuse and mental health issues, family members in prison, and lack of meaningful educational and employment opportunities.

At least I was no longer actively laboring in this death-dealing, dehumanizing system.

The Realization

Although I had left my career as a prosecutor in the Attorney General's Office several months earlier and had felt like a heavy weight had been lifted from my shoulders ever since, I received periodic reminders of the role I had once played in the criminal legal system.

Appellate courts often take months to first review the briefs of the parties and the record of the proceedings in the lower court and then render its written opinion. It's not always easy to get a panel of three judges to agree. Therefore, even after I left my position, I occasionally received copies of court opinions in cases when I had represented the state. When I walked to the mailbox one spring

---

[3] Bryan Stevenson, *Just Mercy: A Story of Justice and Redemption* (New York: One World, 2015), 12.

afternoon and found a thick envelope from the Tennessee Court of Criminal Appeals, it was no great surprise.

Standing on the curb, I tore open the envelope and began to read the decision to remind myself what this case was about and whether the court had ruled in my favor.

But I didn't even make it past the title of the case before I stopped cold. My jaw fell open, and I stared in disbelief at the defendant's name at the top of the page:

Cyntoia Denise Brown.

Chapter 5

A Vision Of Shalom

Cyntoia's name was there in black and white, but I had trouble processing the information. How could that be? Cyntoia was in my class. Then it all snapped into place in one terrible moment of realization: The Cyntoia Brown in my class was Cyntoia Denise Brown, the sixteen-year-old runaway who had killed Johnny Allen after he picked her up for sex, the victim of human trafficking who finally resorted to violence herself. I had been the prosecutor in the appeal of Cyntoia's case.

I had written the brief. I had argued that she was guilty of murder and deserved to spend the next fifty-one years of her life in prison. The details of the case and the issues she had raised flooded into my mind. I had argued that, although she was sixteen years old, she was properly tried as an adult. I had argued that a statement she made to her mother during a secretly recorded telephone call was properly used against her. I had argued that she deserved no mercy, but needed to spend the rest of her life in prison.

I was stunned. Paralyzed. I felt like I had been slapped in the face. I felt panicked and sick to my stomach. My argument had caused my friend to lose her appeal and her chance at a new trial. How in the world could this have happened? What had I done?

I stood at my mailbox, frozen in near disbelief. How had I forgotten this case? How, when I saw the LIFE class roster, did I not recognize Cyntoia's name? Somehow, although it was right in front of me the whole time, I had missed the connection. Never once had it occurred to me that this girl in my class—this witty, sarcastic, exceptional student—was the defendant in a case I worked on.

Cyntoia Denise Brown.

As the horrible realization exploded in my mind, I could see her name printed on the banker's box of records that I reviewed in my office in the John Sevier Building. How did I miss this? Why did I let this happen?

I slowly walked through my front yard to the porch, eyes still glued to the court opinion I was holding. I went inside the house in a daze. I braced myself on the kitchen counter, head spinning. Sherisse immediately saw something was wrong.

"Preston? What is it?"

I could hardly speak. I didn't know how to articulate the devastating news I had just received, devastating news that I helped create. The awful truth stuck in my throat. I was still struggling to grasp it all myself. I finally managed to tell Sherisse that this opinion was affirming the life sentence of one of the students in my class, and I had been the prosecutor on the appeal.

Sherisse was also stunned. We both stood there speechless, reeling from the impact this opinion had. When her words came, they were piercing.

"What are you going to say to Cyntoia?"

Today, maybe tomorrow, Cyntoia would get a call-out and go sign to receive her legal mail. She would nervously open the envelope, trying not to get her hopes up that the Court of Criminal Appeals would finally show her a shred of mercy and compassion, denied her for so long, and grant a new trial or a lesser sentence. She would read through the court's lengthy opinion and see that it denied her appeal, affirming the trial court's decision to keep her in a cage until she was at least sixty-seven years old. Her hopes would be dashed. And she would see my name listed right at the top as the prosecutor who had argued against her.

Preston Shipp, Assistant Attorney General.

A title that used to fill me with pride had become a source of shame. I was a hypocrite, a sham.

I had pretended to be an agent of justice, but all I had done was inflict more pain. I had aligned myself against a broken, traumatized child. I had gone along with a vengeful system that knows only how to hurt, never how to heal. I had judged and condemned people I had never even met. I was a bully.

I couldn't imagine the pain, the sense of betrayal that this would cause Cyntoia. Would she even show up for class on Wednesday night? Would she ever talk to me again? Would she curse me?

She had accepted me as a teacher and friend, not knowing the role I had played in her case. I had unknowingly betrayed her trust before I ever had it. I didn't see any way forward. The damage was done, and it was too great to repair.

The next Wednesday night, I nervously made my weekly trek to the prison. My stomach was in knots.

Would Cyntoia be there? What would she say? What would I?

I made it through the security checkpoint and walked alone across the prison yard. When I got to the hallway leading to our classroom, I saw Cyntoia. She seemed fine.

"Are you okay?" I cautiously asked.

"I'm fine," she said, smiling her usual smile. "How are you?"

She didn't know. She hadn't seen the opinion. My heart sank even lower. I was fully expecting a confrontation. Now what?

My mind raced. Should I be the one to tell her that her appeal had been denied? How could I then tell her that I had been the attorney for the state, arguing against her? I assumed she would be devastated. Should that happen here in the hallway in front of everyone, moments before our class? There wasn't time for this conversation. And I wasn't prepared for it. I just didn't have the words. I wasn't able to tell her.

I tried to keep it together for class, and afterward everyone said their usual goodbyes. I drove home full of regret, first for the role I had played in Cyntoia's case, and second for not knowing how to confess it to her. Now I had a week to dread the way I feared she would look at me the next time we met.

"What did she say?" Sherisse asked when I got home. "Were you able to talk with her?"

I shook my head. "She hadn't received the opinion yet. I didn't know how to tell her."

I had trouble sleeping over the next week. I kept wondering whether this was the day Cyntoia read the opinion, had her hope of a new trial dashed with the words, "the judgments of the trial court are affirmed." My work for the ethics board only highlighted what felt like my own gross misconduct. As a Christian and an attorney, I thought I had all the answers about what justice was and how it was accomplished. Everything fit nicely in its own compartment—faith, family, career—and it all made sense. How wrong I had been. While I hadn't done anything in violation of the ethics rules during my time as prosecutor, the scope of my moral failure, and the betrayal of my friends, felt profound.

I imagined Cyntoia alone in a cold cell slowly reading the 44-page opinion. What must it feel like to have hope snatched away? To be told that there was no merit to anything you had said and that all you deserved was fifty-one long years in prison? How do you get up the next day after receiving that kind of devastating news? Cyntoia was not the only one who had felt such terrible disappointment based on a court opinion in which I had served as the state's advocate. Hundreds of other people, people I didn't know, had received opinions denying them relief that had "Preston Shipp, Assistant Attorney General" at the top. I was ashamed.

Painfully Personal

Since my first coffee chat with Dr. Richard Goode years earlier, I had read dozens of books like *Changing Lenses*, *Just Mercy*, and *The New Jim Crow*, all of which I had used as textbooks, and had countless conversations with people who helped me see that what we call justice is merely institutionalized vengeance. I had walked away from the career I had dreamed of and committed myself to saying yes to every opportunity to stand in solidarity with people who were incarcerated. I believed I had done what I needed to do to be faithful to a vision of justice that is rooted in concern for the healing and well-being of all parties.

The part I played in the denial of Cyntoia's appeal was a horrible reminder that I would not be able to move on so easily.

I had a week to think about how in the world I could face her given this awful chasm between us.

Cyntoia Denise Brown.

In my mind I could still see her name written in black Sharpie on the banker's box in my office. I had read hundreds of pages of trial transcripts and exhibits without ever contemplating, "Who is this Cyntoia Denise Brown, whose life hangs in the balance? What was her life like? What does she need? Who could she be in five or ten years if she experienced love, healing, and support?"

I thought of the hundreds of other cases in which I had argued in favor of condemnation and punishment when compassion and concern might have made all the difference. I wondered, if I had the chance to get to know them, would I consider them friends, like the LIFE students? Would I root for them to get a second chance?

I was finally feeling the concrete harm the criminal legal system causes. The labels, the emphasis on process over people, and the hyper-technical criminal code that only legal professionals can decipher and that tends to obscure the human consequences of a system that seeks only to punish, never to repair what has been broken. I was confronted with the fact that I had been complicit in foreclosing on hope for a young girl who had already suffered so much.

Ministers of Reconciliation

In my studies and early experiences as a judicial clerk and practicing attorney, I approached crime as if it occurred in some kind of social vacuum in which a fully autonomous individual made a choice to break the law and incurred criminal liability. This was my understanding of crime.

While I don't want to diminish the significance of personal agency, many complex factors—such as economics, education, and mental health—create conditions in which crime can fester. Prosecutors and law enforcement officers aren't encouraged to consider the entire human context of a crime. As Zehr outlined in *Changing Lenses*, the system is designed to answer only three questions: what law was broken, who is responsible, and what will the punishment be? The *whys* of crime are far more complicated and messy.[1]

I am not attempting to excuse conduct that creates victims and damages communities. When people cause harm, they must be held accountable. However, accountability and the intentional infliction of more suffering are not synonymous. Our punitive system of mass

---

[1] Zehr, *Changing Lenses*, 237.

incarceration takes people away from their families and communities for years, even decades, weakening those important bonds. Even after the mythical debt to society is paid, discriminatory employment and housing policies leave people who were formerly incarcerated at such a disadvantage that it is almost impossible to thrive. This cycle of retribution must be interrupted by holding people accountable in ways that focus on their rehabilitative potential and lead to a better future. We need a vision of true justice that attempts to repair, not compound the harm.

After his profound experience with the risen Jesus on the road to Damascus, Saul was converted from his violence. He endured a period of blindness until a Christian by the name of Ananias, a member of the very group Saul had been prosecuting, was sent by God to lay hands on him. When Ananias did so, scales fell from Saul's eyes, and his vision was restored. His vision was renewed by spending time with the very people he had once persecuted. No longer did he pose a threat to them. He was no longer antagonistic toward them, and they even welcomed him as a member of their beloved community. He even took on a new title, Paul, leaving his old one behind.

In II Corinthians 5:17–18, Paul writes, "Therefore, if anyone is in Christ, the new creation has come: The old has gone, the new is here! All this from God, who reconciled us to himself through Christ and gave us the ministry of reconciliation."

I relate so much to Saul/Paul because the very people who I prosecuted helped me receive my sight and showed me how to become an advocate and an ally for true justice. I learned from my own Damascus Road moment that proximity is key to both conversion and reconciliation.

For Paul, the ministry of reconciliation is not optional, it is not one possible choice among many, and it certainly does not fit into a tidy little box, separate from other life compartments. The gospel as a ministry of reconciliation wasn't something I learned in church, despite sitting through countless sermons, devotionals, retreats, and camps. I didn't learn it in Christian schools either, even though I had seventeen years of daily Bible classes, quizzes, tests, and chapel services under my belt. No, this was a lesson I learned from people in prison. Their gift to me was a new, rich, beautiful understanding of what it means to be a Christian.

As handy as the old labels and categories can be for successfully navigating institutions and systems, the ministry of reconciliation demands that we let them pass away. Sitting with my friends in a circle in a LIFE classroom, I could no longer regard anyone from a merely "human point of view." I, a former prosecutor, had been loved and accepted by people for whom our society reserves some of its most demeaning labels. I so wanted to experience solidarity with them that I had left my career. Walls had crumbled. The ministry of reconciliation was feeling like a reality.

Yet I could not see how my betrayal of Cyntoia could be overcome. What was the meaning of reconciliation for us?

Her Past Had Followed Her

The next Wednesday finally rolled around. I got ready for work in silence and kissed Sherisse goodbye. She wished me luck and said she would be praying for me. I had trouble focusing on my work. All day I wondered what the moment would be like when I was face to face with Cyntoia. As I drove through the afternoon rush hour traffic to the prison, I kept rolling this all around in my mind. How have I come to the point that I am responsible for a friend getting a fifty-one-year prison sentence? Who am I? I was without answers as I soberly parked my car and approached the prison gates.

I silently made it through the security checkpoint, walked across the yard, and turned the corner to the long corridor leading to our classroom. I immediately saw Cyntoia standing alone in the hallway. The look on her face was clear. She knew. She had seen my name. In her hand she held her copy of the opinion.

I slowly, cautiously approached her, unsure of what was about to happen. "Cyntoia, I don't know what to say. I'm so sorry for the part I played in your case. I feel terrible."

Her eyes searched mine. "When did you know?" she asked.

"I didn't know until I got the opinion. I never made the connection. I worked on your case sometime last year. I had no idea who you were when the class started."

"But you knew last week, didn't you? That's why you were weird and asked me if I was okay."

"Yeah. I had just gotten the opinion. I thought you had, too. And then when I saw you hadn't, I didn't know what to do. I didn't know how to tell you. I'm so sorry."

"You don't need to feel sorry. You were doing your job."

"I never should have been in that job," I said quietly.

"I know. And now you're not. You recognized you were wrong and you quit. That counts for something. I was mad at first, but we didn't even know each other back then. It's okay."

I knew it wasn't, but it seemed like she was ready to be done with the conversation.

"I don't know what else to say, Cyntoia. I'm just so sorry."

Cyntoia said everything she could say. She showed me more grace than I could have ever asked for. In the face of such heartbreak and disappointment from having her appeal denied, compounded by the sense of betrayal she had to feel from the part I played in the case, she showed me compassion. In a moment that beautifully crystallized the wonderful person she is, Cyntoia didn't lash out at me in anger, although she had every right to hate me. She didn't curse me or call me a fraud or a hypocrite. She didn't bad-mouth me to others. Instead, Cyntoia began the process of reconciliation by listening to and accepting my apology for the pain I had caused her.

Reconciliation isn't easy, and it doesn't come fast or cheap. I had hurt Cyntoia, and that hurt had profound legal and personal consequences. I had a hand in making sure her fifty-one-year sentence was not overturned. Without her permission, I was in possession of terrible details about her life—where she had been, what she had endured, and what she had done. An enormous power imbalance existed between us, with her in TDOC denim and me able to walk out of the prison in a few hours. In a real sense, even though I had quit my job and she was a straight-A student, we remained prisoner and prosecutor, worldly designations that are not easily shed. It was like her crime had tracked her down, intruded into the haven of the LIFE classroom, and reopened old wounds that were finally starting to heal.

But Cyntoia had come too far to let anyone label, define, or diminish her.

Or me, for that matter.

She refused to see me as her enemy. She was not going to be reduced to the labels that had been put on her—murderer, monster, prostitute, defendant, or inmate. Neither was she going to reduce me to the label of prosecutor that I formerly wore. We were going to have to figure out how to go forward as Preston and Cyntoia, two people trying to live into the reality of reconciliation. The old things needed to pass away in order for there to be a new creation, a transformed relationship. That was going to take much more than one conversation.

We returned to the classroom and finished the semester, though it was not easy. I was plagued by guilt and regret for what I had done to Cyntoia and so many others, and Cyntoia's confidence was shaken. As the weeks wore on, we nervously found some equilibrium. We remembered how much we enjoyed our class discussions. However, there was still a wide gulf between us, and I knew I needed to try to address it in order to keep the process of reconciliation moving forward.

As our last class of the semester, we had a huge celebration. We ate delicious food, reflected on the remarkable academic journey we had been on for the past sixteen weeks, and enjoyed the relationships that had been forged. Maybe this was the time to address the need for healing in the relationship between Cyntoia and me, I thought.

I asked her if she would be willing to talk for a few minutes, and she said yes. We found a couple of seats away from the rest of the class where we could speak openly. We agreed that we had a long way to go to experience a reconciled relationship and that we needed to be honest about how we were feeling. She invited me to go first. I told her I was having a hard time reconciling the person I knew her to be—gifted, generous, kind, inspirational—with the crime she had committed or the life she had been trapped in at the time. She seemed relieved to hear that I recognized a huge difference in who she was now as opposed to who she had been in 2004 when the crime was committed.

"I'm not the person I was then," she said. I told her I knew that she had worked so hard to overcome everything that had happened in her past and to prove that what was written in the trial transcript and reported in the media was not really her.

"So many people judged me who never even knew me," she shared. "And then I found out that you judged me too."

Her words stung, but they needed to be said.

"I know. I'm very sorry."

I paused.

"I don't judge you now," I offered.

She smiled.

"Thank you. I don't judge you either."

Then she challenged me.

"Now you're going to have to help other people change their minds the way you changed yours."

I nodded and told her I understood. We agreed to correspond regularly in order to keep working on our relationship. Then we hugged and went back to the party.

I hadn't been sure she and I would ever be able to move beyond the human categories that pitted us against each other, but we had made it this far. In the economy of God, adversaries can become allies.

Three Dimensions of Shalom

Cyntoia and I, by no design of our own, became a demonstration plot for what we had been studying all semester and I had been learning for over three years—restorative justice. True justice. Or, as Cyntoia liked to write at the close of her letters, "Shalom." Most of us know *shalom* as a Hebrew word often translated as "peace," but Howard Zehr's writings helped me and my students to recognize its much broader scope. The Christian tradition is the soil in which I'm planted, but teachers from other traditions provide insight into what true justice, shalom, really entails. Because shalom implies a healthy community, the work of seeking true justice belongs to us all. It truly is the first duty of society.

This concept of shalom runs throughout the Bible. Although most often presented in a religious context, shalom should be the aspiration of all our institutions and systems. After all, if the first duty of society is justice, and if justice is best understood as right relationship, shalom should be the goal of every human endeavor.

Shalom is practical. It has an earthy grit to it. It has to do with things being as they should be, being all right in a number of dimensions.

According to Zehr, there are three dimensions of shalom. The first relates to physical conditions and circumstances, things made right though the lack of poverty, sickness, and war. Quite simply, people must be secure and have their needs met. The prophet Micah envisioned a day when everyone would sit, unafraid, under their own vine and fig tree. No lack, no want. If the needs of even one individual or family are neglected, the whole community is affected, and shalom is disrupted.

The second dimension of shalom is one of social connection, with people living in right relationship with one another, free of enmity even amid life's unavoidable conflicts. While conflict between individuals and groups is inevitable, shalom remains so long as all are committed to healed and healing relationships. Right relationship, however, cannot exist where there is gross inequality. As Zehr has warned, "Marked divisions in material conditions and in power which result in the impoverishment and oppression of some cannot exist with shalom, for shalom means the well-being of all in a society."[2]

The third dimension of shalom involves morals and ethics. Greed, dishonesty, and lack of concern for the common good frustrate shalom and poison community. Shalom requires a commitment to truth and concern for one's neighbors. Then society is fulfilling its obligation to promote true justice.

A New Sort of Toughness

Religion at its best promotes shalom. The divine purpose, we might say, is to usher in a vision of shalom, to set right that which is out of balance, to bring about wholeness—or holiness.

Ancient punishments were often drastic, as violations between individuals also disrupted harmony in the larger community. Although examples of retributive approaches to justice can be found in the Bible, from the beginning, it is clear that it is not ideal. Ultimately, Jesus rejects retribution in the Sermon on the Mount (Matthew 5:38-39): "You have heard that it was said, 'Eye for an

---

[2] Zehr, *Changing Lenses*, 133–35.

eye, tooth for a tooth.' But I tell you, do not resist an evil person. If someone strikes you on the right cheek, turn to him the other also."

This does not mean we ignore the wrongs done or fail to hold accountable the people who cause harm, disregard public safety, or trample the rights and needs of victims. The focus of true justice, however, should be on healing the victim and offender, making amends, repairing relationships, and restoring shalom.

The apostle Paul wrote in his letter to the Galatians that the law, with its prescribed punishments, was added because of transgressions—but it was never sufficient to produce shalom. Yet somehow our imaginations failed us, and we settled for punishment instead of the promise of reconciliation that transforms in the way that Cyntoia and I experienced.

Ironically, it is in the areas with highest church attendance that people most stubbornly cling to the notion that justice is synonymous with vengeance. Support for the death penalty is highest in the region of the country known as the Bible Belt, where you can't throw a rock without hitting a steeple, beneath which people confess as their Lord and Savior a man who was condemned as a criminal to the death penalty. How many sermons have you heard naming this contradiction?

Too often it is people who wear their faith on their sleeve who are most resistant to policies that leave room for redemption and second chances. All of us, especially people of faith, should catch a vision of true justice and, to borrow an image from Father Greg Boyle, expand the boundary of our sense of compassion and concern until no one exists outside of its circumference. We can do this by going to where the pain is, which for me was prisons.[3]

Cyntoia and I were committed to erasing the boundaries that had separated us to bear witness to shalom justice. It's not about being "soft on crime" or ignoring wrongs; it's about trying to heal them. Society had failed in its first duty in Cyntoia's case by focusing on punishment instead of restoration. Now it was up to us to embody in our relationship going forward a justice that heals and reconciles and mends what is broken.

---

[3] Greg Boyle, *Tattoos on the Heart: The Power of Boundless Compassion* (New York: Free Press, 2010), 223–24.

Reverse Mission

About a month after our end-of-the-semester celebration, I received in the mail another envelope, which was marked: *The Department of Corrections has neither inspected nor censored and is not responsible for the contents.* I was still committed to my fourfold path of wait, keep doing what you're doing, it won't be long, and it will be clear as day. Yet it was hard not to try to discern my next steps now that I had abandoned my career as a prosecutor and started to make my way out of the valley of my betrayal of Cyntoia. She and I had agreed at the party to correspond via letter as a way to continue the process of reconciliation, and I was the first one to write. I had shared many of my feelings with her about not knowing what I should be doing as a former prosecutor who wanted to work for change.

Now I stood again at my mailbox, tearing open another envelope. This one did not contain a court decision about Cyntoia, however, but my first letter from her. I slowly walked to my front door as I read:

Dear Preston,

It was so good to hear from you. ... Right now you may be uncertain on what exactly you will do, but I am certain it will come to you. ...

Preston, you are a very good teacher. ... You do a very good job, and you force people to think about things from every angle, and in that way you help to change a lot of stereotypes and prejudices. ... I think knowledge and wisdom is not always about knowing all the answers, but rather about forming questions and researching all those issues. All of the questions and all of the facts uncovered in your class all stemmed from one question: *Is our current judicial system fair?* That one little question lead[s] to more questions ...

I was learning that I could count on Cyntoia and my other friends in prison not only to be accepting, understanding, and encouraging but to provide me with wisdom to discern the direction of the current that was carrying us.

I first became involved in prison ministry and the LIFE Program because I wanted to be helpful. I wanted to serve in a meaningful way. I was inspired by the way my parents and Dr. Goode invested in the lives of people who were incarcerated, and I also wanted to help. But I was now convinced that my salvation was bound up with that of people like Cyntoia, people who were judged and discarded and hidden behind razor fences and thick concrete walls. They were helping me redefine salvation.

Overemphasizing the Negative

This may be where I lose some people. It can be difficult in our punitive culture to abandon the institutionalized vengeance that is the American system of mass incarceration and embrace responses to violence that are not rooted in simply inflicting more pain. We are talking here about a fundamental paradigm shift in how we think about the first duty of society, and that takes imagination and courage.

Our minds often go to worse-case scenarios, and some folks ask, "Should we just let everybody go free if they apologize?" Of course not, no restorative justice practitioner is so naive.

One of the most prominent proponents of restorative alternatives was South African Archbishop Desmond Tutu, who was awarded the Nobel Peace Prize for his leadership of the Truth and Reconciliation Commission in the aftermath of the brutal apartheid in his home country. Speaking to a reporter from *The New Yorker*, he said, "Retributive justice is largely Western. The African understanding is far more restorative—not so much to punish as to redress or restore a balance that has been knocked askew."[4]

Although I have not witnessed the atrocities Archbishop Tutu devoted his life to addressing, I have worked on cases involving terrible violence and suffering. Confronted with such shocking cruelty, it can be a challenge not to write offenders off as beyond the hope of redemption.

One case that continues to haunt me involved a man who disciplined his girlfriend's little boy by taping cans of food to his hands and making him stand with his nose against a wall and arms outstretched, a form of torture known as a "stress position." After

---

[4] Tina Rosenberg, "Recovering from Apartheid," *The New Yorker*, November 18, 1996, 86.

many minutes, the boy shook his hands until one of the cans came loose, which he then threw at the boyfriend. Enraged, the boyfriend grabbed the child and punched him in the stomach. The little boy doubled over and crumpled to the floor. The next day, the boy complained of severe stomach pain and intense thirst. He vomited repeatedly and finally had trouble walking. By the time his mother sought medical attention, it was too late. The little boy died at the hospital. The boyfriend struck with such force that it lacerated his spleen, which proved lethal.

What punishment could possibly be enough for such an abusive monster, who tortured and killed a defenseless child?

Then I remember that "monster" was himself once a defenseless child. What was it like for him growing up? What violence and trauma had he endured at the hands of an abusive father or boyfriend?

I think about what would have happened had that little boy not died. What would his life had been like if he had survived, only to endure more torture and abuse for another five or ten years? The trauma would have damaged him in ways he likely would not understand and from which he might never recover. Would any of us be surprised if he grew up and turned all that pain outward by becoming an abuser himself? Would we still feel compassion for him if he hurt someone else?

The knee-jerk response of seeking vengeance can keep us from asking these deeper, harder questions. As a former colleague at the Attorney General's Office once told me, "The easiest way to do the job is by overemphasizing the negative."

But this is not the way of shalom, Archbishop Tutu's kind of justice. To begin to make right what has gone so terribly wrong, we have to cultivate compassion and expand our capacity for concern for all parties. To do that, we must step back and ask better questions than what crime was committed and what the punishment will be.

I'll Accept Nothing Less

Heinous, shocking crimes like these tend to attract the most attention from the media. After all, the news-as-entertainment complex profits off the sensational. As disturbing as these stories are, the majority of people who are incarcerated are actually nonviolent offenders.

In 2010, Michelle Alexander stated that homicides account for less than one-half of 1 percent of federal prison population growth, whereas drug convictions are responsible for over 60 percent. From a public safety standpoint, the criminalization of drug use makes little sense. The annual total of all drug-related deaths, including overdoses and violence, is estimated at 21,000, far less than the nearly 100,000 alcohol-related deaths each year. And while white males are responsible for 78 percent of drunk-driving arrests, they face mostly misdemeanor charges, fines, suspended licenses, and community service.[5] Black males who are arrested for possessing small amounts of marijuana are frequently given prison time.

We devote vast resources to punishing nonviolent drug offenders—and we have become as addicted to punitive policies as any illicit drug user. We seem to think punishment is an appropriate response to every social issue. As the old saying goes, "if all you have is a hammer, everything looks like a nail." Therefore, when looking at crises like addiction, mental illness, poverty and homelessness, gun violence, and even abortion, we think punishment is a panacea.

We judge and condemn without discernment. Punishment is a reaction instead of a calculated response and is therefore not effective as a consequence. When we settle for mere punishment instead of an experience of true justice, what do we hope to gain in return?

Until I was proximate to people who were incarcerated, I felt removed from those who were victims of our system of vengeance, which is precisely how the system is designed. Once I became friends with them, however, and the perimeter of my sense of community expanded, I understood that the perceived distance was a failure of my own moral imagination. With Cyntoia, the failure was especially personal.

In his speeches, Martin Luther King, Jr., called those men who opposed racial justice "victims of spiritual and intellectual blindness. They knew not what they did."[6] This same blindness persists to this day, in me and our faith communities and our nation. We have lost sight of the prophetic vision of shalom and resorted instead to cages and electric chairs.

---

[5] Alexander, *The New Jim Crow*, 101.

[6] Martin Luther King, Jr., *Strength to Love* (San Francisco: Harper & Row, 1963), 30.

Having left my career as a prosecutor, I was committed to keeping that prophetic vision in my mind's eye while helping others do the same. I wanted to take all I had learned from my incarcerated friends and work for meaningful criminal justice reform. When I said yes to teaching that second cohort of LIFE students at the Tennessee Prison for Women, I assumed I was fulfilling the second of my four directives, "Keep doing what you are doing."

Things were certainly not yet "clear as day," but my experience with Cyntoia left me even more profoundly changed. I knew I needed to use my experience and knowledge of the machine's inner workings to reveal its flaws, dismantle its deadly motors, and spring its victims free. I wasn't certain how to go about this or if I would have any support from friends or colleagues, but I trusted that this was the work I was being given to do.

Cyntoia had helped me catch a vision of shalom that was too beautiful to resist and too important to ignore. I didn't know where it was going, but I knew I was in a current.

Chapter 6

From Pews to Death Row

My friends in prison were a tiny microcosm of a much larger community. Approximately 2 million people are imprisoned nationwide, with 200,000 serving life sentences. Approximately 2,500 men and women have been condemned to the death penalty. What could I possibly do in the face of those numbers? What difference could I make against such a behemoth? This was not David and Goliath. It felt like David against all the Philistines. I didn't even know where to begin.

A New Way of Thinking

After my resignation from the Tennessee Attorney General's Office and the ongoing process of reconciliation between Cyntoia and me, I knew I was embarking on a new road, and it continued to erode my faith in the steeples—the insanely wealthy but somehow also allegedly nonprofit institutions that David Woodard helped me see would be unrecognizable as church to early followers of Jesus. After all, there was something terribly wrong if I could be well-regarded, possibly even serve as a leader in church on Sundays, while simultaneously serving as a prosecutor, throwing stones at people I did not know, arguing every day against mercy and redemption. No one in church ever seemed to sense any conflict or tension in me talking and singing about forgiveness on Sunday but acting as accuser the rest of the week. Maybe that grace wasn't so amazing after all.

Church had failed me.

I was convinced that my old friend Hunter was right, that my faith didn't fit in a separate box from career, money, entertainment, relationships, hobbies, and so on. It impacted everything. As professor of religion and fellow LIFE Program instructor David Dark says, "There isn't a secular molecule in the universe." However, church didn't teach me that. Church is where I learned the art of compartmentalization.

I wasn't sure where I fit.

I was reminded again of Nicodemus. I wonder, when he came to visit with Jesus that night, whether he was feeling unsure of himself, of his place within the system. Although he held a respected position, Jesus had a way of disrupting the status quo. For my part, I knew how to do church, but it felt like a house of cards about to tumble. I, as I imagined Nicodemus had, had caught a glimpse of something better, and it had made the gospel come alive for me. Grace, mercy, forgiveness, and redemption were not just abstract theological concepts or lyrics to a praise song; Jesus' proclamation of release for captives was no longer hyper-spiritualized to the point of rendering it practically meaningless; and the command to visit our imprisoned sisters and brothers was not a suggestion that could be discarded in favor of breakfast with Santa. My experience of community with people who were incarcerated made the Christian faith *real*. However, I wasn't sure I could square it with the paradigm of church that I had been working with my whole life. I was hopeful that I wouldn't have to completely begin again.

Still in the habit of trying to forge my own path, I thought that I should try to make my church more what I thought church should be: focused on the counter-cultural, subversive teachings of Jesus of Nazareth, and committed to the work of peacemaking and shalom justice. I had attended a presentation a few months earlier at a Catholic church across town on the genocide in Darfur that was hosted by the congregation's social justice committee. This seemed like an excellent way to help people start thinking about where their faith intersected with real-life issues, so I attempted to start a Peace and Justice Ministry at my conservative church. It did not go well.

The congregational leaders had meeting after meeting during which I was interrogated like a defendant in one of my old cases about my motives for wanting to start such a ministry. One leader accused me of being a socialist. Another said I was trying to convert the congregation to a liberal agenda. It was abundantly clear that I was trying to jam a square peg into a round hole. Rich, complacent people don't like to talk about the people who are being crushed by the systems that have benefited them. One of my college Bible teachers used to compare big, rich, suburban churches to cruise ships. People are there to be entertained, not to serve. They want flashy worship services, fun camp experiences, and trunk-or-treats with bouncy houses in the church parking lot. I was hoping to turn the cruise ship into a rescue boat for people in need. Institutions don't work that way, even the ones that advertise themselves as "church."

As Sherisse and I navigated these waters, we had very open and honest discussions with Lila, Ruby, and Levi. Our kids were learning, as we were, that our faith commitments make certain demands of us, a faith that does not manifest itself in works of justice is dead, and the point of the Christian religion is not believing a set of abstract, manmade doctrines or going to a building adorned with a steeple on Sunday morning. Jesus asked to be followed, not sung to. And from his first sermon in his hometown synagogue to his final moments on the cross, he proclaimed freedom for captives. This was going to be our work, and soon that commitment would put me to another test.

Mutuality Is the Key

Once again, I blame Richard Goode. He seemed to intuit that if I was going to remain in the current, I was going to need trustworthy mentors who knew how to trust it. He introduced me to one of his own mentors, a minister, organizer, criminal justice reform advocate, and the most empowering individual I have ever met—Rev. Janet Wolf. Janet and Harmon Wray established the prison program at Vanderbilt Divinity School that Richard had used as a model for the LIFE Program. Janet is a peacemaker, an educator, and a pastor to many amazing advocates, including *The New Jim Crow* author Michelle Alexander and Naomi Tutu, daughter of South African anti-apartheid activist Archbishop Desmond Tutu. At Richard's suggestion, Janet and I met for coffee.

"You have quite a story," she told me, after learning the details of my conversion experience. "If there's hope for a prosecutor hell-bent on retribution, there's hope for everybody."

I had been reluctant to let too many people know my story, especially criminal justice reform advocates, because I didn't want them to think less of me. I wanted to focus on being an ally, not on having been an adversary. There was no judgment from Janet, however, only affirmation and encouragement. She helped me see that there was power, not shame, in being willing to confess the ways that I had been wrong. This is the significance of repentance. Janet also showed me that my story was still being written, and everything belonged.

"Your story can help people see what grace looks like in flesh." Janet said as we were served our coffee.

"I don't know," I replied. "I sure have found a lot of grace in unexpected places."

"And that's exactly what people need to hear. We're in the business of changing minds, whether we're preachers, professors, or protestors. We need people like you who aren't afraid to show what that looks like. A lot of people will never set foot in a prison. You have to tell them what you found there."

Janet spoke as a person with authority, and her words to me were a challenge, a comfort, and an affirmation. I was about to learn that she, like Richard, had a way of building you up before handing you a parachute and pushing you out of the airplane.

"The people you met in prison," she went on, "those are the folks Jesus identified with, the folks with their backs against a wall. And he expects us to be in solidarity with them too, like you've learned. We can either ignore that or we can be changed by it."

I listened in silence.

"People don't want to change, though. Change is hard. Change involves sacrifice. So instead of being in solidarity with people, we fall back on charity. Charity makes us feel good about ourselves while masking our complicity and cooperation with the very systems that perpetuate poverty and injustice."

I was seeing why Richard wanted me to hear from Janet.

"You can help people see that solidarity and change and repentance should be embraced, not avoided."

"I would love to be involved any way you think I can help," I replied.

She looked pleased. "Good. There's some people you need to meet."

"Where?" I asked.

"Death row."

An Authentic Partnership

Riverbend Maximum Security Institution is the flagship prison in the Tennessee Department of Correction. Situated on the northwest edge of Nashville, twenty buildings spread across 132 acres on a bluff at a literal bend in the Cumberland River. The facility was built to replace the hundred-year-old state penitentiary where *The Green Mile* was filmed. Riverbend is the location of Tennessee's death row, a maximum-security pod of cells located a short walk from the windowed chamber that houses the electric chair and the lethal-injection gurney. Currently, forty-six men are awaiting their state-sanctioned murder. Two of these men have been on death row since February 1983.

Is languishing on death row for three or four decades justice? Under these circumstances, is the death penalty any kind of deterrent whatsoever? Currently, twenty-three states have concluded that the death penalty does not have value as a deterrent and does not promote justice, so they've abolished it. But in my home state of Tennessee—colloquially referred to as the buckle of the Bible Belt, where, I kid you not, the official state book is the Bible—we stubbornly cling to state-sanctioned murder.

Before 1913, hanging was the state's standard method of capital punishment. There were no official records kept up to that point, but of the males whose names are recorded from 1916 to 1921, all eleven were executed by electrocution.

All of them were Black. Five were convicted of rape, in the days before DNA testing. We know that capital punishment is a racist practice, and for every ten people who have been executed in America, one has been proven innocent of the crime for which they were condemned to die. The prolife crowd should be outraged, but often they are the ones most reluctant to abandon this deeply flawed, cruel, and unusual practice.

I had been to Riverbend several times before, although never to the building that housed the men whom the state had condemned to die. Janet Wolf wanted me here, though she never actually told me why.

Passing through the metal detector, being patted down by a guard, having my hand stamped with a mark only seen under a black light, and going through multiple security checkpoints with gates slamming behind me were all familiar. Visiting death row, however, was not. I had changed so much in the way I thought about people who are incarcerated—and myself. But it's hard to shake the popular notion that the people who have been condemned to execution are "the worst of the worst."

It makes us more comfortable with our death-dealing systems to believe that the people it cages and murders are monsters. They are not us—they are *other*. We could never do such horrible things. We are the good guys. In our minds, we need to create distance from the people we determine are not worthy of the life God gave them, to build a protective wall between ourselves and those who would harm us.

I had been involved in prison work for a while, but death row was still outside my comfort. Maybe Janet knew I had another wall that needed to come down.

As she and I made our way through the security checkpoint and began the walk to the high side of Riverbend, which houses death row, we talked about the work she did there.

"Presence is always important," she said, "but it's only a beginning. What we're after is solidarity, and that requires mutuality. We have to acknowledge that everyone brings a gift. Everyone has something to teach, and everyone has something to learn. We don't do ministry *to* the incarcerated; we do it *with* them."

As we entered the small room where our conversation would take place, I was full of anticipation to see what Janet had in mind. We were soon joined by Rev. Jeannie Alexander, the prison's head chaplain. Jeannie is a minister in combat boots. She has been arrested multiple times for her work opposing the for-profit prison industry. She's taught philosophy, ethics, and religion; holds a master's degree in religious studies; and has an impressive canvas of tattoos.

As the men from death-row came trickling into the enclosed space, Janet and Jeannie showed no hints of the nervousness I tried to hide. The men wore white, almost like hospital scrubs, their denim pants bearing the words Tennessee Department of Corrections down each leg. I tried to appear at ease, shaking hands and introducing myself. Eventually, a dozen or so were seated around the room.

Janet was very egalitarian. She didn't presume to lead, and was happy to let the guys set the agenda. These individuals had shown up of their own volition, and eliminating any sort of distance between us was her goal.

One of the men was the facilitator for the day, and he invited us to go around the room and state our name and how we were entering the space. When it was my turn, I said that I was Preston Shipp, and that I was grateful. I probably should have admitted to being nervous.

At the end of the introductions, since I was the guest, I was invited to give more details as to why I was there. I still wasn't entirely sure myself, but I figured I needed to say something more than, "Because Sister Janet told me to come." I suspected that she thought the guys would enjoy hearing about a prosecutor who had changed his mind, so I took a deep breath and started to share my story with a group of men who had been sentenced to death by the system I had once been so happy to serve.

Date with Destiny

Anybody who knows me quickly learns I am a big fan of *Star Wars*. I was born the year the original film came out, and its mythology has always resonated with me. As I addressed these condemned men, confessing my complicity in the system that had banished them and stating my commitment to seek and promote a justice that heals and restores, I felt a bit like young Anakin Skywalker when he went before the Jedi Council for an evaluation of whether he should be allowed to join their work. These men, like a group of wise elders, seemed to be weighing and testing my words, my tone, my body language, and my willingness to meet their eyes. But I didn't feel like I was being judged in a negative way. It was more like coaches sizing up a potential player. It felt like people who knew what's what, looking to see what I was made of.

If I were going to change people's hearts and minds, as Janet said, if I was going to be a credible messenger of the good news of a justice that doesn't compound harm, it would start here. Would this circle of men perceive me as authentic? Genuine? Humble? As an ally?

Would they think I had something of value to contribute? Or would they think I was blowing smoke? On an ego trip? Someone suffering from a white savior complex? They can smell BS a mile away. These elders can't be fooled.

Their collective wisdom was rooted in stark reality. Here within these walls, they were the longest standing citizens of the Riverbend population, the ones who provided stability, while those who cycled in and out were more volatile. In fact, as I learned from Janet and Jeannie, many of these men had studied and been certified in mediation and conflict resolution. They were the prison's peacemakers. They wanted their lives, which the state of Tennessee had determined they did not deserve to retain, to count for something profoundly good.

The strength of their moral character cannot be overstated.

For twenty-three hours a day, each of these men was locked alone in a stark six-by-ten-foot cell. Their view of the larger world came through a three-inch wide, thirty-six-inch high sliver of a window. Although they could see the grass of the prison yard, they might never again be able to touch it. For one hour a day, they were moved from their cells of isolation to a ten-by-ten-foot wire cage that provided no direct view of the overhead sky. They could only eat, sleep, and shower when told, and so much of their time was spent being shackled and unshackled. Yet their wills were solid as a rock.

It was humbling to gaze around the room. One of the men was in his sixties, with a long beard that was almost completely white. One of the men wore a white *Taqiyah*, a short skullcap worn by Muslim men. These were true elders, not the old white businessmen with clean records, big houses, and lucrative careers who are always asked by the steeples to serve as congregational leaders.

It finally dawned on me that Janet had invited me to death row just as much to have these men share with me as for me to share my story with them. She knew I needed them to lay eyes on me, to affirm my testimony and impart wisdom to me.

The Face of the Other

It was an honor to be welcomed in this room, to have these discerning men listen to what I said. I wanted to be engaging and share my journey in a way that they would find compelling and helpful. At one point, I noted how, despite all the external signs to the contrary, we were all fundamentally the same. To make my point, I used an old cliche:

"It could be me in here, under other circumstances," I told them. "There, but for the grace of God, you know?"

"Hold on right there," Janet interjected.

Uh-oh.

"Do you imagine that you have received a special portion of God's grace that these men have not?"

My mouth fell open, but no words came out.

"We have to be careful how we presume to talk about God and grace. We may be saying more about ourselves, our own assumptions, and our own prejudices than we're saying about Him."

I had just received one of the most profound lessons of my life. Sister Janet cared enough to help me see that I had spoken carelessly and with a lack of consideration that often accompanies unexamined privilege. I could almost hear Jedi Master Yoda, "Much to learn, you still have."

After a few moments of silence, I said, "I apologize. That's not what I meant at all. I've never thought about the negative implications of that phrase."

The men in the circle barely moved, though there may have been a flicker of knowing amusement in some of their eyes. I wondered if they had seen other folks from the outside clumsily stumble over their words and get a lesson from Janet. Everyone seemed content to let me continue. Janet gestured for me to do so, as though I was back on the right track. Grace upon grace is what I kept encountering in these places.

Through my contact with the women facing life behind bars and this group of men on Tennessee's death row, I was being converted. Cyntoia, in her letter from June of 2009, had given me my marching orders—to go make a difference in the life of even just one person. Sister Janet had now placed before me an opportunity to have this mission affirmed and validated by gracious men whose very presence on death row exposed the injustice of seeking revenge instead of restoration. The steeples may have failed me, but the beloved community that transcends walls and fences was steadfast.

I felt I was being born again, unlearning things I didn't even remember learning, more certain than ever that the current had me and that all I needed to do was keep doing what I was doing. What had initially felt like an unraveling was starting to feel like coming out of a straightjacket.

Despite the best efforts of our religious traditions, we cannot institutionalize or tame a Spirit that carries us where it will. Instead, we must simply surrender to the divine current that moves us along. When we finally learn to let go of the labels, prejudices, and divisions by which our systems—even religious ones—seek to exert control, we are able to experience righteousness, peace, and joy through alternative communities.

The current, channeled by Sister Janet, carried me to a literal bend in a river. After sitting with a group of elders on death row, I left feeling a little bit more like a new creation.

The Clean-Cut Man in the Booth

Sister Janet wasn't done with me yet. In July 2012, only a few months after my visit to Riverbend, she invited me to Cincinnati, Ohio, to speak at the national conference of the Children's Defense Fund. Janet wanted me to share my story with a larger audience of going from a tough-on-crime prosecutor to an advocate for a justice that heals and transforms in a spirit of shalom.

The conference in Cincinnati was my introduction to the Children's Defense Fund, a national advocacy organization founded in 1973 by Civil Rights activist Marian Wright Edelman to promote policies and programs that provide healthcare to children, reduce the impact of poverty on children, protect children from abuse and neglect, and provide children with educational opportunities. Over four days, I and other speakers would be examining strategies to shut down the well-documented cradle-to-prison pipeline that funnels disproportionate numbers of poor Black and Brown children into the system of mass vengeance that is the multibillion-dollar prison-industrial complex.

After settling into my hotel, I headed to a nearby restaurant to meet Janet for dinner.

"Preston!" she called to me from the booth where she was seated. As I approached, I saw Janet was seated across from a slender, clean-cut man. He seemed familiar, but I couldn't quite place him. When I reached the booth, his dark, kind eyes and laid-back demeanor were unmistakable.

"Ndume Olatushani!" I exclaimed. "What in the world are you doing here?"

He nodded and smiled, as though it was the most natural thing in the world for a man who had spent almost thirty years on death row in Tennessee to now be casually dining in a steakhouse in downtown Cincinnati, Ohio.

An Appalling Miscarriage of Justice

Born in 1958, in St. Louis, Missouri, Ndume was the seventh of eleven children. His father died in 1966, so his mother had to raise him and his siblings on her own. They lived on the eleventh floor of a housing project that was later condemned and demolished by the city. When they moved to a predominantly white neighborhood, Ndume experienced the insidious nature of racism. The verbal and physical altercations that followed resulted in Ndume being labeled as a problem child in his school. He was already caught up in the school-to-prison pipeline.

On October 2, 1983, Ndume and dozens of friends and family members gathered for food, drinks, and dancing in celebration of his mother's birthday. After nodding off late, he made sure to wake up in time for his two sons to attend church.

If he had followed the Mississippi River nearly 300 miles south that morning, he would have ended up in Memphis, Tennessee, where the white owner of a Food Rite grocery was shot dead during an attempted robbery. The culprits fled in a maroon station wagon that was later found by the police and traced back to the St. Louis airport.

Although Ndume had never set foot in Memphis, overzealous police, desperate to solve the crime, alleged spurious connections to the station wagon to name him their prime suspect. As soon as Ndume was targeted, the police neglected to explore other leads. He was eventually arrested, extradited to Tennessee, a state he had never been in before, and charged with homicide. Prosecutors, feeling public pressure to secure a conviction, went along. In December 1985, Ndume stood trial for murder in a windowless Memphis courtroom.

Despite Memphis being a predominantly Black city, the prosecution used its peremptory strikes to reject all Black jurors, likely a violation of his constitutional rights. They made a flippant attempt to discredit Ndume's alibi by claiming he had not proven the date of his mother's birthday, despite having a copy of her driver's license. The prosecutors also withheld mountains of exculpatory evidence, such as eyewitnesses identifying people other than Ndume and reports showing that his fingerprints did not match any of those found on the car. When the prosecution offered him a deal of twenty-five years in prison in exchange for a guilty plea, he refused, knowing he was innocent. He trusted the judicial process and believed no jury would convict a person who was not guilty.

It took the all-white jury only two hours to decide he was guilty of first-degree murder, and he was sentenced to death.

The racism at work in Ndume's case on the part of the police, prosecutors, and jurors was egregious, but not unique. A study conducted in Washington State found that jurors are three times more likely to recommend the death penalty for a Black defendant than a white defendant in similar cases. Today, more than 40 percent of those awaiting execution are Black, even though Blacks make up just over 13 percent of America's population.

When I first met Ndume while visiting with Janet in 2012, he had already spent a quarter of a century in prison for a crime he did not commit.

It was an appalling miscarriage of justice.

During that time, his beloved mother perished in an automobile accident. He spent three days crying in his bed, a two-inch foam mattress over a steel slab. Hopeless, he was convinced his world would come apart. Others had committed suicide in there, and he knew this grief and anger could destroy him.

On that third day, however, his mother appeared to him in a dream. "Get up," she said matter-of-factly. She was not going to have her son surrender to despair.

So Ndume got up and got to work on his future. Although he had never tried his hand at art, he began painting as a way of giving outlet to his emotions, and he found a sense of freedom in his cell. His vibrant colors stood in defiance of his drab surroundings.

Each stroke of his paintbrush was an act of resistance against a racist, corrupt system that elevates procedural rules over just outcomes, going to far as to condemn an innocent man to die. The only power others had over him, Ndume realized, was what he relinquished to them. They might hold him physically, but they could not hold him mentally. He was always free in his mind. This was the hope he clung to and the hope he wanted to share with others who felt broken and defeated.

This was the man I encountered when I visited Riverbend Maximum Security Prison—strong, resolute, unflinching.

In June 2012, with the help of his wife, whom he'd married while behind bars, and the perseverance of his lawyers, Ndume Olatushani was finally able to prove his innocence.

Did the state of Tennessee admit to its wrongdoing? Did the negligent prosecutors and lazy police admit they had acted unethically and created a massive injustice that stole thirty years from Ndume? Did they dismiss the charges? Did they offer any form of compensation for all the suffering they inflicted on an innocent man? Did they expunge Ndume's record?

No, to all of the above.

Memphis prosecutors, confronted with Ndume's actual innocence, endeavored to keep him caged for as long as possible as litigation worked its way through the courts. In order to be released, the prosecutors insisted that he accept what is known as an *Alford plea*, or best interest plea. It was not an admission of guilt, but it prevented Ndume from ever filing a lawsuit against the state of Tennessee for the damages he suffered as a result of the conspiracy its agents had perpetuated against him.

Ndume had already spent over half his life in prison. He took the plea to finally regain his freedom.

The first thing he did after his release was to take off his shoes and walk barefoot on the grass.

There Is Always Hope

There in that Cincinnati steakhouse, we formed an unlikely trio—a reverend, a former prosecutor, and a former death row inmate. I congratulated Ndume and told him how happy I was to be with him on the outside and presenting at the conference. Ndume replied that he was not holding onto anger, but he would use it to fuel his efforts in helping others overcome similar circumstances.

Ndume stands as a testament to hope, to leaning into a future he could not yet see.

He once told me that while he was locked up, whenever he saw an airplane passing over the prison, he would say out loud, "There goes my ride." Over and over again, whenever he saw an airplane, "There goes my ride." Like a mantra or a prayer.

Years after our time together in Cincinnati, he was flying in an airplane and passed over the Riverbend prison. His hope had manifested itself. Such is the power of hope. I wanted it to extend to other people I knew and loved who wanted to experience life outside prison walls.

Chapter 7

The Media's Lens

The criminal legal system and the media are joined together, for better or worse, in an unlikely marriage. Unfortunately, for some, this can lead to till-death-do-us-part.

Take my friend Ndume, for example.

Barring the millions of dollars of *pro bono* work done by a New York law firm, Ndume would likely have been murdered by the state of Tennessee, convicted on fabricated, bogus evidence with no consequences for the unscrupulous, unethical cops and prosecutors who had betrayed their sworn duty to uphold justice.

Although the Constitution's Sixth Amendment guarantees citizens the right to a fair and impartial jury, it is not always easy to procure, particularly in high-profile cases. While true impartiality can only happen when jurors approach a case with no biases or preconceived opinions, the media circuses that took place around O. J. Simpson and Richard Jewell remind us how susceptible all of us are to snap judgments about the persons accused and their alleged crimes.

My friend Cyntoia Brown had also been labeled a monster by some news outlets. Without knowing the details of a person's background and the full context surrounding the events, it's easy for us to go along with these negative portrayals because they fit so neatly into our black-and-white, good guy/bad guy view of life.

Most people are almost wholly ignorant about the criminal legal system and the complex network of laws and punishment, the politics, and economics around the largest system of mass punishment in the history of the world. Ironically, their ignorance does not interfere at all with their conviction that America has the best system in the world.

Good triumphs over evil. Wrongdoers are punished.

Faith in our legal system, even when that faith is almost entirely blind, makes us feel safe, secure, and protected, and that all is pretty much right in the world. An ignorant but trusting citizenry makes it easy for cops, prosecutors, judges, wardens, and executioners to do their jobs without being questioned, as we saw in the case of Ndume.

If we get a little closer to the system, however, and learn a little bit more and hear a few disturbing stories of gross miscarriages of justice from people like the women in the LIFE Program and Ndume, our belief in the system may be severely shaken. Things are not always as the media presents them. They are certainly not as they should be.

The Criminal Justice Building in downtown Nashville, a portion of which is depicted on the cover of this book, and the Tennessee Supreme Court building, where I argued so many cases, are majestic and impressive. A visitor would assume that the justice carried out there is as firm and trustworthy as the foundations and walls that support the massive structures. However, such ornate, imposing buildings may mask systemic corruption and rot. When Jesus' disciples were in awe of the splendor of the temple in Jerusalem, he cautioned them against placing their trust in such institutions: "Not one stone will be left on top of the other. Every one will be thrown down."

The Footage Is Compelling and Heartbreaking

Cyntoia Brown was still a child at the time of her arrest in August 2004, unable to do any of the things the law permits adults to do. Yet in one of those impressive courtrooms, a judge and a prosecutor decided, under the guise of justice, to pretend she was an adult and condemned her to serve fifty-one years in prison.

The unfairness and downright absurdity of it all made a deep impression on prominent Nashville attorney Charles W. Bone.

Cyntoia wasn't a small adult, he reasoned. She was a traumatized child.

A pillar of the local legal community, Mr. Bone was cofounder and chairman of Bone McAllester Norton PLLC, and had practiced law for forty years, handling mostly business and corporate issues.

He did not practice criminal law.

Well, that was about to change.

On a Saturday afternoon, April 17, 2010, Mr. Bone sat in the Green Hills Regal Theater for a screening of *Me Facing Life: Cyntoia's Story*, a documentary by filmmaker Dan Birman highlighting the layers of injustice in Cyntoia's case. Mr. Bone had been invited to the screening at the Nashville Film Festival by his longtime friend Judge Patsy Cottrell, who sat on the Tennessee Court of Civil Appeals.

The documentary began with previously unseen footage that Birman recorded only days after Cyntoia's initial arrest. It followed her personal and legal struggles, while providing insights into her family history and the hell she endured as a victim of sex trafficking. This marked the first time that the public heard another side to Cyntoia's tragic story. A film critic for the *Nashville Scene* wrote,

> There's no denying the violence of the crime ... as Dan Birman's documentary shows, however, it's difficult to understand why Brown was tried as an adult and how the murder could have been premeditated. Nashville's juvenile justice system allowed the filmmaker generous access to Brown, and the footage is compelling and heartbreaking. Particularly devastating are the early interviews, which show that Brown was clearly still a child.[1]

Although the media had vilified Cyntoia years earlier, Birman's camera brought to light her humanity, her vulnerability, and her unrecognized potential.

Charles Bone was deeply moved by the film. A sixteen-year-old child had slipped through the cracks, was preyed upon and victimized in ways most of us cannot imagine, and when she had finally endured all she could stand and determined to not let herself be abused again, the gatekeepers of our system of laws and punishment conspired to lock her in a cage for the rest of her life.

"I was really stunned by the fact that even though she was the victim, she became the convicted felon," Mr. Bone later told the

---

[1] Jack Silverman, "Sentenced for Life: Cyntoia's Story," *Nashville Scene*, https://www.nashvillescene.com/news/sentenced-for-life-cyntoias-story/article_45b450db-b8ed-5cdc-91de-8d6600aad89c.html.

Business Journal. "That just did not seem right to me. ... I just didn't think that was what America was all about."[2]

He was so moved by the mountain of injustice in Cyntoia's case that he committed to using his own resources to fight for her freedom. He would represent her for free. I told him how much it meant to me to see a seasoned, esteemed lawyer like him try to remedy the injustice that I now saw in Cyntoia's case, an injustice that I had helped bring about.

Mr. Bone seemed to understand.

"You know," he confided, with a hand on my shoulder, "this will be my first criminal case."

When the Lights Came Up

A few months later, in October of 2020, I attended another screening of the documentary on the Lipscomb University campus. As *Me Facing Life* walked us through Cyntoia's heartbreaking story, I was flooded with memories of my classroom interactions with this remarkable young woman.

I had come to know that she was so much more than her worst mistake. She was gracious and forgiving, intellectually gifted, and desperate for an opportunity to help at-risk kids.

It felt almost voyeuristic to watch Cyntoia's case unfold through recorded interviews and scenes in courtrooms and prison cells, when she was prohibited by the prison from attending the screening of the film that bore her name. Dr. William Bernet, a renowned juvenile forensic psychiatrist from Vanderbilt University, was featured explaining his evaluation of Cyntoia. Her adoptive mom, Ellenette Brown, discussed her daughter's troubled childhood and teenage years. And her biological mother, Georgina Mitchell, admitted to being diagnosed as bipolar and manic depressive, and to struggling for years with an addiction to alcohol and crack cocaine. All of these factors contributed to her giving Cyntoia up for adoption when she was two years old.

---

[2] Adam Sichko, "NBJ Reports: Pursuing Freedom for Trafficking Victim Cyntoia Brown Lit a Fire in Charles Bone," *Nashville Business Journal*, https://www.bizjournals.com/nashville/news/2020/09/22/charles-bone-law-cyntoia-brown-trafficking-case.html.

Birman's film exposed three generations of sexual violence and trauma in Cyntoia's maternal line, which figured into her psychological makeup and complexity. Cyntoia was a victim many times over before she was ever pushed to the point of resorting to violence herself.

When the lights came up, the audience was clearly impacted. The film's emotional power came from its use of timelines, interviews, and facts instead of sentimentality.

I was asked to be part of a panel discussion. Also on the panel was one of Cyntoia's former attorneys and her adoptive mother, Ellenette Brown. We had seen Ms. Ellenette in the footage, a kind and resilient woman who cared for her garden and kept an orderly home, who wondered if she would still be alive when her daughter was finally eligible for parole in over four decades.

When I was able to speak with Ms. Ellenette, I told her how deeply sorry I was for the role I had played in her daughter's case, for the arguments I had made, and for the terrible outcome of a fifty-one-year sentence being imposed against a child.

In response, she gave me a hug.

She looked in my eyes and told me she was proud of me. As tears rolled down my face, she told me that she was so thankful that I had the opportunity to see the good in Cyntoia and that I allowed my experience with her to change the trajectory of my life.

Grace upon grace upon grace.

The Fight for Cyntoia

An accomplished and well-respected founding member at a prestigious firm, Mr. Bone was a great person to represent Cyntoia. But when he agreed to serve as Cyntoia's *pro bono* counsel, he could not have predicted where it would lead, particularly as he did not regularly practice criminal law.

Any lawyer in his position would have their work cut out for them. But Mr. Bone was focused, determined, with a will to do whatever it took to accomplish what he set his mind to do.

To get Cyntoia's conviction overturned now that the Court of Criminal Appeals had ruled against her in the opinion that I received, Mr. Bone would have to convince a court that an error of constitutional magnitude had compromised the fairness of the process. Having worked for years as an appellate prosecutor who toiled daily to defeat such postconviction attacks on a judgment, I knew this was extremely difficult. Once a person is convicted in our system, it is very hard to have the judgment reversed, even if the person is, like Ndume, innocent. In Cyntoia's case, her guilt was not in question, and the passage of time only made it more difficult to have the conviction set aside.

The media presented Mr. Bone with another significant challenge by having already dismissed Cyntoia as a teenage prostitute who'd killed a john. First impressions are often lasting. Much of this prejudicial content airs on the nightly news and gets posted on social media.

The court of public opinion is quick to pass judgment—no time to waste, because new sensationalized stories will be appearing within days, hours, even minutes. News outlets compete for viewers and clicks, and they are quick to portray a defendant as evil, monstrous, and subhuman. Grabbing viewers' attention often outweighs sticking to proven facts before trial. To compound the problem, police and prosecutors are usually first to present their case to the public, framing it for the media.

Combating these initial impressions is not easy, even if they are wrong, as is often the case. Judges, juries, and parole board members are certainly human, making them just as susceptible to preconceived notions about a defendant and a crime.

Even so, my hope that Mr. Bone would obtain relief for Cyntoia was boosted when he solicited help from one of his best friends, J. Houston Gordon. Mr. Gordon was a highly respected attorney from west Tennessee with a robust criminal practice.

Cyntoia now had two of the most committed, highly regarded lawyers in the state representing her.

I was cautiously optimistic.

The Best Legal Strategies

Over the next eighteen months, Mr. Bone and Mr. Gordon met with Cyntoia's original defense attorneys to develop a strategy for attempting to win her freedom. They did a deep dive into Cyntoia's background to ask for the first time what factors were at work when she pulled the gun from her purse and ended Johnny Allen's life.

They wanted to explore every possible issue that might entitle Cyntoia to relief.

- There was the issue of Cyntoia's young age when she committed the crime.
- There was the life sentence without any possibility of relief until after she served fifty-one years, which should be considered excessive punishment in the case of a minor.
- There was the largely unexplored element of Cyntoia suffering terrible violence as a victim of sex-trafficking. Before that, she had a history of being subjected to physical and sexual abuse dating back to when she was a small child.
- There was the issue of Cyntoia waiving her constitutional rights at the time of arrest, in the absence of a lawyer, parent, or guardian.

The problem was that these issues either were or should have been raised by Cyntoia's previous legal team during her initial appeal. At this stage, the only issues that were available to Cyntoia were those that implicated a constitutional right, most notably whether her previous attorneys had been ineffective in violation of her Sixth Amendment right to counsel.

There was one other issue that had not been explored at all, but that was hinted at in the *Me Facing Life* documentary. When Cyntoia's birth mother, Georgina Mitchell, spoke of her alcohol abuse and use of crack cocaine while she was pregnant with Cyntoia, she laid the groundwork for a legal tactic that Cyntoia's trial attorneys had completely overlooked.

Cyntoia suffered from fetal alcohol syndrome, or FAS.

If Cyntoia's lawyers had presented the jury with evidence of the impact of FAS on her cognitive functioning, would the jury have concluded that she was not capable of acting with premeditation, thereby rendering her conviction for premeditated murder unconstitutional?

After Dr. William Bernet's original mental evaluation of Cyntoia, her trial counsel described her as "brilliant" but said she was "all over the place ... like there was something wrong that we couldn't figure out what it was." Yet Cyntoia's trial lawyers did not explore her mental condition or whether she had the mental capacity to commit first-degree murder. fetal alcohol syndrome was never part of their defense strategy.

Mr. Bone arranged for Cyntoia to be evaluated by Dr. Richard Adler, a clinical and forensic psychologist from Seattle. Cyntoia was twenty-three years old at the time. Although she was highly intelligent, the Vineland Adaptive Behavior Scales showed her functioning at the level of a thirteen- or fourteen-year-old.

"Alcohol is a particularly heinous poison to the developing fetus," Dr. Adler told Mr. Bone and Mr. Gordon. He explained how it affects every cell and does damage to a baby's developing brain. The effects of FAS include diminished capacity to effectively regulate emotions, control impulses, and appreciate the risks and consequences of conduct, all of which was extremely relevant to the issue of whether Cyntoia had acted with premeditation. Given that Cyntoia's trial lawyers never investigated this possible defense, it seemed like a promising basis for seeking postconviction relief and a new trial.

Still preparing their postconviction petition strategy, Mr. Bone and Mr. Gordon were presented with another option in June 2012, when the U.S. Supreme Court decided the case of *Miller v. Alabama*, in which it ruled that a mandatory sentence of life without the possibility of parole was unconstitutional for anyone younger than eighteen years, under the Eighth Amendment's prohibition of cruel and unusual punishment.

Cyntoia was not serving life without the possibility of parole, so *Miller* was not directly applicable to her case. But she was serving a mandatory sentence of fifty-one years before she would be eligible for parole, which, as a practical matter, didn't sound so different from life without parole. Mr. Bone and Mr. Gordon saw this ruling as another arrow in their quiver.

They filed a petition for postconviction relief on Cyntoia's behalf and were granted a hearing in November 2012.

Fetal Alcohol Syndrome

Robed in black, Judge Randall Wyatt, Jr., presided over the postconviction hearing in the Criminal Justice Building, where "The First Duty of Society Is Justice" is engraved on the outside wall. Behind the judge, a small statue of a familiar figure, Lady Liberty, stood with her scales in her hand. Many teachers and students from the LIFE Program who had come to know and love Cyntoia attended the hearing to support her. She was transported from the Tennessee Prison for Women in handcuffs and ankle chains. She sat in her blue denim prison uniform, her hair pulled back and eyes downcast.

From the witness stand, Dr. Adler described his evaluation of Cyntoia for fetal alcohol syndrome. He detailed how the U.S. Surgeon General began warning the public of the negative effects of alcohol on pregnancy in the early 1980s, and how the Institute of Medicine gave guidance for diagnosing the disorder in the mid-1990s. He stated that Cyntoia had facial characteristics consistent with the disorder, such as the flattened philtrum between her nose and upper lip, and spoke of her central nervous system abnormalities. He then pointed out her cognitive deficiencies, ranging from visual/spacial planning to impulsivity to motor coordination. He shared the results of a brain scan, which revealed further evidence of impairment.

Cyntoia, who was well on her way to completing an associate's degree with a 4.0 grade point average, sat in stunned silence as legal and mental health professionals discussed her disorder as if she were a laboratory test subject.

"She has alcohol-related neurodevelopmental disorder," Dr. Adler stated. "She is seriously impaired, and this leaves her with a diminished ability to cope with stress, control her emotional impulses, and appreciate the consequences of her conduct."

Cyntoia lowered her tear-filled eyes. This trained expert, this doctor hired by her legal team, made it sound as though she could barely function. She had overcome so much and was investing so heavily in every opportunity to better herself in the hope of being a free woman and living the normal life she had never enjoyed. Yet he was speaking of her as though she was incapable of anything normal.

Tears rolled down Cyntoia's cheeks.

"And that is not inconsequential. People suffering from fetal alcohol syndrome have markedly higher rates of problems with the law."

Once again, the system reduced Cyntoia to a label, this time by diagnosing her with a mental disorder.

As a legal tactic, I understood the strategy of demonstrating that Cyntoia was not capable of forming the requisite mental state required for a conviction of first-degree murder. Not only was she still a teenager who, like all people her age, did not yet possess a fully developed brain, she was also hampered by severe mental issues out of her control that had plagued her since birth.

Watching her listen to what was being said about her almost broke me. We weren't able to speak in the courtroom, but when our eyes met I could tell she was embarrassed and in pain. Once again, she was being made to feel like a pariah, this time in front of her friends. As we left the courthouse after the hearing concluded, I hoped it would be worth it.

A few weeks later, the answer came. Judge Wyatt denied Cyntoia's petition for postconviction relief. He concluded that Cyntoia had failed to show that, had the jury been presented with evidence of her fetal alcohol syndrome, the outcome of her trial would have been different. It was another devastating blow.

To their credit, Mr. Bone and Mr. Gordon were undeterred. They knew it was an uphill battle, and they were committed to appealing Judge Wyatt's ruling to the Court of Criminal Appeals, the Tennessee Supreme Court, and even the U.S. Supreme Court, if necessary. However, with every defeat, the chance of success seemed to grow more slim.

The Media: Can't Live With 'Em, Can't Live Without 'Em

The media, more than ever, is a window through which the public views crime and justice. Breaking news reports and social media accounts give us updates in real time about school shootings, high-speed chases, and police violence against Black people and shape the way we process these events. We are glued to our phones and televisions, but we are not always mindful that the corporations making information available to us are doing so to make money. They need ratings and clicks to be profitable to advertisers.

We, the viewers—the consumers of their product—may not always be able to discern truth from fiction, to sift through embellishments and exaggerations, and to reject misleading or downright false information.

Technology, in its various forms, has potential to both aid and hinder the legitimate search for truth and justice. Were it not for social media, the white men who murdered Ahmaud Arbery while he was jogging never would have been held accountable. Local police and prosecutors had determined to take no action in a dereliction of duty reminiscent of law enforcement looking the other way after white mobs lynched Black victims. It was only after video of the murder went viral and caused widespread outrage on social media that the Georgia authorities got involved, arrested the men, and had the case transferred to a different prosecutor's office that did not have a conflict of interest. Without cell phone video and social media, the men who performed a modern-day lynching would have gone free.

On the other hand, at their worst, media outlets appeal to our fear and anger, exploiting our worst biases and prejudices to keep us coming back for more. I am reminded that the Fox News channel recently agreed to pay Dominion Voting Systems almost $800 million to settle the voting machine company's lawsuit over the network's promotion of lies that there was fraud in the 2020 presidential election. The damage, however, was already done. Millions of Americans believed the "fake news" and remain convinced of the lie that Donald Trump defeated Joe Biden. It was only one of the 30,000 documented lies that Trump told while he was in office—likes that outlets like Fox News were all too happy to amplify for ratings.

When media obscures the truth, it poses a threat to authentic community and shalom, and our smart phones become what Will Campbell has called "electronic soul molesters."

This phenomenon predates iPhones and Twitter, however. In the early 1980s, the Reagan administration launched a war on drugs at a time when American public opinion polls indicated drugs were low on the list of important issues to be addressed. To fuel his agenda and secure funding from Congress, Reagan employed the newshounds always looking for a story.

Television networks, newspaper editors, and magazine publishers grabbed hold of this opportunity and ran with it, drawing in consumers with sensationalized accounts of crack cocaine in urban areas.

The nightly news could scarcely end without a story about the drug epidemic, which was always tied to poverty-stricken, marginalized communities. Soon, illegal drugs took center stage in voters' minds, and lawmakers promising to implement tough-on-crime policies that drastically increased prison sentences for drug convictions were elected to positions of immense political power.

The average sentence for possession of crack cocaine is around ten years, which is more severe than the sentences given for many violent crimes. Black people, who were always the target of the drug war, went to prison in unprecedented numbers to serve sentences that spanned decades.

We care about what the news-as-entertainment complex tells us to care about. It is complicit in the explosion of America's prison population over the past four decades.

Sex-Trafficking and Its Victims

Certainly, the news has changed public perception about what used to be commonly referred to as "prostitution." In the past twenty years, we have begun to better comprehend the nature of the power imbalance between traffickers and their victims, as well as the trauma, addiction, violence, and threats that keep victims trapped in a cycle of sexual abuse.

Here, we can thank the media for its role in bringing these issues to the fore. It has shone a spotlight on sex trafficking and its victims. Those once dismissed as willing participants in the sex trade are now recognized as often being victims of sex-trafficking, and our legislatures have passed laws in response.

When Cyntoia was arrested, tried, and convicted, Tennessee's system of laws was not prepared to address the nature of the hell she was trapped in. It has since taken steps to treat sex-trafficking for what it is—slavery—and to hold accountable the people who profit from it—the traffickers.

Yet many people, so far removed from this violent, exploitative practice, have trouble humanizing the issue.

The media had demonized Cyntoia as a teenage prostitute-turned-murderer who deserved to grow old in a cage. However, Dan

Birman's riveting film showed her to be a vulnerable, victimized child in need of compassion, care, and community.

I had seen her in both lights. More than anything, now she was simply my friend, and I desperately wanted to see her receive a second chance outside the prison walls. In reality, given what her life had been like before, she needed a first chance.

My Fifteen Minutes of Fame

Through people I'd met when I attended the Children's Defense Fund conference in Cincinnati with Sister Janet, I was presented with an opportunity to be part of another film project to raise awareness of the need for criminal justice reform, using my conversion experience and reconciled relationship with Cyntoia as a backdrop. For several days, my family welcomed a film crew into our home to document the journey we had been on together.

In July of 2013, the short documentary *Redemption of the Prosecutor*[3] was screened in Washington, D.C., for criminal justice reform advocates and faith leaders. It was then released to the public and promoted to faith communities, schools, and civic organizations as a tool for building grassroots support for reform efforts.

The film marked a rare and valuable opportunity for me to step back from my life and observe the profound changes I had experienced in my career, my faith, and so many of my assumptions about the way the world works that might otherwise have gone unquestioned.

At one point, my eight-year-old daughter Lila tells the camera, "My dad's name is Preston Shipp. He does law. I think he was working as an executor for a judge."

"You mean, prosecutor?" the interviewer asks off-screen.

Lila scrunches her face. "I guess so."

It was humbling to see my children talking about my mistakes. I may not have been an executioner, but my kids knew I had passed judgment on people I didn't know and helped condemn them to prison.

---

[3] *Redemption of the Prosecutor*, Brave New Foundation, https://www.youtube.com/watch?v=dQpQlqN8EY0.

"You were the one that put her in prison," Lila continued.

"It would be hard to know that your teacher put you in prison," added six-year-old Ruby.

It wasn't easy to hear my children so clearly and concisely articulate my failures.

The Grind of Criminal Justice

The legal timeline of Cyntoia Brown's case now extended from her arrest in 2004, to her conviction in 2006, to the denial of her direct appeal in 2009. In 2010, she filed a petition for postconviction relief, in which she was represented by Attorneys Charles Bone and Houston Gordon, and which Criminal Court Judge Randall Wyatt denied after the hearing in late 2012. Mr. Bone and Mr. Gordon promptly appealed this decision.

In March of 2014, I attended the argument before the Court of Criminal Appeals, the same court where I had clerked for Judge Welles at the beginning of my career. The argument was heard in the same courtroom where I had argued against Cyntoia six years earlier. The setting was so familiar—the rows of wooden benches, the deep red carpet, the dark wooden walls and crown molding, the giant Seal of the State of Tennessee and the U.S. and Tennessee flags that adorned the bench where the panel of judges sat. Everything in the room reflected the gravity of the decisions that were made here. It was a place where, as a young lawyer, I had felt honored to be.

Now I felt like a different person. Now I sat in the public gallery instead of at counsel's table. Another lawyer with the Tennessee Attorney General's Office stood at the podium where I once stood and argued as I had that Cyntoia needed to spend fifty-one years in prison. Would that lawyer ever experience the same regret for making that argument that I now carried? Why is there never a shortage of lawyers who are willing to advocate for the destruction of the futures of people they don't know? Why do so few of us ever stop long enough to ask what in the world we are doing?

Mr. Bone and Mr. Gordon persuasively argued that Cyntoia was denied her constitutional right to effective counsel by her trial attorneys' failure to explore and present to the jury evidence of her fetal alcohol syndrome. Had the jurors been able to consider this evidence, they likely would have viewed Cyntoia in an entirely different light and concluded that she was not able to form the mental state needed to sustain a first-degree murder conviction.

When the appeals court rendered its decision seven months later, it was another heartbreaking blow. The court again denied Cyntoia any relief.

The gears of injustice kept grinding forward, with no one willing to acknowledge the terrible problems in her case. She was quickly running out of options.

In June 2015, Mr. Bone and Mr. Gordon filed yet another petition, this time a petition for a writ of habeas corpus in federal court. In Latin, *habeas corpus* literally means "you have the body," and a habeas corpus petition is a vehicle for attacking the legality of a person's detention. They listed twelve claims for the court to consider, including the lack of evidence presented at her original trial regarding fetal alcohol syndrome and other mental health issues, her family history of trauma, and the prior sexual, emotional, and physical abuse—all of which her trial lawyers should have presented to the jury.

The federal court quickly disposed of the petition that Mr. Bone and Mr. Gordon had filed, however, concluding there was not even cause for a hearing.

This federal court rendered its brief decision in late 2016, twelve years after the news of Cyntoia's arrest was first aired on the news. It felt like the final nail in the coffin. In all likelihood, Cyntoia would die in prison.

Part Three

Restitution:
Right Community

Chapter 8

Contemplating Awareness

While Cyntoia and her dedicated team of legal experts kept fighting for her freedom, I was still trying to find my own footing.

Thanks to Janet Wolf, in early 2012, I'd been to death row to meet with what were for me a council of Jedi Masters, men who had gained deep wisdom and compassion through decades of rigorous self-evaluation, study, and reflection.

Ndume and the other men I met on death row had moved beyond the seemingly endless attachments and distractions that characterize life in the free world. They had let go of what is false and illusory and were manifesting their true selves, to use Thomas Merton's language.

Having spent so much time in a religion in which comfort, prosperity, and entertainment were taken to be Christian values, and a career in which the intentional infliction of suffering was presented as justice, could I put aside my attachments to such illusions?

I had made a significant career change, and my faith had evolved to something that would have been unrecognizable to me a decade earlier. I think I had naively assumed that once I quit being a prosecutor, I was done. However, after meeting the elders on death row, I was beginning to see that was only the first step on what was looking to be a very long journey. There was no quick fix.

Howard Zehr's writing and my friendship with people who were incarcerated helped clarify for me this idea of justice as a covenant community, in which everyone functions together in rightness and wholeness. It was a vision of stability and strength, encouragement and vitality. It was a vision large enough to embrace marriages, families, cities, and nations. It could offer healing in cases ranging from vandalized church buildings and stolen cell phones to the aftermath of South African apartheid. The goal should always be to restore. If even one person is cut off, it impacts the entire community. This is the kind of justice that is the first duty of society, to repair the harm that is done.

My passion for justice was still there. However, my experiences at the Turney Center, in the LIFE Program, and on death row had taught me a deeper, truer, more compelling vision of justice that I wanted to share.

Being born again is a life's work. Maybe Nicodemus knew that's what Jesus was driving at. We don't just seek the kingdom of heaven once and then move on. Loving our neighbors as ourselves isn't a one-time thing. Laying down the heavy burden of judging others and embracing the ministry of reconciliation are daily, life-long practices, not singular events.

I was still working for the Board of Professional Responsibility, investigating ethics complaints against attorneys. Yet these experiences were making me feel like I was caught up in a current that might eventually require another career change. I wanted to know where it was leading and what I needed to be doing, but I couldn't see how the different views I was catching along the way could fit together into a coherent whole. I still had to wait. I had to trust that if I kept doing what I was doing, it wouldn't be long, and it would be clear as day.

What would happen next? I had no clue. How should I proceed? I had no idea.

I was learning, albeit very slowly, that I didn't need to know. Looking back, none of the good things that had happened to me were by my design. Yet I could see that I was being carried. I had to continue to trust that what needed to happen would come to pass.

The current flows wherever it will. We often can't tell where all of the twists and turns will lead. As Thomas Merton prayed, sometimes the best we can do is trust that we will be led in the right direction, although we may know nothing about it.

There is tremendous freedom in admitting that we don't know, that we don't have it all figured out. What a blessed relief to admit that our feigned certainty is a sham and that the control we like to think we have over our lives and futures is an illusion. Here again, politics and religion are of no help. Politicians view repentance, a change of mind and heart, as a liability, a weakness. Institutional religion foolishly claims to have concrete, simple answers about a reality more vast than our incomprehensible universe and more intimate than the tiny, subatomic particles that make up our human cells.

We are invited to rest in the unknowing.

For me to even begin to do so, it took a Damascus-road-type conversion experience that knocked me off my chosen path of self-assured, carefully laid plans, into a current not of my making or choosing. My only responsibility was to stay in it and keep my eyes open so I didn't miss anything important that it brought my way.

I needed to wait. I needed to focus on what I was doing. I had to trust that it wouldn't be long, and that it would be clear as day.

Finding Acquaintance with Silence

Some Christian folks are suspicious of contemplative practices, or anything that sounds mystical, Eastern, or new-agey. The disciplines of silence, solitude, and meditative prayer, however, are not new to the Christian tradition. Rather than ways to escape from an active life of service and ministry, they are meant to equip us for it. We must remember that Jesus himself often spent time in solitude and prayer in lonely places before facing the crowds again.

Sherisse and I had seen several men and women burn themselves out in ministerial and other leadership roles, sometimes wounding others in the process. But the contemplative disciplines serve as anchors that can keep us from being tossed about by the many demands on our time. Contemplation, as I understood it from teachers like Richard Rohr, should be the solid ground in which we remain rooted, lest our action devolve into mere busy-ness. However, without corresponding action, times of quiet meditation and study can devolve into navel-gazing. As Rohr is fond of saying, "We do not think ourselves into a new way of living, we live ourselves into a new way of thinking." Action and contemplation are two sides of the same coin, and we must take care to honor them both.

Opportunities for action, such as engaging with advocates for justice reform, were coming more regularly. I was humbled and grateful when Janet Wolf invited me to share at the Children Defense Fund conference in Cincinnati about the ways my experiences in prison classrooms had propelled me into a new way of thinking. There I met Jody Kent Lavy, the young, enthusiastic director of the Campaign for the Fair Sentencing of Youth (CFSY), a D.C.-based organization devoted to ending life without parole as a sentencing option for children. Jody invited me to speak at the CFSY's annual conference. I knew if I was going to keep sharing my story in an authentic way with advocates, people whose family members were incarcerated, and people who have directly been impacted by our system of mass punishment, I had to prepare myself to speak humbly, honestly, with courage and transparency.

Times of being still, prayerful, and silent provide us with the strength, wisdom, and perspective necessary for meaningful social action.

To nurture our inner life, Sherisse and I committed to attending a liturgical service on Wednesday nights in which, in addition to singing songs and reading scripture, we practiced ten minutes of silence. Sometimes even ten minutes of silence once a week felt like a lot. Our lives and minds seem so resistant to even a little silence. As I tried to sit still, my monkey brain leapt from one compulsive thought to the next. My mind was like a movie projector that didn't have an off switch. Yet Sherisse and I noticed that carving out even a little time for being deliberately still kept us steady and centered during this chaotic time of transformation; it helped us be okay with not knowing where we were going.

We also decided to take an annual self-care retreat together. Several times we visited the Sacred Heart Monastery in Cullman, Alabama, where we were able to join the daily rhythm of Benedictine nuns. We learned from them how to write prayer journals, craft pottery, and—most importantly for me—walk a labyrinth.

A labyrinth is an ancient tool, a practice in which we pray by walking. A labyrinth looks similar to a maze, but there is only one path in and out. The way winds around, twisting and turning, sometimes close to the center, sometimes out at the perimeter, before opening up to the space in the middle. It is a powerful metaphor for the inner and outer journey we are all on. We seldom can anticipate the bends and curves. At times the path takes us so close to the center in which everything feels like it belongs, but then we make a quick, unexpected turn, and we feel like we are out on the fringes. We must trust that the path will take us exactly where we need to go, which is symbolized by the stillness of the center. After a time of rest, we resume our journey, making our way back out to engage once more with the sufferings and injustices of the world. The stone labyrinth at the Sacred Heart Monastery in Alabama was the first one I ever walked, and it is still my favorite.

After almost two decades, I am still trying to learn the lesson of being quiet and trusting the path. If my words and actions are to have any value, they must be grounded in stillness. There are so many distractions and so many versions of the false self. Contemplation is the counterweight to keep ourselves true, centered, focused, and authentic.

I still wanted to know where it was heading. I spent my days working for the Board of Professional Responsibility, but I felt a deep, strong calling to use my story of repentance to help others rethink our punitive approach to justice and invest in change. Should I try to get more speaking engagements? Might there be a way to make prison ministry and education a full-time job? Should I try to be a college professor like Richard Goode? An advocate like Janet Wolf? Should I go to seminary and start a ministry that imagined restorative alternatives to our system of institutionalized vengeance?

Nothing was clear.

The word "vocation" is derived from the Latin *vocare*, meaning "to call." We can't manufacture a call. I once felt called by God to work as a prosecutor, protecting society and vindicating victims by being an agent of retribution against people who broke the law. But I had learned that call was counterfeit.

A List of Incredible People

In the spring of 2013, a friend named Thomas Kleinert—the progressive, socially-conscious pastor of Vine Street Christian Church in Nashville—wanted to commemorate the 150th anniversary of the Emancipation Proclamation. President Lincoln's announcement of freedom for enslaved people hadn't been as far-reaching as originally believed, and the Thirteenth Amendment, which allowed incarcerated people to continue to be subjects to slavery, undermined some of his nobler goals. It was, nonetheless, a pivotal point in our nation's continuing march toward justice.

Thomas decided he would host an open forum for the community, a symposium with various speakers and panels addressing the Christian church's complicity in slavery, Jim Crow, and mass incarceration.

I admired Thomas's openness and zeal for truth-telling and repentance. A wise, sensitive, and courageous leader, Thomas was a kindred spirit who longed to see his church embrace justice work.

My mom's sister, Sara Harwell, was also involved in the project. Sara had served as an archivist for Vanderbilt University and a historian for the Christian Church (Disciples of Christ), the denomination to which Vine Street Christian Church belonged. She was an expert in both church history and the Civil War and Reconstruction eras. She understood well that if we do not reckon with our dark history, especially our complicity in racial violence and injustice, we may be doomed to repeat it.

Rounding out the organizing team was none other than my mentor, Sister Janet Wolf. She observed that if we were going to talk about the church's complicity in mass incarceration—the most recent manifestation of systemic racism in America—we needed to hear directly from people impacted by it. Because people who were incarcerated could not attend our church conference, Janet arranged for us to visit the Riverbend prison for several listening sessions to learn from the true experts and document their insights into the ways that racism is endemic in the American system of laws and punishment. We would then share their accounts with the conference attendees.

One of the men who volunteered to participate in the listening sessions was Rahim Buford.

If I am ever asked to list the impactful people I've met over the years, women and men who embody their deeply held beliefs and truly walk the walk, without hesitation, Rahim would be at the top of the list.

A native Nashvillian, Rahim had a trimmed goatee and warm, bright eyes behind his fashionable glasses. He was in his early forties, steady as a rock, confident but humble, with an unquenchable thirst for new experiences. His sense of wonder and awe kept him networking, seeking new opportunities, and looking for ways to learn. His desire to learn, to forge new relationships, and his openness to new ideas made him an ideal participant for our listening sessions.

In the late 1980s, Rahim was a teenager living in a poor, crime-ridden neighborhood. He had fled an abusive home and was living on a friend's couch. He had no money and no way of providing for himself. He did not feel like a man. However, he had a gun. He decided to use it to rob a fast-food restaurant. He told the attendant behind the counter to empty the cash register. When the clerk didn't move fast enough, Rahim fired a shot at the floor to scare him.

Tragically, the bullet ricocheted off the floor and struck the clerk.

Two days later, twenty-five-year-old Barry Latham died.

Rahim pled guilty to first-degree felony murder, and in 1990 was sentenced to life in prison with eligibility for release after twenty-five years. By the time I met him, Rahim had spent more than half his life caged in seven different prisons across the state. Had he committed the crime five years later, under the stricter sentencing laws that applied to Cyntoia Brown, he would have had to serve fifty-one years before having any chance of release.

During our session at Riverbend, Rahim and I immediately hit it off. We quickly developed a sense of kinship. He was deeply remorseful for the pain he had caused the Latham family, as he lost his own sister to violence while he was behind bars. He desperately wanted to show that was worthy of a second chance.

"Preston," he asked, "would you speak on my behalf at my parole hearing?"

I was honored.

Rahim Faces the Parole Board

When I arrived for the parole hearing in the large visitation gallery of the Riverbend prison, more than sixty individuals had gathered to support Rahim's release. There was his yoga instructor, an ex-cop, a former prison guard, and a college president who said Rahim had a full scholarship waiting on him if he were released.

I had never seen so many people at a parole hearing.

The parole board listened to Rahim's compelling presentation of the considerable efforts he had made to better himself during his years of incarceration. He had a long list of programs he had completed, certificates he had earned, and honors he had received. He had invested heavily in his education, earning college credit through Lipscomb University, Ohio University, and Vanderbilt University Divinity School. He had done everything he could to prepare himself for a successful, productive life outside prison walls.

Unfortunately, as with every other parole hearing I've ever been to before or since, Rahim was essentially put on trial again. The parole board reviewed every detail of the twenty-five-year-old case as though it had just happened. The board members elevated what Rahim had done when he was a teenager over the man Rahim had become over the past quarter century.

The victim's family opposed granting Rahim parole. Their hearts were still broken by the loss of Mr. Latham over two decades earlier. His adult daughter, who was only a year old when he was tragically killed, shared what it was like growing up without a father. Every Christmas, every birthday, every father-daughter dance was tinged with pain and emptiness because of Rahim's actions so long ago.

After hearing all the testimony, the parole board rendered its decision. "Mr. Buford, you are the picture of rehabilitation. You have done everything you could be expected to do. But in light of the testimony of the victim's family, we believe release at this point would depreciate the seriousness of your offense. We will review your case again in one year."

Another year. The words fell like a hammer, smashing our anticipation of Rahim's release. The parole board did not even make any recommendations for programming or classes Rahim should complete. They knew he was ready to come home. They put him off for a year simply in the name of retribution. They wanted him to suffer more.

Rahim and all of us who had gathered to support him were devastated. People cried and hugged. I stood alone almost in disbelief.

If this remarkable man was not deserving of a second chance, who is? What hope do others have who face this same group of hard-hearted parole board members? We barely had time to tell Rahim how sorry we were before they rushed him back into the bowels of the prison where he would be caged for another year for no reason other than pure vengeance.

As the shock of the irrational decision wore off, I became furious. I felt the injustice and unfairness of it all in my chest. I wanted to put my fist through the concrete wall that would separate my friend from his loved ones for another Thanksgiving, another Christmas, another round of birthdays. The parole board had the power to do the right thing, to give a second chance to a man they recognized as deserving. Instead, they told him that his rehabilitation did not matter. They were cogs in a wheel that crushes people, families, and entire communities by robbing them of hope. The process they presided over knows only how to hurt, never to heal.

As we all left the visitation gallery in silence, retrieved our IDs, and made our way to our cars, the heartbreak we carried was heavy. No justice was accomplished that day. No one was vindicated. No one had benefited. The grieving family gained nothing from institutionalized vengeance against Rahim. It didn't matter that Rahim had pled guilty, received a lengthy sentence, and spent twenty-five years investing in every opportunity for rehabilitation that came his way while exhibiting exceptional character. The victim's family and the parole board defined justice as punishment, as the intentional infliction of more suffering. They, like so many in our retributive society, mistakenly thought that compounding the harm would balance the scales.

Why call it a Department of Correction if it's nothing more than a Department of Vengeance?

As much as the Latham family had suffered, subjecting Rahim to the violence of a cage for another year would do nothing to alleviate their grief, bring back their loved one, or help them see Rahim as he really was—a person with profound potential to do good.

The Stormy Question Symposium

On a Saturday in May of 2013, the Stormy Question Symposium kicked off at Vine Street Christian Church to celebrate the 150th

Anniversary of the Emancipation Proclamation. Thomas Kleinert, my Aunt Sara, Janet Wolf, Ndume Olatushani, and I all spoke, and my parents, Sherisse, Lila, Ruby, and Levi were present. The interviews with Rahim and the other men from Riverbend were shared, detailing their experiences of the racism that spreads like an insidious virus across American history and institutions, manifesting itself first as Antebellum slavery, then as Jim Crow laws and the terrorism of lynchings, and most recently as mass incarceration.

We reevaluated the meaning of church in light of a gospel that proclaims freedom for the captives, and in the context of a country in which racism keeps reinventing itself. It was not enough to abolish slavery and end Jim Crow. We must cultivate a prophetic imagination and form beloved community with those who have been condemned to mass incarceration.

Again, this is getting down to the brass tacks of the ministry of reconciliation, in which human categories like "prisoner," "felon," and—I would argue—even "pastor" have passed away. This is the mystery of the gospel, that God restores unity where we have created division.

Being there among kindred spirits—many of whom had been invaluable guides on my journey, all of whom believed that the work of the church is dismantling every oppressive, dehumanizing domination system—was inspiring.

Not long thereafter, I began volunteering with the education program at Riverbend, which meant I got to spend more time with friends like Rahim.

The beloved community the current had brought me to seemed to be thriving.

As time went on, I was becoming more aware of more challenges and opportunities. The LIFE Program was wonderful, but there were so many more people in need of support and community.

What for them?

Sunday School Lessons

"I want to get in the habit of saying yes," I told Sherisse.

"Yes to what?" she asked.

"Anything. Everything. I feel like I need to take advantage of every opportunity to be with people who are working for real justice. I think I have something to offer, and I know I have so much to learn from people who are trying to tear down this system. I want to be in prison classrooms, speaking at parole hearings, any opportunity the current brings my way to share all I've experienced. I think that's how I go forward."

"You know I will support that as much as I can," she replied.

I always tried to be mindful that every "yes" I said to an invitation to speak or teach left her alone with our three kiddos. Even so, she was with me one-hundred percent in every way.

In fact, Sherisse had been caught up in her own current for a while that was pulling her away from the congregation we had loved and served for well over a decade. First there was the fiasco with the Peace & Justice Ministry, which led to me being called a socialist. Then a woman whom Sherisse and I greatly admired, who had been a guide for both of us, was denied a leadership position merely because of her gender. Finally, a friend of Sherisse who was trying to escape an abusive marriage with her teenage daughter and special-needs son went to the all-male eldership to ask for financial assistance. They offered to pray with her, of course. They'll always say a quick prayer. They were unwilling to provide any financial support, however. This was the straw that broke the camel's back. Sherisse decided she would not ever return to that church.

"We're not on the same path. It doesn't make sense for us to stay."

I agreed. The current seemed to be carrying us away from institutional religion toward something more authentic.

As Sherisse and I attempted to let go of years of being conditioned to think that being a good Christian meant going to church, it was a challenge to know how to replace the community we had lost. Some folks, even family, wondered what was going on with us. My parents—so proud of my academics, career, and recent teaching—were concerned with the unfamiliar nature of this current I was in. My mom even called Sherisse wanting to know why I couldn't just keep doing Christianity as we'd always done it. Was one of these mentors leading me away from the faith? Was I even still a Christian?

It was a hard reminder that when we answer a divine call, others may not understand and may even doubt us. When we begin to ask hard questions that start to cause the old wineskins to crack, even those closest to us may think we've gone off the deep end.

Sherisse and I remained committed to trusting the current, however. Sherisse especially was convinced that God would send us where we needed to be, and would bring us what we needed in the meantime. At the end of the day, the best Sunday school lesson I ever saw Lila, Ruby, and Levi receive was while we were volunteering at the Nashville Food Project on a bitterly cold winter day. A teenage girl came to our distribution truck barefoot. When Sherisse asked where her shoes were, she replied that she didn't have any. Without hesitating, Sherisse took off her warm winter boots and gave them to the girl.

Doing "small things with great love," to use Mother Teresa's famous words, is the essence of the faith that I want to pass down to my kids.

Seeing Secret Beauty

The contemplatives have a knack for breaking it down like that. They see things a little more clearly, as they really are. Thomas Merton had a famous contemplative experience when he stood on a busy street corner in a shopping district in Louisville, Kentucky, and saw how beautifully connected we all are: "I was suddenly overwhelmed," the monk wrote, "with the realization that I loved all these people, that they were mine and I theirs, that we could not be alien to one another even though we were total strangers. It was like waking from a dream of separateness, of spurious self-isolation."[1]

During my time as a prosecutor, I had failed to appreciate that I was connected to all the defendants in my cases. I was kept at a dehumanizing distance from them, which is how the system is designed. The disconnection obscured their status as bearers of the divine image. Only becoming friends with people who were incarcerated led me to seeing more clearly how connected we all are.

Merton was clear that this way of perceiving others doesn't just happen—and certainly not by accident. Jesus and other wisdom

---

[1] Thomas Merton, *Conjectures of a Guilty Bystander* (New York: Doubleday, 1966), 140.

teachers repeatedly tell their followers to wake up, be alert, and cultivate awareness. In my own life, even short times of quiet in the morning or a walk in the woods helps me catch a glimpse of our interconnectedness. We are not separate, even from people who live behind razor-wire fences. Our dignity, our humanity is bound up with each other's. In the words of Archbishop Desmond Tutu, "We can only be human together."

Rooted in the Will of God

Nouwen, Merton, and so many others invite us to transcend the illusion that we are disconnected from God and from one another. Through contemplative reading and practices, I have become more aware of the dualistic thought processes and false dichotomies that so grip our world. Systems and institutions depend on them. For example, I was once so confident that I, as a law-and-order prosecutor, was good, and that people who had broken the law were bad. However, proximity to people who were incarcerated and times of reflection have revealed that we are all the same and all connected. That's the "scoop."

"Therefore from now on we have stopped evaluating others from a worldly point of view" (II Corinthians 5). No more of the self-serving us-versus-them divides in which our group is always good and right and included, but the people in prison—or people from other denominations, traditions, religions, political parties, nations, races, sexual orientations, genders, or whatever else—are in various ways and degrees bad, wrong, lost, less than, and excluded. The contemplative, the one who has the scoop, recognizes that we are all of us capable of great good and great evil. We are, all of us, caught up in a web of mutuality and interdependence.

The only people Jesus seemed to exclude were the people who clung to labels and divisions to exclude others. Even then, I'm not aware of him ever turning one of them down for a dinner invitation. If his famous parable of the good Samaritan is any indication, he seemed to desperately want people to embrace the truth that the one we are tempting to exclude may end up saving us.

I am convinced this is the way of God's peaceable kingdom, the kingdom that Jesus said is already in our midst. We experience this kingdom when we are reconciled to and stand in solidarity with anyone who is overlooked, discarded, marginalized, and scapegoated.

Vanderbilt University Professor of New Testament and Jewish Studies Dr. Amy-Jill Levine, who has taught many divinity classes inside Tennessee prisons, observes in *Short Stories by Jesus*[2], that one of the most critical questions that our faith traditions should compel us to ask is, Who is not being counted?

In Luke 15, Jesus presents a triad of parables about lost things—a wayward sheep, a missing coin, and a rebellious son. Dr. Levine has pointed out that the only way a person can know whether they have 99 or 100 sheep, or 9 or 10 coins, is to count each and every one. And even if a father has only two sons, one of them—or both of them for different reasons—may feel as though he is not being counted. In God's economy, everyone single one counts.

Although contemplative practices such as silence, times of solitude, simplicity, meditation, and study may at first appear to have little to do with being in community with people who are pushed to the margins, the German philosopher Meister Eckhart reminded us, "What we plant in the soil of contemplation we shall reap in the harvest of action.[3]" Before we can effectively serve others, speak prophetic truth to the dehumanizing powers, and work for justice, we must learn to discern who is not being counted.

When we are committed to making sure that all are counted, the narrative of offense and retribution is quickly exposed as incapable of producing true justice because it also perpetuates the cycle of violence. None should perish under the unfair weight of dehumanizing labels or be sacrificed to the spirit of institutionalized vengeance that robs people like Ashlee, Cyntoia, Sarah, Ndume, and Rahim of their dignity as unique, precious bearers of the divine image.

Waking from a Dream

After being denied release in 2013 and 2014, Rahim Buford was finally granted his well-deserved freedom in 2015. He would be on

---

[2] Amy-Jill Levine, *Short Stories by Jesus* (Nashville, TN: Abingdon Press, 2018).
[3] L. J. Milone, *Nothing but God: The Everyday Mysticism of Meister Eckhart* (Eugene, OR: Resource Publications, 2019), 116.

parole for the rest of his life—forfeiting his right to vote, checking the felon box on job and housing applications—but he was no longer in a cage.

One of the first things Rahim did was take Dr. Forrest Harris, president of American Baptist College, up on his offer of a full scholarship. Not only did he earn his bachelor's degree, he gave the commencement address. Freedom looked good on Rahim.

Eager to put his second chance at work for others, Rahim started working with Janet Wolf at the Children's Defense Fund, speaking to at-risk youth and trying to disrupt the cradle-to-prison pipeline. He also expressed an interest in going with me to the Turney Center, the prison an hour west of Nashville where I still conducted church services.

"You think you can get me in?" he asked.

It was an unusual request. It isn't often that someone who has just gotten out of prison tries to go back in, especially to the exact prison where he spent the first eleven years of his sentence.

"The prison may not allow it," I admitted, "particularly since you haven't even been out a year."

"Well, see what you can do."

As luck would have it, it worked.

On March 27, 2016, which happened to be both Easter Sunday and my thirty-ninth birthday, Rahim and I drove out to what felt like the middle of nowhere in rural Tennessee to visit the guys at the Turney Center.

As we pulled up to the imposing complex, I wondered what must be running through my friend's head. What would it feel like to voluntarily return to a place where he had been held captive for so long? Was there any apprehension about not being allowed to leave when the time came? What nightmares did he associate with this place? What violence had he witnessed here?

"Wow. I used to live here," Rahim said, almost overwhelmed as he looked up at the fences and walls and towers on our way in. He was like a man waking from a dream.

"You know, when my family came on visitation days, I used to try to picture where they were as they were waiting to be admitted," he reflected as we arrived at the first visitor checkpoint. "This is it. I'm standing in the very spot I tried so many times to imagine."

Once we cleared the security checkpoint, Rahim and I made our way across the compound toward the chapel. He pointed out to me where he used to jog for exercise and play basketball. He also showed me where a fight once broke out and a man was stabbed.

Later, Rahim told me another story about violence at the Turney Center, this time involving him.

Old Friends (and Enemies) and New Life

In 1996, Rahim was locked up at the Turney Center, and so was one of his brothers. His brother developed a conflict with a gang member and, although Rahim had nothing to do with the controversy, both his brother and he were targeted by the gang. A few days later, one of the gang members confronted Rahim; then two others, one of them armed with a homemade shank, jumped him from behind. Rahim avoided serious injury in the ensuing fight, but everyone involved was thrown into solitary confinement for several weeks.

When Rahim was finally released back into the general population, it was universally understood that he had been wrongfully targeted, assaulted, and punished for something that had nothing to do with him. As such, he was entitled to vengeance. To keep things from escalating, however, a rival gang mediated the dispute and arranged for Rahim to be compensated in the form of drugs.

"I haven't always been a good person," he said with a little embarrassment as he told me the story.

Once this restitution was made, the issue was considered resolved, and both Rahim and the gang were expected to drop the issue. However, the hard feelings remained between the men involved in the fight.

Two decades later, on this Easter afternoon, Rahim returned a changed man, and a free man.

As we across the prison yard, Rahim saw two men with whom he had served time years earlier. They hurried over to us and hugged him, almost in disbelief that he had come back to visit them. So few ever do.

Stepping into the chapel, he saw three more guys he knew. These were his neighbors, whether he still lived here or not. He knew from experience how much it would mean to them for him to return and show them he had not forgotten them. His trip was already impactful.

I was inspired by Rahim's example and honored and humbled to lead that Easter evening service with him. We did many of the things that had occurred earlier in church buildings across the world: sang hymns, shared the Eucharist, and read the gospel account of Mary Magdalene discovering the empty tomb. Rahim preached a powerful sermon about all people being made in the image of God and being God's children. This is our deepest, truest identity.

"God's power is at work in all of us," Rahim said, "and we can have new life as a result of that power."

Heads nodded. Amens were offered.

Rahim continued, drawing from his experience as a captive to encourage these men who were still, in a sense, entombed, with the good news that prison and death would not have the final word.

After the service, many of the men thanked him for returning to that dark place with a message of hope. One man lingered, nervously awaiting his chance. When he and Rahim locked eyes, Rahim instantly recognized him. He was one of the gang members who had jumped him twenty years earlier. He had shown up at the chapel that evening without any idea of who would be speaking.

The man hung his head and apologized for acting violently against him.

Rahim—embodying his lesson on the power of God at work in dark, death-dealing places—told the man that was in the past and that all was forgiven. Rahim hugged and forgave his former enemy.

That Easter evening, Rahim's words took on flesh as resurrection broke through in the form of an apology, forgiveness, and reconciliation.

Easter truly happened.

But we weren't in some opulently decorated church building with multicolored lighting rigs, jumbo screens, and a state-of-the-art sound system. No, to experience this powerful, dramatic manifestation of resurrection, Rahim and I had to venture away from the world of pretty clothes and egg hunts to go to that place of suffering where Rahim was held captive for so long. Like Mary Magdalene, we had to go to a place of pain and grief, a place where it appears death has won, a place where people are made to feel they do not count, to bear witness to Easter.

Had Mary not gone to the tomb, she would have missed the miracle. We have to leave our comfort zones to see violence be overcome by peace, animosity by reconciliation, hostility by friendship, hatred by love, death by life. Easter is not about going to church. It is about going to a tomb.

A Justice That Really Sees

Were we seeking true justice, transformative justice, we would not banish from our sight the people who have caused harm. Banishment only causes more harm to individuals, spouses and children, and communities. We know that people better themselves in prison. Rahim did. And Ashlee. And Sarah, Cyntoia, and so many others I have not yet mentioned.

Many people who cause harm are themselves victims of physical, emotional, or sexual abuse and endure further trauma behind bars. My friend Eric Alexander, who cofounded the Incarcerated Children's Advocacy Network (ICAN), was locked away at the age of seventeen. He recounts how every day for the first two weeks he had to fight to protect himself from men seeking to take advantage of him. Fourteen straight days of prison fights. Our so-called justice system subjected a child to this horrific violence, and had he lowered his guard for even a moment, he would have become easy prey. The system didn't care, however, because Eric didn't count.

We treat people who are incarcerated as throwaway people, as damaged goods to be discarded and forgotten.

It is incumbent on all people of faith and good will to show them otherwise.

On an Easter Sunday at the Turney Center Prison, Rahim showed through his simple presence to both his old friends and his old enemies, "You are counted."

Gospel moments such as these help us see a little more clearly the true nature of reality, the interconnectedness we all share. They bolster our senses of calling and compassion. In these thin places, where we start to see through the veil and taste a new kingdom and economy of shalom, our perspective broadens, the perimeter of our sense of kinship expands, and we understand justice is created when we recognize ourselves in others.

We are all pretty much the same.

This way of seeing ourselves as infinitely complex, of eternal value, and having the capacity for both good and evil actions is what makes beloved community possible. And it helps us answer the old question, "And who is my neighbor?"

This is a vision of justice that is rooted in shalom, in the conviction that all people are made in the divine image and should be counted, in the practice of beloved community, which sees every human being that dehumanizing systems try to hide.

This is the first duty of society.

I believed it. I was about to find out I was a long way from living it.

Chapter 9

A Reckoning with Racism

It was November of 2016. Donald Trump had just won the election to be president of the United States. Trump campaigned under the standard law-and-order rhetoric, which has served as an anti-Black dog whistle since the Civil Rights Movement. Nevertheless, white Christians overwhelmingly supported his candidacy. Trump's success among white Christians was largely due to the latent racism that had always lurked just under the surface but had grown in intensity for the eight years that a Black family lived in the White House.

For my part, I was convinced it was a moral imperative to speak loudly and often against Trump's thinly veiled appeals to racism and white supremacy. Formerly, I may have been tempted to believe that racists were confined to groups like the Ku Klux Klan. But now, with anti-Black and anti-immigrant rhetoric coming from the Oval Office, they were emboldened. All people of conscience—especially white Christians—had to resist their attempt to undo the racial progress of the last sixty years.

Healing and Hope Get Personal

I had been invited by the Campaign for the Fair Sentencing of Youth to return to Washington, D.C., to speak on a panel at the Healing & Hope gathering it was hosting for formerly incarcerated youth, family members of people serving time, people who have lost loved ones to youth violence, and other advocates. The topic of the panel discussion was racism in the criminal legal system.

Although I was trying to cultivate the habit of saying "yes" to every opportunity the current brought my way, I would have to let this one pass by. I was not the person for the job. Even as a beginner in the contemplative task of seeing things as they truly are, I saw myself clearly enough to know I could not speak credibly about racism. This time I had to regretfully decline.

The CFSY's communications director, James Ross, who had always been supportive and encouraging of me, asked me to reconsider. "We really think you'd be a great addition to the panel." But I knew something that James and the CFSY didn't know. Something that, if they knew, would have kept them from inviting me. I was still a no.

James was persistent and persuasive, however. He finally convinced me to join the panel. I knew the only way I could speak with any credibility and integrity was if I gave an honest account of my own history.

The event arrived, and I took my seat as the only white panelist speaking to a racially diverse audience. I looked at the crowd and saw people I had known for a few years now, people I loved and respected, including Jody Kent Lavy, Rahim Buford, Eric Alexander, and James Ross. I saw people who admired me for the change I had experienced and for leaving my career as a prosecutor. I wanted them to think well of me. Yet I knew that all I could offer as a member of this panel discussing racism was a public confession.

If healing and hope were going to be personal, I had to tell the truth.

"My name is Preston Shipp," I told the audience of a couple of hundred people whose lives had been impacted by this racist system of punishment. "I used to be a prosecutor, but now I support criminal justice reform. And as much as I would like to think otherwise, as a white man raised in the South, I am guilty of being a racist."

The silence was deafening.

My mouth went dry. My heart pounded. My stomach hurt and I started to sweat.

There was no going back now.

The Power of the Symbol

My family's roots go deep into Southern soil. My Dad's family is from a town called Bell Buckle in rural Rutherford County, southeast of Nashville. Mom's family is from Pulaski, Tennessee, where former

Confederate General Nathan Bedford Forrest and others founded the Ku Klux Klan the year after the Civil War ended.

As kids, my sister Emily and I often heard about our ancestors who fought in the Civil War. Sometimes it was even called the "War of Northern Aggression," implying that the South had been the innocent victim of the North's violence, which forced everyday people to take up arms to defend their families and homes from the invading Union Army. To this day, across the South you can see Confederate flags flying, statues honoring Confederate soldiers, and people wearing clothing with Confederate symbols.

Raised with a white-washed, romanticized version of Southern history, I was not encouraged to think of brutal slave traders, families ripped apart, kidnapped Africans chained in ship holds, and human beings bought and sold at auction like farm animals or machinery. I didn't imagine that the "way of life" Southerners fought to preserve amounted to forcing men, women, and children to work in brutal conditions, then return to miserable quarters with only scraps for sustenance. We didn't talk about the abuse, rape, and severe torture in the form of whippings and amputations. I wanted to believe that my ancestors were good, fair, honorable people.

This revisionist history is still being reinforced in history classrooms throughout the South, as we have recently seen in states like Florida, where the teaching of critical race theory has been banned and new standards promote the idea that slavery was of some benefit to Black people because it taught them useful skills.

There is so much about life in the South that I love—giant magnolia trees like the one in my front yard, lightning bugs on summer nights, fried foods and sweet tea, and SEC football. I grew up listening to music by bands like Lynyrd Skynyrd, the Allman Brothers, and Alabama, who sang "Song of the South," "Dixieland Delight," and "Mountain Music." I've raced down dirt roads and jumped railroad tracks on the way to a swimming hole, just like Bo and Luke did on *The Dukes of Hazzard,* in their orange Dodge Charger named the General Lee, complete with Confederate flag painted on the roof.

When I saw that flag, I didn't think about the murderous violence, terrorism, and injustice of white supremacy. I was thinking of some of my favorite bands and TV shows, all of which tapped into a nonconformist, rebel spirit. Fellow Southerner and Rock and Roll

Hall of Famer Tom Petty used the Confederate flag onstage at some of his early concerts, for which he eventually issued a public apology.

I, too, was ignorant. And ignorance breeds racism.

Nothing in my experience of Christian churches and schools helped me overcome that ignorance. Attending predominantly white congregations and almost exclusively white schools is an effective way of protecting the ignorance that is a hallmark of white privilege. White people like me have the luxury of not learning about the insidious, even lethal effects of racism on the lives of Black Americans.

As I spoke to the attendees at the conference hosted by the Campaign for the Fair Sentencing of Youth, I confessed to my hurtful ignorance. I was filled with shame, as I am now, to admit that I told jokes about Black people, thinking it was good-natured, harmless fun. To celebrate that rebel spirit that I admired in people like Tom Petty, I hung a Confederate flag in my college dorm room, never once considering how offensive it would be to the Black people who saw it. (Please know I have since apologized personally to the Black students who lived in my dorm for harboring racism in my dorm room and in my heart while I was in college. They responded with grace and forgiveness.) I bought a t-shirt in Gatlinburg, Tennessee, a popular tourist destination in the Great Smokey Mountains, that depicted the Confederate flag and the words: "Heritage Not Hate." As an ignorant white person, I was blind to the fact that the heritage *was* hate.

I had not yet confronted the symbolic power of the Confederate flag and its connection to an evil history of slavery, burning crosses, and lynching. I had not yet read James H. Cone's assertion in *The Cross and the Lynching Tree*[1] that, in light of the history of racial violence in America, it is impossible to not see Jesus' crucifixion as an ancient lynching. The lynching tree in the United States is like the cross in Roman culture. Victims of lynchings were stripped of their humanity, and the secondary victims—the terrorized communities—were reminded what could happen to them if they in any way offended the white power structure.

The flag of the Confederate States of America cannot be separated from this history of racist brutality. Yet when I was eighteen years old, I had the letters "CSA" tattooed on my right shoulder.

---

[1] James H. Cone, *The Cross and the Lynching Tree* (Maryknoll, NY: Orbis Books, 2011).

Marginalized Life Experiences

As I publicly confessed my most shameful actions and attitudes, my eyes filled with tears. I scanned the audience, which listened in total silence, and saw the faces of people I held in such high regard. Many of them I thought of as sisters and brothers, despite the different color of our skin. Now I was having to own up to things that I wished weren't true, ways I had betrayed their friendship before I knew them. It felt like my reckoning with Cyntoia all over again.

My voice started to crack and tears streamed down my face. I apologized first to the other panelists, then to individuals I saw in the audience trying to make sense of what they were hearing. I was invited to be on this panel because they perceived me as an ally in the struggle for racial justice. Instead, they were hearing that I was now doubly guilty of contributing to the indignities that they had suffered.

Would I have ever before called myself racist?

Of course not.

As I saw justice more clearly, thanks to my friends who were or had been incarcerated, I also began to perceive the myriad ways that America's original sin of racism infects every aspect of the judicial process. It had infected me as well. My friendship with gracious people from different races and backgrounds gave me a broader perspective and helped me recognize the plank that had always obscured my vision. My friends referred me to books and documentaries by African American authors and filmmakers that helped me recognize my own racist tendencies and the need for repentance and confession.

Richard Rohr often refers to the margins of society as "liminal space," which he has described as "an inner state and sometimes an outer situation, where people can begin to think and act in genuinely new ways."[2] In his reflections on social justice, Mark Longhurst stated, "For white people coming from privileged backgrounds, this may mean non-defensive, open-hearted listening to the marginalized life experiences of black and brown Americans."[3]

---

[2] Richard Rohr, *Adam's Return: The Five Promises of Male Initiation* (Chestnut Ridge, NY: Crossroad Publishing, 2004), 135.
[3] Mark Longhurst, "Transformation at the Margins," *Oneing* 5, no. 1 (2017): 108.

This described so well my friendship with many of the amazing individuals gathered in this room.

Longhurst added, "Once hearts are cracked open, for example, to hear the horror of African American experiences, first of slavery and lynching, and now of incarceration, the war on drugs, and gun violence, it becomes a transformative human response to affirm with weeping, prayer, solidarity, and action that black lives matter."[4]

I very much felt like I was being cracked open. I had spent the last several years acknowledging the role I had played in America's broken system of retribution. It can be hard enough to acknowledge injustice in an institution like a police department or in a system like the prison-industrial complex. Now I was having to confess to the injustice in my own heart.

The Primary Predictor of Violent Crime

A justice that restores is possible. We can imagine and develop alternatives to retribution that seek the well-being of all affected parties, that do not perpetuate the cycle of racism. They can break forth like a flower through concrete. However, as long as we allow overwhelming numbers of Black Americans to be regarded as disposable, with no hope of restoration, our society will remain sick unto death.

Poet Adrienne Rich said that war represents "an absolute failure of imagination," and I believe the same can be said of our criminal justice policies and the fifty-year-old war on drugs. Rather than imagining healing paths that lead to wholeness, we have limited ourselves to acts of punishment and revenge that disproportionately impact Black and Brown individuals, families, and communities.

Instead of facilitating rehabilitation, imprisonment—and all its collateral consequences of employment and housing discrimination—creates more crime than it prevents. My friend Rahim Buford coined a term to describe this blatant affront to the spirit of the Civil Rights Movement: *felonism.*

The casual, unexamined racism that might lead an ignorant college kid to hang a Confederate flag in his dorm room—or cause a voter to cast a ballot for a blustering, immoral con man promising

---

[4] Longhurst, "Transformation at the Margins," 108.

to Make America Great Again—also insidiously infects our criminal justice policies and courtrooms. For most of my life, my unacknowledged white privilege allowed me to ignore uncomfortable facts about myself, my family, and my country, and my own moral imagination was compromised.

Each of us has a choice to expand our understanding and grow, or to stay mired in the ignorance that makes bigotry possible.

The choice is up to us, and we must keep making it.

So Accepting and Affirming

On that chilly afternoon in Washington, D.C., in front of a room full of the CFSY's staff, partners, supporters, and friends, I had to muster the courage to be honest about my own history of racist attitudes and actions. It went completely against my tendency to protect my self-image as a good, moral person. When my priority is keeping my mask on, I lose the truth. There was no other way for me to speak truthfully and with any integrity about the racism inherent in our system of laws and punishment. I was hoping that the saying of Jesus recorded in the gospel of Thomas was true: "If you bring forth what is within you, what you bring forth will save you. If you do not bring forth what is within you, what you do not bring forth will destroy you."

As I concluded my remarks and dried my eyes, I felt intensely vulnerable and afraid of how the people in the audience might be thinking differently of me. Had I just done permanent damage to my friendships with people like Rahim, Eric, and James Ross, who might well be regretting his invitation to have me join the panel?

As the session ended, a member of the CFSY staff approached me to thank me for what I had shared. Instead of shaking my hand or giving me a hug, he put his hands on my face, thanked me for my courage, and told me he forgave me. His words and actions felt pastoral and healing.

Grace upon grace upon grace upon grace.

First, I was forgiven by the women in the LIFE Program for being a prosecutor. Then I was forgiven by Cyntoia and her adoptive mother for specifically arguing in her case that she should spend fifty-one years in prison. Now I was being forgiven for years of neglecting to reckon with my own racism.

Others expressed their thanks and forgiveness as well, their words like a healing balm after confessing my own deep brokenness. Two weeks later, I received an email from James Ross, whose insistence that I serve as a panelist helped channel the current in this direction of healing:

My friend, my brother—I just wanted to drop you a note of thanks . . .

Your voice was critically needed on the panel on race. I think it is a mistake to talk about race without including white folks. In addition, you have the experience of working as a prosecutor, so you understand that mentality. And you offered a level of honesty about whiteness, white sensibilities and the lack of awareness that often accompanies it. That knowledge will pay dividends for many years. ...

I will never forget the power of hearing your story, of what contributed to your racial formation, of the ways in which you were participating in racist practices, generally without realizing it. Your humility in sitting before a group of people of varied races ... and apologizing for your behaviors was transformative and restorative. It reminds me of the potential that we all have to bring forth goodness. And it affirms for me that often, what people want more than anything else, is for someone else to acknowledge their pain . . .

I have found that many white people become enraged when they are accused of engaging in racist behaviors. I find that highly problematic because it forestalls the possibility of real engagement. ... I don't think it is possible to live as a white person in this society and not take on some white supremacy. It is core to our society. Yet, it is possible to be intentional about confronting it. ...

Anyway, none of this is the reason for my email. ... I really just want to thank you for your presence and witness during the convening. ...

Blessings to you, today, and always,

James

In late 2016, when an unrepentant white supremacist had just been elected president of the United States based largely on his inflammatory racist rhetoric, I felt the current carrying me toward deeper unity and kinship. Dear friends like James Ross, Eric Alexander, Rahim Buford, and many others had accepted and affirmed me in ways I couldn't have imagined possible prior to the Healing & Hope gathering. Having confessed some of my worst sins, I experienced both.

America's Original Sin

I know from experience that it is tempting for white people to speak against racism on a systemic level and advocate for racial justice without acknowledging our complicity in racial injustice or engaging in the hard work of repentance. Repentance is, I think, the beginning of moral seriousness, and it's the first word of the good news announced by Jesus of Nazareth.

This kind of specific, granular repentance—when we open ourselves up publicly and expose our most hidden realities, the parts of ourselves we'd rather keep hidden and pretend don't exist—can feel a bit like jumping off the high dive. I had to work up my courage before I took the plunge in front of that room full of people. Now, in this regard at least, I don't have to pretend to be something I'm not. I was so scared, but the water was fine.

Every time I've admitted to being wrong, every time I've mustered up the courage to honestly confront my own shadowland, it has made the next time a little easier. Confession, repentance, and apology open the door to moments of healing that otherwise wouldn't have been possible.

One of those opportunities came three years later, in November 2019, when I had an opportunity to visit The Legacy Museum, in Montgomery, Alabama. Developed by Bryan Stevenson's Equal Justice Initiative (EJI), the museum is situated on land by the Coosa River where African Americans were once bought and sold as slaves. Using interactive media and jarring visuals, it chronicles the insidious history of racism in America, from the unspeakable horrors of the slave trade, to the terrorist violence and dehumanizing indignities of the Jim Crow era, to the racial disparities inherent in the war on drugs and mass incarceration.

Less than a mile away sits the National Memorial for Peace and Justice, also founded by EJI. As I approached the Memorial, I saw more than 800 black pillars rising from the foundation to support the structure—or so it appeared. Drawing closer, I realized stairs worked their way down several levels below the pillars, which were actually suspended from the roof. Every county in which a Black person was lynched is represented by a column, and the names of the victims and dates of the murders are also engraved on the pillar. Each act of terror is documented by tedious research, and soil samples are collected from each site and put on display.

The Memorial offers a gut-wrenching, visceral, physical lament and remembrance in honor of the victims of lynchings. Observing the thread that runs from slavery to the horror of lynchings to the modern era of the prison-industrial complex makes an indelible impression on all who bear witness to it.

The sheer scale and numbers are staggering, with columns representing counties in more than a dozen states—not all in the South. The victims number more than 4,400, all murdered between 1877 and 1950. Some were beaten to death or hanged, others shot or stabbed, and others drowned or burned alive. The names and stories are haunting and heartbreaking, a damning indictment of our failure to reckon with and atone for America's original sin.

I saw a column representing Rutherford County, where my dad's family came from.

There was Giles County, where my mom was born.

There was Davidson County, where Sherisse and I lived with our sweet children. Horrors happened here that white people have refused to talk about.

As I walked down into the center of the memorial, columns hanging over my head, I thought about the thousands of families who had lost loved ones to these acts of racial terror and the systems of injustice that refused to hold the white terrorists accountable, right up to the lynching of Ahmaud Arbery in February of 2020.

As theologian David Dark says, "America is a crime scene."[5]

The poison of racism has infected every aspect of our common life.

---

[5] David Dark, "Dark Matter," accessed February 22, 2024, https://daviddark.substack.com/p/the-new-seriousness.

Racism did not end when slavery was abolished in 1865, or when the Civil Rights Act was passed in 1964. It has reasserted itself in the form of mass incarceration, a fact illustrated at the EJI Legacy Museum in Montgomery. It has caged and killed far more Black people than all of the decades of unchecked lynchings.

As much as we would like to think that our house has been swept clean, the evil of racism was never exorcised from our hearts or our institutions, as we've seen numerous times over the past few years:

The murder of nine Black church members at a Bible study in Charleston.

The marching of white supremacists in Charlottesville.

Eleven people killed and six wounded in a Pittsburg synagogue.

A controversy over removing monuments to Confederate soldiers.

Vilifying NFL players kneeling in protest of police brutality against Black people.

Like a diseased man who foolishly assumes he has been cured merely because the symptoms have changed, many of us have been horrified to see white supremacists emboldened to speak and act in ways that we hoped died decades ago.

One of the most urgent tasks we face is to stop living in denial about the racism that sickens our systems, institutions, and hearts, and to commit to changing ourselves and our society.

The Church Has Failed Miserably

Perhaps part of why it was so difficult for me to own up to my own racism is because that kind of confession and repentance was not modeled for me. The white church is as complicit in America's original sin as any institution in the nation. After all, the largest Protestant denomination in the nation, the Southern Baptist Convention, was founded in 1845 as a white supremacist haven for enslavers. Not only did it teach that the gospel of Jesus Christ had nothing to do with the dehumanizing practice of treating other human beings as property, it affirmatively baptized slavery as an expression of the divine will for humanity.

Many have noted, including Dr. Martin Luther King, Jr., that Sunday morning is the most racially segregated time of the week.

This trend of racial division within the church continues, as shown by the recent research of Robert P. Jones in his book *The End of White Christian America.*[6]

White Christians do not merely worship in segregated churches, however. We live in racially segregated neighborhoods. We send our children to racially segregated schools. This is all by design.

Is it any wonder that, during the Civil Rights era, white Christians were overwhelmingly opposed to the work their Christian brothers like Dr. King and John Lewis were doing to promote racial justice? The white church in America has failed to bear witness to the gospel, the ministry of racial reconciliation.

In his book, *Race and the Renewal of the Church,*[7] Will D. Campbell lamented that the church "has waited too long to carry out its mandate, and to a large part of the world, what we Christians do from here on out really does not matter very much."

The book was published in 1962.

Has anything really changed?

Are white Christians in America embracing their vocation to be ministers of reconciliation? Or are they overwhelmingly still supporting a white supremacist who slanders immigrants by calling their countries "shitholes" and warning they will "infest" the United States?

If we're honest, we have to admit there has been no confession and no repentance, which I learned as a child in Sunday school are both necessary to an experience of salvation.

We have not, despite all our religious rhetoric, been born again.

A Rude Awakening

Our stubborn refusal to be converted to a compassion that will not tolerate the evils of racism was brought home to me in a series of events in late 2019 and early 2020 that left me both furious and heartbroken.

My alma mater, Lipscomb University, which had such a profound impact on my formation, most immediately through my involvement

---

[6] Robert P. Jones, *The End of White Christian America* (New York: Simon & Schuster, 2017).

[7] Will D. Campbell, *Race and the Renewal of the Church* (Louisville, KY: Westminster Press, 1962).

in the LIFE Program, had just hired a brilliant young Black woman to serve as its first ever Dean of Intercultural Development. White parents, who no doubt attended white churches in the white suburbs, were immediately suspicious.

When a history teacher, a white man, assigned a reading about America's shameful history of racism, the white parents wrongly assumed he must have done so because of the influence of the new Black dean. Although they both refuted this claim, the mob of parents would not be deterred. Someone was going to pay for their white children learning about the reality of racism, and they had found a perfect scapegoat.

Led by John Rich—a Trump-supporting, country singer who once upon a time won the Celebrity Apprentice—the parents demanded that Lipscomb fire the new dean. Otherwise, they could easily send their children to any of the other numerous private Christian schools in Nashville, many of which were founded in the 1970s as "segregation academies" in direct response to the desegregation of public schools. They knew that if Lipscomb would not budge, plenty of other schools would be glad to take their tuition dollars and never say anything that might challenge latent racism and bigotry.

Lipscomb eventually capitulated and fired its brilliant Black dean, sacrificing her to an angry white mob.

The disgraceful incident made the national news, including *Sojourners* magazine and *Christianity Today*. It wasn't the first time that Lipscomb found itself in the national spotlight because of its racist actions. In 2017, the university president was forced to apologize to Black students after inviting them to his house and serving them macaroni 'and cheese, collard greens, and cornbread, on tables decorated with cotton stalks as centerpieces, and to Latinx students after serving them fajitas the previous night.

I reached the disappointing conclusion that my alma mater was an institution that, while marketing itself as "Christian," was unwilling to reckon with the deep-seated racism in its midst. I spoke as loudly and often as I could on behalf of the dean, who was a friend. In doing so, I knowingly burned a bridge that meant a great deal to me. I have not been invited to teach or speak in any capacity at Lipscomb University since.

White supremacy is a hell of a drug, and sometimes, for institutions like Lipscomb, it pays the bills.

It's Hard to Acknowledge Sin

I was greatly humbled and encouraged by the gracious email from the CFSY's James Ross thanking me for participating in the panel. Soon after, I sent him my reply:

> I hardly know what to say. Thank you for your kind words . . .
>
> I found the conference to be inspiring, and I was in need of some inspiration. I have told a number of people how remarkable it was to have such a diverse crowd in terms of race, gender, and background, people who have served long sentences, families of victims of violence, all dedicated to reconciliation, healing, and justice. It was beautiful. ...
>
> It was healing for me to get to share the culture I grew up in and try to humbly acknowledge ways in which I am a "recovering" racist, to use your pastor's terms. As I am coming to terms with the racism in our society and in my own heart and history, I am convinced that confession and apology and repentance are essential before any reconciliation can begin. ... I needed to do that publicly, but don't know when I would have otherwise had the guts. It's hard to acknowledge sin, especially such an ugly sin, which is probably why so many white people are in denial. So thank you for giving me the opportunity to reckon with some of the sin that is so hard to root out. I am so thankful to have friends like you.
>
> I'm excited to stay involved with your good work. ... As always, let me know if there's anything I can do.

Growing up in church and Christian schools, I learned that two things were of highest importance. The first was obeying rules, mostly about not drinking or having sex before marriage. The second was believing all the right things about everything from the significance of Jesus' death to how to read the Bible to the role of women in the church to whether we could have instruments playing during the service. I was not taught to question how my faith affects my thinking about and work for racial justice. I was certainly not encouraged to confront, as a matter of Christian discipleship, the racism baked into our most trusted institutions—like the criminal legal system, the Southern Baptist Convention, and Lipscomb University—much less my own heart. Yet after that moment of confession during the panel on racism, I recognized that sharing my weakness had not created despair — it had instead created hope.

Chapter 10

A More Promising Path

It is infuriating to me that my home state of Tennessee, where there's a church building on every corner and politicians routinely tweet out Bible verses, has some of the most draconian sentencing laws in the country, including far and away the harshest mandatory sentence for murder in the country. Tennessee still stubbornly clings to the death penalty and will condemn to life without the possibility of parole a child who legally cannot do any of the many things we reserve for adults.

The judges who impose these harsh sentences, many of whom occupy the most honored positions in their Christian congregations, seemingly cast away the gospel values of mercy, forgiveness, and redemption when they wrap themselves in their black robes, and instead place their trust in a retributive system that institutionalizes violence.

Our entire system of laws and punishment, every aspect of the billion-dollar prison-industrial complex, is constructed on the myth of redemptive violence. It is so prevalent and ubiquitous that it largely goes unquestioned. Trying to discern the myth of redemptive violence in all its manifestations is like a fish trying to notice water.

One might presume that our society thinks its first duty is redemptive violence.

As Wink and many others have observed, this myth that violence is redemptive is very dangerous for people who claim to follow One who taught that our highest calling is to love our neighbors as ourselves, who cautioned against seeking eye-for-an-eye vengeance, and who observed that those who employ violence will be destroyed by it.

In hundreds of cases, I argued for eye-for-an-eye retribution, and I did so thinking it was God's will. Raised with a picture of God as a righteous judge who would dole out eternal punishment to wrongdoers, I saw no conflict in serving in a role centered around judgment and punishment. Every time I signed my name to a brief, I affirmed my moral and legal belief that justice was synonymous with punishment. The government that I worked for did not bear the sword in vain.

We Don't Mean What We Say

The myth of redemptive violence has so captured our collective imagination that many Americans actually believe we are too soft on crime. This despite the United States having the largest prison population in the history of the world, being the only country in the world known to condemn a child to die in prison, and remaining the only advanced Western democracy that maintains capital punishment. We lock away more of our citizens than the very nations we condemn for human rights violations.

Punishment—specifically, prison—remains our default response even to nonviolent property and drug crimes. Lawmakers, prosecutors, and judges, all of whom are popularly elected, want to avoid any hint of appearing soft on crime, and can derive some cheap political capital by letting voters know they are being hard on lawbreakers. Again, the good/bad, us/them dichotomy is always self-serving.

While other developed countries measure the success of their criminal justice policies by their ability to effectively rehabilitate and return to society people who have broken the law, here in the alleged Land of the Free, where we euphemistically refer to our prison system as a department of "correction," we measure success in terms of how much time we can make someone serve, often with no regard to whether the person has experienced rehabilitation.

As in the case of Rahim Buford's parole hearing, we will tell a fully rehabilitated individual for whom continued incarceration will serve no constructive purpose, "We just want you to suffer more."

It is as though violence is the point.

Why? Why are we so hellbent on vengeance?

Why are we proving incapable of learning the lessons that other civilizations have mastered? After all, if punishment could make us safe, ours would be the safest society in history. Yet our rates of violence crimes far exceed those of countries whose criminal justice policies we would dismiss as soft and unrealistic.

As the saying popularly attributed to Albert Einstein goes, "Insanity is doing the same thing over and over and expecting different results." Our continued overreliance on incarceration, our stubborn clinging to the death penalty, and our racially disproportionate prison population clearly demonstrates that we have collectively lost our minds.

In Their Defense

We are clearly doing something wrong, when our unprecedented investment in systemic punishment causes more harm than it addresses. From the comfort of our offices, sofas, and pews, most of us still claim to value forgiveness, redemption, and second chances. Talk is cheap, however. The sentencing policies we have tolerated or even supported are rooted firmly in the myth that the solution to violence is more violence.

Cyntoia Brown, reflecting on her own experience of our institutionalized vengeance, has written, "I believed a juvenile court prosecutor should seek to reposition misguided youth onto a more promising path—to issue tickets of transfer from the train of perdition to the train of promise. The sad reality I witnessed was that the prosecutor was out for blood and intent on sealing off the path to the 'land of second chance.'"[1]

It is worth noting here that in the Bible, the name Satan literally means "accuser." And when the Accuser approaches God in Job chapter 1, he does so as a prosecuting attorney before an impartial, aloof judge.

This spirit of accusation animates our criminal legal system, and for a time, I was quite comfortable serving as its host body. My

---

[1] Cyntoia Brown and Preston Shipp, "Misjudging: A Reconciliation Story" in *And the Criminals with Him: Essays in Honor of Will D. Campbell and All the Reconciled*, eds. Will D. Campbell and Richard C. Goode (Eugene, OR: Wipf and Stock, 2012), 226.

parents were proud of me. No one in my church circles ever seemed to notice any tension between being a prosecutor and following Jesus, who was a victim of that same spirit of accusation.

Yet Jesus warns us, "Do not judge, or you too will be judged. For in the same way you judge others, you will be judged, and with the measure you use, it will be measured to you. Why do you look at the speck of sawdust in your brother's eye and pay no attention to the plank in your own eye?"

I had read these words many times but I didn't know how to apply them to my life until I was in close proximity to people who had received our society's harshest judgments.

Only then did I begin to understand that we are not called to be accusers, but to stand with those who are accused, marginalized, scapegoated, and made into objects of condemnation and scorn.

When people are ready to throw stones of accusation, Jesus disrupts the violence. Here is one who does not offer condemnation, even where guilt is not at issue. We are called to stand with those who are being judged and condemned.

But don't hold your breath waiting to hear that message from many other pastors. Steeple management tends to obscure these truths that only tend to come into focus when we heed Jesus' command to visit the places that scare us.

Recognizing Ourselves in Each Other

More than anything else, this is what I hope folks who read this book will understand—I have learned more from people who either are or have been in prison about the nature of God—about the gospel of joy, peace, justice, forgiveness, reconciliation, redemption, and second chances—than in all my years of religious education and going to church. When it comes to true, deep, humble, Godly wisdom, professors and pulpits don't hold a candle to the men on death row. And it's not even close.

My story is about the ongoing conversion I experience by associating with people who often exist outside the sphere of our concern. It is through those friendships that I gained an enlightened gospel perspective. Although I had always "believed," it took going into prisons to convert me from a superficial, self-satisfied faith that was focused on pretending to have all the answers to abstract theological questions, to a deeper, compassion-focused faith that actually makes a concrete difference in my life and the lives of others. Just talking and singing about God Sunday after Sunday after Sunday is a clanging cymbal. Faith that doesn't manifest itself in works of true justice is worthless. Sensing this, people are leaving the steeples in droves, as Sherisse and I did when our congregation's elders refused financial aid to an abused woman in need. Authentic faith, faith that saves, is not aloof. It bandages the wounds of the broken.

I am slowly learning the lesson Jesus laid out in Matthew 25, that my salvation is bound up with that of people who are suffering in dark and lonely places. In my mind, this is the key to understanding true justice.

When President Obama noted that "justice grows out of recognition of ourselves in each other," he was delivering a eulogy for Reverend Clementa Pinckney, who, along with eight other Black people, was murdered by a white supremacist as they held a Bible study. In the wake of that unfathomable racist violence, we seek a justice that does not in any way minimize the nature of the tragedy or the grief and trauma of the victims, their loved ones, and their communities. We seek a justice that can help begin the process of healing. We do not settle for the popular myth that more violence is redemptive. We embrace a new vision of justice, which consists of recognizing ourselves in each other.

This is true justice, biblical justice, shalom justice. This is the justice prophets through the ages have prayed to roll down like waters. And it "grows out of recognition of ourselves in each other."

I would not have understood these words had I not learned their meaning from my friends in prison.

Cyntoia and I needed this experience of true justice, of recognizing ourselves in each other, putting aside human labels, and being reconciled. Rahim and his attacker needed an experience of shalom justice in that prison chapel, of recognizing themselves in each other despite the violence that had divided them twenty years earlier, to forgive and embrace.

Justice like this is the core of the gospel, and it is the antithesis of the myth of redemptive violence because it always seeks to heal. It's like a treasure hidden in a field where most people never even think to look. It's like a pearl of great price that, once you understand its value, you're willing to give up just about anything, even a promising career, to experience it more fully.

Reconciled To Each Other

Learning to renounce the myth of redemptive violence, to abandon the spirit of accusation, and to recognize ourselves in each other is a life's work. Every step we take along the journey opens us up to experiencing true justice and beloved community.

This should be the work of the church, but I'm afraid it is not. In the twenty-plus years I've been volunteering in prisons, I have had a preacher join me only once. I have never had an elder go with me. More times than I can count, out of a congregation of more than 1,000, I was the only person volunteering with the prison ministry. Fewer than a third of people who are incarcerated receive a monthly visit from a friend or family member.[2]

On the back of every pew in every sanctuary in every one of America's 300,000 church buildings is a Bible, in which Jesus' words are written, "I was in prison, and you visited me." However, many Christians aren't leaving those pews. Perhaps they think sitting there on a cushion for an hour a week is the point. We are left with churches that fail to take seriously the words of the One they sing to, and two million incarcerated people who are under no misapprehension about how Christians feel about them. The lost sheep can remain lost while the ninety-nine listen to praise and worship music.

Prison abolitionist and preacher Will Campbell opined that if every Christian congregation in America committed to regularly visiting one, two, or three people who are caged, "this elementary act of charity alone would provide all the prison reform that society could tolerate."[3] But it's mighty hard for Christians to echo Jesus' proclamation of release for prisoners when they don't even know any prisoners.

---

[2] Bernadette Rabuy and Daniel Kopf, "Separation by Bars and Miles: Visitation in State Prisons," Prison Policy Initiative, accessed Jan 26, 2024, https://www.prisonpolicy.org/reports/prisonvisits.html.

[3] Will D. Campbell, "Law and Love in Lowndes," in *And the Criminals with Him: Essays in Honor of Will D. Campbell and All the Reconciled*, eds. Will D. Campbell and Richard C. Goode (Eugene, OR: Wipf and Stock, 2012), 19.

As a Christian, I believe all people of faith must take this calling seriously. It's also the work of civic organizations, sports teams, and universities. Small business and multi-billion-dollar corporations can make a huge difference if people of conscience in positions of influence will simply ask what they can do where they are.

Imagine the impact on our justice system and on our communities if we actually invested in the lives of people who are incarcerated. If we treated them as people in need of a helping hand, some guidance, and support, rather than monsters to be banished, the rate of recidivism would plummet. College initiatives like the LIFE Program would be the norm rather than the exception. Upon their release, employment, housing, and transportation needs would be addressed. Counseling and self-care to heal the pain of prior trauma and abuse would be encouraged and available because, as we know that hurt people hurt people, we also know that healed people heal people. As we sought to provide a network of support that is so desperately needed by people who are incarcerated, we would find a network of support for ourselves. We would leave behind the spirit of accusation and embrace the vision of beloved community.

"Come and See"

When Philip told his friend (or possibly brother) Nathanael about Jesus of Nazareth, Nathanael replied, "Can any good thing come out of Nazareth?" Knowing that some folks may likewise be wondering whether anything good can really come out of a prison, my answer is the same as that of Philip: "Come and see." See if these aren't some of the most brilliant, resilient, compassionate, motivated, inspirational people you've ever met.

James "Jamo" Thomas was condemned to die in prison when he was a fifteen-year-old child. After serving thirty years in prison, he was given a second chance. Today, Jamo runs a nonprofit food ministry called Rising Sun Ink that feeds seven hundred needy families a week. He dedicates his life to tackling poverty and inequities in his community, mentors youth, organizes back-to-school supply giveaways, and helps returning citizens in Michigan transition to life after prison.[4] He is driven to give back, to be "an agent of change."

---

[4] Schultz Family Foundation, "This Former Juvenile Lifer Is an Agent of Change," posted October 24, 2022, https://www.youtube.com/watch?v=zopaoEEYAXI.

Lorenzo Harrell was sentenced to life without parole when he was seventeen. He was caged for twenty-six years. While he was locked up, he taught himself Braille because he wanted to stop hurting people and start helping people. He now "gives back" by transcribing books into Braille so that blind people can read.[5] (I'm hoping he'll translate this book!)

When Jesus came on the scene, he told folks that one of the telltale signs that the kingdom is breaking forth is that blind people begin to see. Lorenzo is doing his part.

Ashlee Sellars, my friend from the LIFE program at Tennessee Prison for Women, was finally released after twenty-one years after being imprisoned at seventeen. Since her release, Ashlee has been prolific in her community advocacy. She works with a number of organizations promoting restorative justice for youth involved in the criminal legal system, most notably Raphah Institute, which diverts kids out of the punitive system into a process that actually focuses on problem solving.

Donnell Drinks was sentenced to death as a child, before the barbaric practice was finally ruled unconstitutional in violation of the "cruel and unusual punishment" clause of the Eighth Amendment. He was then sentenced to life without the possibility of parole, or death by incarceration. But when the U.S. Supreme Court ruled that mandatory life without parole was likewise unconstitutional for children, he finally received a parolable sentence and was eventually given a second chance. Donnell now runs a violence intervention program in Philadelphia. He is out on the streets late at night trying to keep young people out of bad situations that could take them down the road he had walked.[6]

Ndume Olatushani was set free after nearly twenty-eight years, twenty of them on death row at Riverbend, for a crime he did not commit. He received no compensation for this injustice. Ndume now lives in Colorado, shares his stories with audiences around the world, and his art has been featured in museums, universities, and even courthouses.

---

[5] Campaign for the Fair Sentencing of Youth, "Lorenzo's Journey: The CFSY," posted May 12, 2023, https://www.youtube.com/watch?v=3ACpaNKm1RU.

[6] Issie Lapowsky, "Sentenced to Life as Boys, They Made Their Case for Release," *New York Times*, August 15, 2023, https://www.nytimes.com/2023/08/15/headway/prison-life-sentence-release.html.

After serving ten years for essentially being in the wrong place at the wrong time when he was seventeen years old, Eric Alexander, reflecting on the child he remembers being, developed programs for at-risk youth that were implemented by the YMCA and Metro Nashville Public Schools.

Edward Sanders, another life-sentenced child, became such an expert in the law while he was locked up that, after his release, he served as a consultant in a reform-minded prosecutor's office.

My friend Eddie Ellis was arrested and charged with murder at age sixteen. At his sentencing hearing, the judge read from the presentence report that Eddie was a "menace to society" who simply could not be rehabilitated. Labeled irredeemable and discarded, Eddie served ten long years, a full decade, in solitary confinement. He was eventually released into the general population and ultimately given a second chance at life outside prison walls.

Eddie invested himself in criminal justice reform initiatives, and he began receiving speaking invitations. He was even asked to speak at Georgetown Law School. Joining Eddie on the panel was the judge who had sentenced him, and the judge brought with him Eddie's presentence report.

The judge again read from the report the same words he had used to condemn Eddie fifteen years earlier. Menace to society. Incapable of rehabilitation.

Before a conference full of law school professors and students, the judge repented. "I want everyone here to know that was wrong. We never should have talked about Eddie that way."

Eddie now leads self-care retreats for formerly incarcerated people. During the pandemic in 2020 and 2021, Eddie called me at least once or twice a week to make sure I was doing all right and taking care of myself.

After serving over twenty-one years, Dolphy Jordan became a reentry specialist for folks who have been diverted to drug court, connecting them with health and housing services and employment opportunities.

Sarah Bryant, the poet from the LIFE Program who impressed Nikki Giovanni, earned her degree in social work and became a drug and alcohol treatment counselor.

Upon his release, Brandon Harrington was working fourteen-hour days in a factory. But he saw a commercial on television for becoming a commercial truck driver. He obtained his commercial driver's license and is now filling an important economic need for truck drivers in rural Michigan.

Barbi Brown completed her bachelor's degree in the LIFE Program. After she was released, she became the director of policy and practice for the Tennessee Higher Education Initiative, which makes it possible for other incarcerated people to benefit as she did from ongoing education.

After finally being released on parole after twenty-six years, Rahim Buford went to work as the manager of the Nashville Community Bail Fund, which provides small loans to people who cannot afford bail and would therefore be forced to remain in jail, awaiting a court date, despite the fact that they were presumed innocent. A loan as small as $300 means some of these folks can continue working, helping support their families, and not languishing behind bars before even being found guilty.

Rahim also earned a bachelor's degree from American Baptist College and founded a nonprofit called Unheard Voices Outreach, which seeks to empower people who are returning to their communities after long prison sentences. His goal is to remove the stigma of "felonism" and bear witness to beloved community, where everyone belongs.

Each one of these remarkable individuals has been a light in dark places. Each of them has refused to allow their future to be defined by the worst moment in their past. Each of them has refused to allow an unjust, racist system built on the myth of redemptive violence and the spirit of accusation to rob them of their dignity and personhood.

Our Personhood Is Our Greatest Asset

Meeting such outstanding people and feeling my sense of connection to them expand caused me to continue to trust the current that was carrying me. I felt like it was taking me to new places and exposing me to views that I never would have imagined possible. Since I could not anticipate the next twist or turn, I simply remained committed to saying yes to whatever opportunities it brought my way, believing it would carry me where I needed to go.

Oddly enough, a nun who saw *Redemption of the Prosecutor* ended up getting me involved in an organization called Theology & Peace. Focused on connecting progressive theology to active peacemaking, the organization acts to subvert the human tendency to violence, specifically in the form of the scapegoat mechanism. I traveled to Chicago to share my conversion experience with the group in a presentation titled, "When Prosecutor Meets Defendant: Moving from Retribution to Reconciliation." Later, I was asked to serve on the board, which meant I helped plan the next conference, and we chose as our theme, "Beloved Community as the Way from Scapegoating to Ubuntu." One of our keynote speakers was Naomi Tutu, daughter of South African Archbishop Desmond Tutu.

Like her father, Naomi suffered through the age of apartheid as a child in Cape Town, South Africa. Racial injustice and inequality were not only condoned but enforced by the government. Archbishop Tutu was a powerful figure in the nonviolent campaign to heal the terrible national wounds that white South Africans had ignored.

Among proponents of nonviolent resistance and practitioners of restorative justice, Archbishop Tutu's leadership of the Truth and Reconciliation Commission stands as a powerful reminder that we can resist the myth of redemptive violence and disrupt the spirit of accusation and retribution.

Sister Naomi is just as committed to true shalom justice, peacemaking, and the ministry of reconciliation as her father was. She is a teacher with authority, full of grace and truth, and I felt so fortunate to spend time listening to her.

During her presentation at the Theology & Peace conference, she explained to us a concept dear to her heart:

> Ubuntu is the highest compliment you can pay someone in African culture. It is to be recognized as fully human. We were taught to strive for this goal, even in a land where our political and religious structures did not treat us as fully human. Even though my father had inferior pay, housing, and opportunities compared to white leaders in the Anglican church, we nurtured the spirit of Ubuntu.

Where, I wondered, do people find the moral will and courage to resist systems of death without dehumanizing the managers of those systems? How do we undo the myth of redemptive violence?

"Our personhood is our greatest asset," Naomi said. "A true human being looks at others with eyes of respect and concern, with the idea of living out a connection which is already there."

Her wisdom would change the world if we all had ears to hear it. She learned it from one of the greatest peacemakers of our time, whose interfaith friendship with the Dalai Lama has inspired millions, including a *New York Times* bestselling book and a Netflix documentary. But when I mentioned them to Sister Naomi, she just rolled her eyes.

"Oh, those two," she said with exasperation. "When they get together, they're incorrigible. Like a couple of bad little boys."

I laughed out loud. I wanted to talk about two of the most revered religious figures in the world, but she just compared them to mischievous kids.

Naomi wasn't regarding them from a human point of view, as if they were superheroes. They were just people, like all of us— profoundly gifted, flawed, of infinite value, and members of the beloved community, which extended all the way into the Tennessee Prison for Women.

None of Us Had Any Idea

In September of 2017, the federal district court denied Cyntoia's petition for habeas corpus relief. But she could appeal to the Sixth Circuit Court of Appeals. The hope was that the federal appeals court would conclude that her life sentence was unconstitutional or that by not presenting evidence of her fetal alcohol syndrome, her trial lawyers had rendered a constitutionally deficient performance. Either way, she would get relief from her sentence.

It was a long shot, and everyone knew it. So few cases are successful this late in the process.

In mid-October, Mr. Bone and Mr. Gordon filed Cyntoia's appeal to the Sixth Circuit, while I drove to Asheville, North Carolina, to share our reconciliation story at a conference of Lutheran pastors. None of us had any idea of the firestorm that was about to break.

In the end, it had little to do with lawyers or appeals or habeas corpus petitions or hyper-technical legal arguments. The media, so often complicit in miscarriages of justice, started prying open the prison bars by shedding a helpful light on Cyntoia's case.

On Friday, November 17, 2017, Nashville news anchor Stacy Case presented an investigative report on the local evening news. The segment was less than four minutes long.

Drawing from Dan Birman's documentary footage, Ms. Case explained how Cyntoia had been abused as a child, arrested for murder in 2004, and viewed at the time as a prostitute. Ms. Case delved into her mother's drug and alcohol abuse and Cyntoia's fetal alcohol syndrome. Video was shown of her in yellow prison garb and handcuffs, followed by photos of her college graduation in a black cap and gown.

Dan Birman appeared and said, "This is a young girl who is at the tail end of three generations of violence against women. ... She had no chance." It was explained that Cyntoia, her mother, and grandmother were all victims of rape. The jury never learned the extent of the prior trauma in Cyntoia's life.

"If Brown's case were heard today," Ms. Case declared, "the court would treat her as a child sex-trafficking victim."

For the first time, the public was presented with a picture of Cyntoia that was heartbreakingly accurate. She was no monster. She was not an adult capable of making cold, calculated decisions. She was a child—a poor, abused, frightened child who had been abandoned by her mother, preyed upon by a sex trafficker, and picked up for sex by a pedophile. When she finally stood up for herself and refused to be victimized one more time, we judged her, condemned her, banished her, and forgot about her. Because that's what our broken system of laws and punishments is designed to do.

"I want a second chance," Cyntoia pleaded over a prison phone.

The world heard her.

Social Media Gets Its Day in Court

The days following Stacy Case's news segment were a whirlwind. Over the weekend, the story went viral and created a social media firestorm. International pop star Rihanna seems to have ignited the blaze with an Instagram post that received more than 1.7 million likes, asking:

> did we somehow change the definition of #JUSTICE along the way?? cause. ... Something is terribly wrong when the system enables these rapists and the victim is thrown away for life! To each of you responsible for this child's sentence I hope to God you don't have children, because this could be your daughter being punished ... #FREECYNTOIA BROWN #HowManyMore

It wasn't easy reading these words, because I fell into the "responsible" category, and I would certainly never want anyone passing judgment on Lila, Ruby, or Levi the way so many people had judged Cyntoia. However, the attention seemed like a welcome opportunity to elevate the need for Cyntoia to obtain relief from her excessive sentence, which popular opinion was showing to be a gross miscarriage of justice. And the attention was only beginning.

Kim Kardashian, who has one of the largest social media followings on the planet, weighed in forcefully. She would later pursue her own law degree, motivated by stories of women facing injustice throughout the prison system. She voiced her outrage on Twitter:

> The system has failed. It's heartbreaking to see a young girl sex trafficked then when she has the courage to fight back is jailed for life! We have to do better & do what's right. I've called my attorneys yesterday to see what can be done to fix this. #FreeCyntoiaBrown

More music stars fanned the flames, including T.I. and Lana del Rey. People from across the entertainment industry responded, with celebrities like Amy Schumer and Ashley Judd also making their voices heard.

NBA superstar LeBron James had over 439,000 likes after tweeting:

> What's really going on here man!?!? Like seriously though. Guess she didn't have the RIGHT to finally defend herself huh?!? ... Doesn't make any sense at all ... #FreeCyntoiaBrown

Every post by a celebrity generated hundreds of comments. Soon an online petition was generated demanding that Cyntoia be released.

Charles Bone told Stacy Case in an interview, "You know, it just breaks your heart. ... I talked to Cyntoia about noon today. She's very shocked and surprised and thankful, as we all are for the interest of these celebrities."

Who possibly could have guessed that a four-minute news segment would go viral? Who would have thought that #FreeCyntoiaBrown would be trending? Who could have anticipated the role that pop stars and professional athletes would play in undoing the spirit of accusation that had swirled around Cyntoia all these years?

I was reminded that the current flows where it will.

Pressure From Behind the Scenes

With Cyntoia's story blowing up on a national level, it didn't take long for reporters to dig into her background and discover that the prosecutor who handled her appeal, yours truly, had experienced a change of heart, quit his job, and became a criminal justice reform advocate. I got a few interview requests, including one a few days before Thanksgiving from Stacy Case, who was working on a follow-up segment.

Since I was still working for the Board of Professional Responsibility, I went to my boss' office to make sure she was comfortable with me being interviewed in conjunction with Cyntoia's case. I had no reason to think she would have any problem whatsoever. She had always supported me sharing my story in various settings and even had me do so in partnership with one of the board members at ethics seminars across the state highlighting lawyers' responsibility to work to improve the justice system.

This time was different, however.

After I explained that Stacy Case wanted to interview me, my boss said, "Please don't."

I told her I didn't understand.

"Please decline the interview."

"Why?" I wanted to know.

"Preston," my boss said, "You and I have worked together for a long time. You're a good attorney, and I have nothing but respect for the work you do at the prison. But I'd appreciate it if you'd avoid contact with the media for a while."

"What has changed?" I asked. "There's never been any kind of problem before."

She asked me to close the door, then filled me in.

"I've recently received calls from two Tennessee Supreme Court Justices, asking me why they keep seeing your name in connection with all this Cyntoia Brown stuff and wanting to know why you're working here."

My mouth went dry.

"I think it would be best if you let things quiet down for a while."

Stunned, I told her I would think things over very carefully. I left my boss's office and tried to make sense of what had just happened. Were two Tennessee Supreme Court Justices coming after me? Was I being targeted for my advocacy? Was I about to be fired? What about my right to free speech? My head was spinning.

I made one phone call to a retired judge I knew from fifteen years earlier, when I clerked for Judge Welles. This former judge knew about the politics at play in these kinds of situations, and he knew about my work both with the ethics board and Cyntoia's case. I needed someone who could quickly size up the matter and tell me what I had just gotten myself into.

When the judge answered, I quickly explained what had happened and asked what he thought. He whistled and said, "Oh boy."

"Preston," he began, "You need to be very, very careful."

"Are you serious? Do you think they might fire me?"

"I do."

"But I haven't done anything wrong! Certainty not in the work I do for the Board. And they can't fire me for exercising my First Amendment rights on my own time."

"Of course they wouldn't fire you for that. They'd fire you for something else."

"Like what?"

"They'd find something."

I couldn't believe my ears. "You really think they'd go that far?"

"Yes sir," he said matter-of-factly.

It seemed like Cyntoia might finally get an opportunity to prove that she deserved a life outside prison walls, but I suddenly felt like the walls were closing in. At the moment when I thought my voice might have the most impact, I was being gagged. I sensed the familiar tension of being trapped between doing my job and doing what I knew was right.

Part Four

Redemption:
Doing Justice

Chapter 11

The Victims' Shoes

This seemingly impossible situation weighed heavily on me over the Thanksgiving holiday. More than ever, I felt compelled to keep saying yes to every opportunity to share all I had learned and experienced as a prosecutor who had a conversion experience, especially now, when it mattered the most to Cyntoia's chances for freedom. With all the media swirling around Cyntoia's case, I wanted to do anything I could to change people's hearts and minds. This was the best way I knew to try to make right what I had gotten so wrong. This was what my advocacy was going to look like, and how I was going to continue the process of being reconciled to Cyntoia and all my other friends in prison.

However, if the judge I spoke to knew what he was talking about, I was on the verge of being fired due to public statements I had already made. I feared this calling to be in solidarity with people in prison was about to cost me another career and a potential blacklisting by the Tennessee Supreme Court.

I was not in a very celebratory mood when we gathered for Thanksgiving with Sherisse's family.

During the meal, I received a text from a friend. Glancing at my phone, I saw it was a link to an article in *Newsweek*. When I opened it, I felt like my heart stopped. The headline read: "Prosecutor in Cyntoia Brown Case Quit After Learning He Helped Keep Her in Prison."[1]

---

[1] Christal Hayes, "Prosecutor in Cyntoia Brown Case Quit After Learning He Helped Keep Her in Prison," *Newsweek*, November 22, 2017, https://www.newsweek.com/prosecutor-who-helped-keep-cyntoia-brown-prison-quit-after-case-720324.

I felt sick.

I did not agree to the publication of the article or have any advance knowledge of it. Yet there my name was in a national magazine, in plain view of any Tennessee Supreme Court Justice and anyone else who could read. Not only that, but the story explicitly mentioned my work for the Tennessee Supreme Court: "Shipp now works at [the] Board of Professional Responsibility, which is a watchdog organization that supervises the ethical conduct of attorneys. He has also become a criminal justice reform advocate, who has written pieces in the *Huffington Post* arguing for changes in the juvenile justice system."

No more turkey for me today.

Sherisse and I spent the next several days talking at length about where the current seemed to be carrying us, and we agreed the time had come to find a job that did not prevent me from speaking about the matters that were of utmost importance to me. I couldn't keep quiet. I also couldn't stay in a situation where powerful people were waiting for a chance to fire me for publicly indicting the corrupt, unjust, racist system they proudly presided over and profited handsomely from.

Where could I go? What could I do? Nothing was clear except that the current had turned into dangerous whitewater rapids, and I was just trying to keep my head above water.

Lord, I thought being a Christian was supposed to make life easy.

As the new year came around, the attention surrounding Cyntoia's case only intensified, with calls for Tennessee Governor Bill Haslam to exercise his executive clemency powers and grant her early release from her fifty-one-year sentence.

The Moment of Truth

By early 2018, the Free Cyntoia Brown petition had garnered approximately half a million signatures. Every online signature, every tweet and Instagram story ratcheted up the pressure on the governor to seriously consider the petition for clemency that Attorneys Bone and Gordon had filed on Cyntoia's behalf.

There were still so many questions.

Would the parole board grant a hearing? If so, when?

Would this unexpected public outcry finally result in Cyntoia going free?

In the meantime, Sherisse and I decided that this moment was too important for me to sit on the sidelines, silently watching as so many others invested so much in trying to reverse the damage that I had contributed to in Cyntoia's case. If the divine reality of reconciliation was waiting to be actualized in our lives, me speaking up on Cyntoia's behalf was critical to the process. I had learned enough about restorative justice to know that when we cause harm, as I had, it creates an obligation to do what we can to rectify it. We must take concrete steps to heal and restore the relationship. This is fundamental to the ministry of reconciliation, to *ubuntu*, to shalom, to beloved community, to everything that I wanted to stand for. All the classes and conferences in the world wouldn't mean anything if I failed to take this exact step at this exact time. I had to speak loudly on behalf of Cyntoia's freedom.

If I got fired for it, so be it. Sherisse assured me we would think of something.

Jesus said that nobody who puts a hand to the plow and then looks backwards is fit for the hard work of seeking true justice.

In March, I flew to Pasadena to speak to a group of advocates at a prison ministry conference, and I encouraged them to support the movement for Cyntoia's release in any way they could. I presented alongside two of my heroes—Sister Helen Prejean, the author of *Dead Man Walking*, and Father Greg Boyle, founder of Homeboy Industries. I knew how boldly each of them had spoken for decades on behalf of people who are demonized—death row inmates and inner-city gang members. It affirmed that now was the moment of truth for me as a friend and ally. The current had brought me this far. There was no backing down now.

By the time I returned to Nashville, the Board of Parole had scheduled a clemency hearing for Cyntoia.

The Clemency Hearing

After years of failed filings and disappointing appeals, Cyntoia finally had a real shot at proving she deserved to be released. Mr. Bone asked me to serve as a witness and testify at the hearing. A decade earlier, I had argued in court that Cyntoia needed to spend the rest of her life in prison. Now, ten long years later, I was being given the opportunity to argue the opposite, to admit that I had been wrong, to stand with my friend and ask that she be set free.

It had been nine years since Cyntoia forgave me for the role I played in her prosecution. In those nine years, I had done everything I could think of to make up for the harm I had a hand in bringing about. I had taught five more cohorts of students at the Tennessee Prison for Women, visited the Turney Center Prison at least a hundred times, spoken at churches, universities, and conferences, written op-eds and book chapters, and told pretty much anyone who would listen that we need a justice system that transforms and restores, not damns and kills.

But every time I passed through the razor-wire fences and steel doors at the Tennessee Prison for Women to visit Cyntoia, I was reminded that it hadn't been enough. She was still where I helped put her. She was still praying for an opportunity to get out from under the judgment I helped impose. Nothing I had done in those nine years had done anything to change her circumstances.

Now, however, she had the best opportunity for a second chance that she was likely ever going to get.

I wanted it to count.

On May 22, 2018, hoping to harness a little of the power of social media that had gotten us to this point, I posted my thoughts on Facebook:

> I am not big on prayer requests, and I know that many of you aren't either. But I would appreciate any prayers/ thoughts/positive energy you can spare.

> Tomorrow morning, the Tennessee Board of Probation and Parole will conduct a clemency hearing for Cyntoia to evaluate whether she should be granted early release. The final decision will be made by the Governor. Tomorrow morning, a decade after arguing that she needed to spend the rest of her life in prison, I will have the opportunity to argue that Cyntoia deserves a second chance. Time and proximity are funny. They can turn adversaries into allies. ...

Pray that our penchant for retribution might give way to something more life-giving, more beautiful and compassionate.

On the morning of Wednesday, May 23, I parked my Jeep at the Tennessee Prison for Women as I had on so many Wednesday nights when I was teaching in the LIFE Program. Wearing a gray pinstripe suit, I walked past the television news vans and rows of cameras lined up to film the glistening razor wire. After passing through security, I joined others in the room where Cyntoia's attorneys, Mr. Bone and Mr. Gordon, faced the six-member Board of Parole. The mood was solemn. It would remain that way for the next three hours.

Cyntoia was brought in, hair pulled back in a ponytail, handcuffed and wearing the familiar blue denim uniform, her only fashion option for the past fourteen years. Prison officials situated her between her attorneys. A box of tissue sat waiting on the table.

From his chair, Mr. Bone faced the four men and two women of the board. He was calm and composed, his gray hair and easy smile lending him an air of authority. "We're not here to argue the facts of the original crime," he said in his soft Southern drawl. "We are here with a story of transformation ... transformation in the life of a wasted child who has become a beautiful, intelligent, caring, educated woman who can make things better in the world."

He turned the microphone over to Cyntoia. She thanked the board members for granting this hearing, which she characterized as an act of mercy on their part. Cyntoia's voice quivered as she accepted responsibility for killing Johnny Allen when she was sixteen years old. She acknowledged the pain that she had caused his friends and family.

"I have no choice but to live a different life," she said. "There are people who I've hurt. They've been hurting for fourteen years, and I did that. I can't fix it. I can't go back. The only option I have is to change. I could not live with myself being the same person who did that." She paused for a deep breath. "Whatever you decide, I respect it, but I do pray that you show me mercy and give me a second chance. That is my prayer. ... I won't let you down."

A parade of people came forward and Cyntoia's eyes welled with tears as professors, fellow students, and individuals from within the penal system shared about the positive impact Cyntoia had in their lives. The depth of love and support for her was profound.

Ashlee Sellars, who was in the LIFE classes with Cyntoia and went on to lead a restorative justice organization, spoke about their friendship and how deserving Cyntoia was of a second chance. Next came Dr. Richard Goode, the founder and director of the LIFE Program. He outlined Cyntoia's tremendous academic achievements since her first semester in the program in 2009. Her commitment to education demonstrated how invested she was in her own rehabilitation.

Prison officials spoke about the dramatic change they had witnessed in Cyntoia over the fourteen years of her incarceration. A local nonprofit director informed the board that from inside the prison, Cyntoia telephonically served as a mentor to at-risk girls who had gotten caught up in the juvenile justice system. She was already doing everything in her power to serve her community and make her experience count for others.

Then my name was called. The past nine years of trying to be an effective advocate for criminal justice reform, of helping people imagine a justice that doesn't throw people away as disposable but cultivates hope and holds open the door to redemption, had culminated in this moment. I stood and buttoned my suit jacket as I used to when I was about to argue on behalf of the Tennessee Attorney General. Today, however, I finally had the opportunity to argue on behalf of my friend.

I took my seat beside Cyntoia. She smiled at me.

I introduced myself to the board and explained that a decade earlier, I had reviewed every page of the transcript of Cyntoia's trial. I had studied every exhibit. I had carefully crafted an argument that Cyntoia's conviction and fifty-one-year life sentence were proper. I did all this because I worked as a prosecutor in the Tennessee Attorney General's office. Like every other person whose cases I worked on, I didn't know her.

But now I did. Now I knew her and I could say with confidence that I had been wrong to ever argue against her. Now I knew that she was an outstanding student, she was committed to making a difference in the lives of others, and she possessed a kind and generous spirit. Now I argued that she deserved to be free.

I looked into the eyes of each board member and reminded them that the remedy of executive clemency exists for a reason.

Sometimes justice, true justice, demands that we reconsider our harsh judgments. Sometimes justice requires that we show mercy. "And I say this," I concluded, "because I have borne witness, along with all these other people, of the exceptional person that Cyntoia is."

I will never forget that liminal moment sitting next to Cyntoia, hoping that the Board of Parole would listen to my call for mercy as carefully as the court had listened to my earlier call for punishment.

I went back to my seat in the audience and took a deep breath. I had been waiting nine years to speak that truth when it really mattered, when it could really make a difference and set things right. I just hoped that I had said enough. I hoped that I said what I needed to say to undo some of the damage I had helped cause when I, on behalf of our society, told a broken, desperate, sixteen-year-old girl that we were unwilling to do anything for her but throw her away.

His Life Mattered

Only two people spoke in opposition to Cyntoia's release, the detective who, in 2004, convinced that frightened, abused sixteen-year-old child to waive her constitutional rights and confess to killing the man who had picked her up for sex, and Anna Whaley, a friend of Mr. Allen. Neither of them knew Cyntoia.

"Johnny has a voice," Ms. Whaley stated. "And Johnny's family has a voice. It has not been heard in all these years, but today I am that voice. Cyntoia has done great harm, and Johnny did not deserve to die." She paused to collect herself. "I hope, I hope sincerely, God has transformed her life. I do. I am here to make sure he isn't forgotten and to say that Johnny's life mattered. Johnny was loved and he is missed dearly."

Even after fourteen years, grief was written across her face.

Cyntoia had a moment to respond before the hearing concluded.

"His life mattered," she whispered. "It did."

Watching her, I knew how difficult it was to once again confront the gravity of her worst mistake and the consequences that could not be undone. She had wanted to speak with Johnny Allen's mother years ago. She, like most people who commit violence, never had a chance to engage one-on-one with those whom her actions had harmed. Our adversarial systems of sterile rules and procedure prohibits it. Even a simple apology could be used against her.

"I don't want anyone to go through what his family has gone through," Cyntoia concluded. "They've grieved for fourteen years. I think about that every day. ... Whether I'm in here or out there, I will think about that and I will live differently."

The Parole Board members took a brief recess, then came in and faced Cyntoia and her attorneys. They took turns declaring their votes out loud.

Later in the day, I posted the results in a follow-up Facebook post:

> No clear decision from the parole board. Two votes in favor of granting Cyntoia's petition straight up. Two votes to deny it outright and have her serve 51 years. And two votes to lower her sentence to 25 years, making her eligible for release in 2029. No idea in the world what the Governor will do.

Our Penchant for Retribution

None of us—me, Cyntoia, Dr. Goode, Charles Bone, Houston Gordon, or any of Cyntoia's scores of friends and supporters—was under any misapprehension about our chances. We were asking the Tennessee Board of Parole—the notorious arbiters of a draconian, retributive system—to break with its institutionalized vengeance and show mercy. This was a Hail Mary pass.

It shouldn't be this hard, I thought, for such an exceptionally gifted person who had the potential to do so much good, who had invested so heavily in her own rehabilitation, to get a second chance. All around the country, five decades of mass incarceration has shown that punishment as an end goal, particularly in the cases of young people like Cyntoia, has failed miserably.

Scientific research is finally able to confirm what parents have known forever—children are fundamentally different from adults. The minds of young people have not yet fully developed. Consequently, kids are not able to fully appreciate the consequences of their actions. They are more susceptible to peer pressure. They are not as capable of regulating their emotions, and they lack impulse control. For these reasons, we don't let people younger than eighteen drink, smoke, vote, gamble, get married, join the military, serve on a jury, or enter into a contract. We recognize that they don't have the judgment of an adult. Yet we pretend that children like Cyntoia are just as culpable as adults.

On the other hand, once their brains fully develop around age twenty-five, former juvenile offenders show remarkable rehabilitative potential. A recent study by professors at Montclair State University found that among former juvenile lifers, the rate of reoffending is only 1.14 percent.[2]

We should not have to seek an extraordinary remedy and beg for Cyntoia to have a second chance. Every kid should have the opportunity to prove they have changed.

In a later interview with *Oxygen* television network, I said of children sentenced to life, "We can give them second chances. It's not a threat to public safety. It doesn't diminish our concern and compassion for victims, because we have to think about victims as well, but second chances are not some kind of affront. They don't diminish our compassion for victims; it recognizes that a lot of the people who commit these crimes are victims themselves, and so we need to cultivate that sense of understanding and compassion when we deal with these folks because we know that they can change. Children have the capacity to make positive change."

We have to finally move past the notion that justice is a zero-sum game. We can invest in age-appropriate alternatives to lengthy adult sentences without compromising the safety of our communities or weakening our concern for the healing and well-being of victims. To do so, we must repent of the myth of redemptive violence that says the only way to balance the scales is to inflict more suffering.

Giving Victims More Consideration

This ubiquitous myth of redemptive violence—institutionalized in our state capitols, courtrooms, and prisons—preponderates against an experience of justice, as Cyntoia's clemency hearing and Rahim's parole hearing made painfully obvious.

---

[2] "Resentencing of Juvenile Lifers: The Philadelphia Experience," The Legal Decision Making Lab, accessed January 26, 2024, https://www.msudecisionmakinglab.com/philadelphia-juvenile-lifers

The people who sustained the harm often still seem as raw after fourteen years, as in Cyntoia's case, or twenty-six years, as in Rahim's, as they were in the immediate aftermath of the crime. Nothing has occurred that could facilitate healing. Their many questions have gone unanswered. There has been no opportunity for an apology or restitution, no chance for dialogue, no concrete taking of responsibility. Consequently, the victims have trouble imagining, even after many years, that the person who hurt them or their loved one may have changed and be ready for a second chance. The criminal legal system makes promises to victims that it can't keep, as there is no punishment, no period of time that can make things right or heal what has been broken.

The very concrete human pain on both sides is abstracted by legal jargon and the substitution of the state as the victim.

An adversarial system presided over by detached legal professionals who are obsessed with the process, not the outcome, renders true justice an impossibility.

If the first duty of society is justice, we don't have to keep settling for vengeance that neglects the needs of both parties.

Years ago, I heard about a vehicular homicide that occurred in Japan. Instead of shuffling the responsible person through an impersonal, sterile process that essentially asks only what law was broken and what the punishment is going to be, the judge's first order was for the defendant to attend the funeral of the victim. The judge understood that crime is not first and foremost a violation of a hyper-technical legal code, but a violation of relationship. Therefore, crime creates relational obligations.

The judge recognized that the first step the defendant needed to make was to pay his respects and see for himself the harm he had caused. Legal abstractions are no substitute for witnessing the heartbreaking, tragic consequences of violence.

The judge attended the funeral as well. He wanted to observe how the defendant interacted with the victim's family, and vice versa. The judge's goal in all of this was not merely to punish, but to discern what true justice required. What was needed in order to nurture accountability on the part of the defendant, to promote him taking full responsibility for the harm he had caused, to have him feel and express remorse and apologize? What was needed for the victim's family to begin the process of healing, to express their grief and anger, to have their questions addressed, to be compensated for their loss, even in a symbolic way, and to accept the apology?

If justice is about attempting to make right what has gone wrong, then the goal of a justice process should ultimately be reconciliation. I wonder whether reconciliation might have been possible for Cyntoia and Rahim and the people who suffered because of their actions when they were teenagers.

Embodying Transformative Justice

I've seen breathtaking reconciliation between people before. I once spoke at a conference in St. Louis with Sharletta Evans, who lost her three-year-old son, Casson Xavier Evans, when he was caught in the crossfire of a drive-by shooting. The shooter was sixteen-year-old Raymond Johnson.

At the time of his arrest, Raymond read at no more than a third-grade level. Both of his parents had abandoned him, forcing him to raise himself with the help of grandparents. Despite these mitigating circumstances and his youth, Raymond was condemned to life in prison. Ms. Sharletta did not question the prosecutor's decision to make an example of Raymond.

Over the years, however, Raymond earned his GED, maintained a clean prison record, and invested in his Islamic faith. In Raymond's words, "That night, it changed me, by pulling the trigger, doing everything I did, it changed me. When you take another human being's life, you lose a part of yourself, you're never the same, and that night, I think of that part did I lose, and how can I heal while in that process."

Eventually Raymond expressed his remorse to Ms. Sharletta in a letter. "My focal point was to heal her from the wounds and the pain that I caused her and her family, to heal my family, and as a byproduct of their healing, to heal myself."

Raymond understood that we cannot heal what we do not acknowledge.

Ms. Sharletta decided to write back. As they corresponded, her perspective changed. She wanted to meet Raymond face-to-face.

Our punitive, adversarial system is not designed for such meetings. But through Ms. Sharletta's advocacy, the Colorado Department of Corrections began a pilot program to allow mediation between people who have caused harm and their victims. Ms. Sharletta and her surviving son, Calvin, were the first victim's family to participate in the restorative justice process. On May 23, 2012, Ms. Sharletta and Calvin met with Raymond for the first time. Many more visits, calls, and letters followed.

Ms. Sharletta emerged as a leader in the movement to abolish life without parole as a sentencing option for children, and in November of 2021, Raymond was released from prison after serving twenty-six years.

About Raymond's release, Ms. Sharletta said, "I feel accomplished. I feel like all the work was not in vain."

Sharletta and Raymond experienced a reconciled relationship and a future that was not held captive by the past.

When I spoke to Ms. Sharletta and Raymond on a Zoom call to plan our conference session, as we ended the call, Ms. Sharletta said to Raymond, "Good morning, son," and he answered her, "Good morning, mother."

I'm a Christian. I've been taught since I was a child that we should walk in love as God loves us, that we should love even our enemies, that we are called to be compassionate as God is compassionate, and that it is according to how we forgive others that we will be forgiven. Even so, when I heard Ms. Sharletta refer to Raymond, who was responsible for the death of her sweet child, as her son, and when he called her mother, I could hardly believe what I was witnessing.

The world is not accustomed to that level of forgiveness, mercy, grace, compassion, and reconciliation. It's so radical as to scandalize our sense of "justice." It cannot be forced or insisted upon. When we encounter it, it is breathtaking. When we settle for mere retribution, however, we miss out on so much beauty and healing.

Ms. Sharletta and Raymond stand as powerful witnesses to what anti-death penalty lawyer and author of *Just Mercy* Bryan Stevenson is often known to say: "We are all of us more than the worst thing we have ever done." And they also bear witness to the truth that we are all of us more than the worst thing we have ever suffered.

In Ms. Sharletta's words, "I've learned no one is a throwaway. I've learned that even the hugest mistakes in our lives, we can redeem ourselves."

Ms. Sharletta and Raymond show us the power of cultivating compassion through listening.

Restorative or transformative justice aims to help people who have caused harm understand in concrete terms what they have actually done to their victims and what steps they can take to make it right, beginning with an apology. It empowers victims to become survivors by voicing their questions and needs and helping determine the outcome of their case.

This is a long view of justice, rooted in the power of shalom and the possibility of beloved community. Transformative justice is not about forgetting what was done or acting like it didn't matter. Instead, it opens up a future that is not hemmed in by the past.

Taking on the Cruel System

Ashlee Sellars, the former LIFE student who spoke on Cyntoia's behalf at the clemency hearing, was released from prison in 2017, after serving twenty-one years. Instead of seeing them as lost years, she considers them twenty-one years of experience she can use to shed light on the brutal realities within the justice system. She is a member of ICAN— the Incarcerated Children's Advocacy Network—and serves as the director of restorative justice initiatives at Nashville's Raphah Institute.

Raphah interacts with justice-involved youth and gives them meaningful ways of understanding their actions and the effects of the harm they have caused. Its restorative process places victims at the forefront. Many people who have suffered harm feel victimized yet again by the criminal legal system, which reduces them to bystanders in an impersonal process, where they have little say in what charges are filed, whether a guilty plea offer is made, or how the person who harmed them will be held accountable. Raphah, on the other hand, facilitates voluntary conferences between victims and young offenders. A trained facilitator helps people who have been harmed express how the crime affected them for so that the people who caused the harm can accept responsibility for their actions. If possible, the parties agree on an accountability plan to attempt to repair the damage.

Both sides get to tell their story. Both sides gain newfound appreciation for the other as human beings. Their stories heard, they are free to move forward

Young people heading down a dark path are shown a better option.

Victims are able to share their pain and heal.

Ashlee experienced something similar as a teenaged girl, when she asked after her trial to meet with the parents of the victim. Healing happened for all involved, and it gave Ashlee hope that she could be restored. After two decades of incarceration, she is now helping to create an alternative to the cruel system that grinds so many kids beneath its wheels.

Batman's View of Justice

In his book *Insurrection*, Peter Rollins wrote, "[R]evolutionaries are always untimely—for the simple reason that they can never be deemed reasonable or right by the present system because it is the present system that they critique."[3]

I think of revolutionaries like Martin Luther King, Jr., and Nelson Mandela, both of whom famously suffered for critiquing their culture's racist systems.

Echoing Paul in his letter to the Ephesian church, Rollins added,

> But this is not a battle against people; rather it is one that sets itself against systems that oppress people, preventing their development into fully responsible, ethical individuals. It is this direct attack against prevailing structures, such as ineffective school systems or unjust legal structures, that can facilitate real change in society.

We need revolutionaries who stand up and make themselves heard over the grinding cogs and broken gears of our injustice system. We need morally serious individuals, groups, and congregations

---

[3] Peter Rollins, *Insurrection: To Believe Is Human To Doubt, Divine* (New York: Howard Books, 2011), 173.

to oppose the proliferation of new prisons operated by private companies that lobby for harsher laws so they can profit by locking away our citizens.

I hear Brother Will Campbell's voice echoing from the past and Bryan Stevenson's in the present, but they must be reinforced by a prophetic chorus of Sharlettas and Raymonds and Ashlees who will no longer accept "justice" as shorthand for the vengeful infliction of more violence.

In making a similar point, Rollins drew on the mythology of Batman. Batman felt the trauma, pain, and loss that violent crime brings about. He channeled his hurt into a drive for revenge, hoping in vain to heal his wounds. He is a vengeful crusader.

Not surprisingly, the cycle of violence is only perpetuated, not interrupted and sent in a new, healing direction.

Consider the real dilemma: Bruce Wayne, multi-billionaire, has all the resources needed to support positive change across his city. He could invest in schools, public transportation, affordable housing, job creation and training, libraries, substance abuse programs, mental health treatment, and more. In short, he could cure the real illnesses instead of fighting a symptom.

But then where would this leave Batman?

Bruce Wayne's purpose is tied directly to his unquenchable desire for vengeance. He finds meaning in inflicting violence. He is more focused on exacting revenge than on healing the wounds in his city. Unwilling to walk the hard road of compassion, healing, and reconciliation taken by Ms. Sharletta, he stands with people who oppose second chances for people who have spent decades investing in their own rehabilitation.

As Rollins pointed out,

> Bruce Wayne needs the criminals in order to experience the cathartic release of directly attacking them. ... Bruce Wayne is able to look and feel like he is part of the solution when, in his overall material practices, he is really part of the problem. It is one thing to beat up a criminal; it's another to commit oneself to the difficult task of transforming society.[4]

---

[4] Rollins, *Insurrection* 142–43.

Our criminal legal system has a Batman complex. Reflecting on my time as a prosecutor, I see how often we are committed to vengeance under the guise of public safety. We perpetuate the myth of redemptive violence when what we need is true justice that heals harm and transforms the world into something better, more whole, more like shalom.

If We Do Not Speak

Whether we are Christian or Muslim, agnostic or Jew, Catholic or atheist, we all have something to gain by investing in communities that are whole. To really invest in true justice and work for beloved community, however, we must be willing to leave our insulated places of privilege and be agents of positive change.

If Jesus is to be taken seriously (and literally) in Matthew 25, God is most present among people who are vulnerable, people who have been pushed aside and told they don't count, people who are outcasts, people who are despised and targeted, people who are scapegoated and excluded. This can include both people who suffer harm and those who cause it. To the extent that I am not present with them, I cannot meaningfully be said to be following Jesus.

The real liturgy, the real work of people of faith and good will, takes place outside the walls of our opulent buildings. What often passes for a successful congregation—lots of bottoms on padded pews, multi-million-dollar building projects, state-of-the-art lighting and sound systems and smoke machines, exciting youth group trips——may well contribute to the downfall of institutional Christianity within a generation. People are looking for authentic expressions of faith that actually make a difference in the world, not a religious-entertainment complex that looks more like an exclusive social club than a countercultural movement of radical love inspired by Jesus of Nazareth.

The question that first hounded me over twenty years ago when I was a law school student continues to demand a response: Do my religious beliefs intersect in any meaningful way with my regular life?

This is a question for all morally serious people.

Faith, morality, and ideals without corresponding actions are dead.

Martin Luther King, Jr., warned us, "If the church does not recapture its prophetic zeal, it will become an irrelevant social club without moral or spiritual authority." Six decades later, I dare say we are there. The white church in America has been blinded by its comfort and privilege. The world is in desperate need of authentic expressions of the ministry of reconciliation, like that modeled for us by people like Ms. Sharletta and Raymond, but the church is complacent, self-satisfied, and lukewarm.

As it happens, we are seeing that the church is expendable.

When the church was unwilling to speak about extreme poverty in Africa—about people who perished simply because they did not have access to clean drinking water or basic medical care, about tens of thousands of children who starved to death every day—then God, in God's infinite sense of irony, raised up a celebrity like Bono to speak the word of the Lord and jar the conscience of wealthy, complacent Christians.

If the church refuses to speak, the rock stars will cry out.

When the church refused to speak honestly concerning America's history of racial violence and injustice, which continues right up to the modern lynchings caught on cell phone videos and broadcast on social media, the prophetic spirit that the church quenched fell on millionaire professional football players. By kneeling in protest during the national anthem, they bore witness that racism and white supremacy violate the core of the gospel.

When the church lacks the courage to speak truthfully about America's addiction to violence and instruments of violence in the aftermath of the seemingly endless mass shootings, then someone else, such as late-night comedians, will be chosen to do the work of the Lord.

As the church has failed in its mandate to expose the myth of redemptive violence as a falsehood, we must imagine and bring forth alternative expressions of beloved community in which everyone is counted. In the prophetic words of Jesuit priest Greg Boyle,

> [W]e imagine, with God, this circle of compassion. Then we imagine no one standing outside of that circle, moving ourselves closer to the margins so that the margins themselves will be erased. We stand there

with those whose dignity has been denied. We locate ourselves with the poor and the powerless and the voiceless. At the edges, we join the easily despised and the readily left out. We stand with the demonized so that the demonizing will stop. We situate ourselves right next to the disposable so that the day will come when we stop throwing people away.[5]

Reviewing the Facts of the Case

Cyntoia Brown was still in prison. Governor Haslam gave no indication of when or how he would respond to her petition for clemency, and Cyntoia's legal team pressed on with other attempts to gain her freedom.

In June of 2018, the Sixth Circuit Court of Appeals heard arguments on whether her life sentence was constitutional in light of the U.S. Supreme Court's ruling against mandatory life without parole sentences for children. Though there is little practical difference between fifty-one years and life without parole, the court ruled that Cyntoia was not entitled to relief because there was technically a possibility of parole, provided she lived to be sixty-seven years old. Whether or not she would survive for fifty-one years in prison was not for the court to decide.

In July, Governor Haslam received all the materials related to Cyntoia's clemency petition, which was thousands of pages. Somewhere in that mountain of paperwork was my letter asking him to grant Cyntoia release, which was the only outcome that was truly just. I wondered whether he would ever actually read it. He had only six months left in office, and he was not required to make any decision at all.

On Thursday, December 13, 2018, CNN reported that Governor Haslam was doing his best to "review every aspect of her case ... talking to everybody involved."

One week later, the governor's office released a list of individuals to whom he was granting clemency, as an act of mercy and leniency. It included eleven names, with offenses ranging from embezzlement and DUI to forgery and cocaine possession. Governor Haslam

---

[5] Boyle, *Tattoos on the Heart*, 223–24.

pardoned seven and commutated sentences for the other four. "These individuals have made positive contributions to their communities," he said in a statement.

Cyntoia Brown's name was not on the list.

Less than a month remained in the governor's term.

Chapter 12

Becoming an Ally

Nurturing hope inside prisons is a unique discipline. It is extraordinary the countless ways people cultivate life in places of death. Day after day, week after week, month after month, years turn into decades, yet like a thistle stubbornly growing through cracked concrete, the hope of freedom, of a redeemed future remains. Sometimes it is little more than a smoldering wick, but it is not extinguished.

We probably all tend to view ourselves as the heroes of our own stories, and since boyhood I had wanted to be one of the good guys. It's why I became a prosecutor in the first place. I wanted to do the right thing. My idea of what is right had changed, but my desire to see true justice done was as strong as ever.

It began with my amazing friends at the Tennessee Prison for Women, including Cyntoia Brown.

I wanted so much for her to walk free from that prison, where I had helped to banish her before I even knew her.

On January 7, 2019, Charles Bone texted me. He wanted me to join him and twenty or so others in his office overlooking downtown Nashville. I parked in the garage and took the elevator up. Circling the conference room table were men and women I had come to greatly admire—Ellenette Brown, Richard Goode, Kathy Sinback, and many others. This group of people had invested so much legally, materially, educationally, and emotionally in Cyntoia's life and her quest for freedom from the confines and indignity of prison.

It was just after 11 a.m. when Cyntoia called from the prison and was connected through the speaker phone in the center of the table. Mr. Bone shared the good news we had all been praying for, that Governor Haslam had decided to commute her sentence from fifty-one to fifteen years, meaning she would be moved into the prison transition group, for release in nine months, on August 7, 2019.

Everyone clapped and cheered and cried. I hugged Ellenette, who had loved Cyntoia since she was a little girl, and Kathy, who had been working to free Cyntoia longer than anyone else. I thanked Richard Goode for his vision of a community that would bring people like Cyntoia and me together in a classroom. I shook Mr. Bone's hand and thanked him for seeing to it that a tremendous wrong I had a hand in bringing about was finally being undone. I turned and looked out the window at downtown Nashville and wiped away tears of relief and gratitude.

So many people had worked so hard and kept the faith for so long, and it culminated in this surreal moment.

Only twelve days before leaving office, Governor Haslam had chosen mercy over more retribution, compassion over ongoing vengeance.

"Cyntoia," Mr. Bone said, "I wanted you to be able to say hello and thank you to some friends of yours. I won't try to tell you all the people who are here, but you can guess."

"Awww," she rejoiced through the speaker. "I love you all."

"We love you too," we echoed back. "We love you, Cyntoia."

A public statement by the governor read:

> Cyntoia Brown committed, by her admission, a horrific crime at the age of 16. Yet, imposing a life sentence on a juvenile that would require her to serve at least 51 years before even being eligible for parole consideration is harsh, especially in light of the extraordinary steps Ms. Brown has taken to rebuild her life.

Cyntoia would have to serve ten years on parole, with the conditions that she maintain employment or educational enrollment, participate in regular counseling sessions, and perform at least fifty hours of community service, including work with at-risk youth.

Cyntoia released her own statement: "I am thankful for the support, prayers, and encouragement I have received. We truly serve a God of second chances and new beginnings. ... I would have never made it without him."

"You know," Ellenette said later, "she has everything she needs to be successful. How she uses it will be up to her."

After working on Cyntoia's case since 2010, Charles Bone had accomplished what he set his mind to when he first encountered her story in Dan Birman's compelling documentary. He'd taken on his first and last criminal case. J. Gordon Houston would return to his home and law office in Covington, Tennessee.

Their belief in a justice that heals and restores and their years of Herculean efforts had finally paid off. Ten years after Cyntoia was a student in my Judicial Process class, she was free. But in many ways, my work was just beginning.

Changed People Can Change People

On March 1, 2019, less than two months after Governor Haslam announced that Cyntoia was receiving a second chance, I was working in my office at the Board of Professional Responsibility when I received a text from my friend Eric Alexander, who was now working for the Campaign for Fair Sentencing of Youth:

> Hi Preston. The Campaign for the Fair Sentencing of Youth is seeking to hire an attorney/lobbyist to work on the issue of sentencing reform/juvenile life without parole at the national level. Drafting policy, lobbying, testifying before state legislative committees, coordinating with advocates in those states to apply pressure on individual legislators, etc. If you know someone who is passionate about this kind of work, please share my info with them and have them reach out to me. Thanks.

Everything stopped.

If I knew someone who is passionate about this kind of work?

Could this be it? Was this what I had been waiting for? Was this what was going to be clear as day if I just kept doing what I was doing?

I had known Eric since 2012, when Janet introduced us at the Children's Defense Fund conference in Cincinnati. Eric had been in the audience in 2016 when I confessed my sin of racism to the crowd that had gathered for the CFSY's Healing and Hope celebration.

Was this where the current had been carrying me all along? Was this my opportunity to finally lean fully into the work of criminal justice reform?

I had loved the CFSY since 2012, when they first invited me to share my journey as a former prosecutor, and I told them that the people we might be tempted to dismiss as "devils" could end up being "angels."

Given that my advocacy-as-hobby had pissed off two Tennessee Supreme Court justices, the timing couldn't have been any better.

I reread Eric's text.

They were looking for an attorney to lead their legislative advocacy work.

Did they know I had exactly zero policy experience? I had never drafted a bill, registered as a lobbyist, or testified at a legislative hearing.

But boy, it seemed like a perfect fit.

I rushed to tell Sherisse about the door that I sensed might be opening. She was elated. However, I had so many questions: Could I even do this job, given that I had no prior experience? What about all the travel to different states? What would it be like working remotely with no office? Sherisse, on the other hand, was confident that this was where the current had been leading for years. She offered me the same encouragement she had twelve years earlier when I was first presented the opportunity to teach at the women's prison.

"We're doing this," she said resolutely.

I texted Eric back:

"Hey Eric, thanks for sending this my way. Ever since 2012, when I spoke for the first time at the CFSY conference, I have been consistently impressed and most grateful for the work y'all do. I would love to learn more about the position."

With that, Eric started making things happen.

I soon found myself accepting a position as the CFSY's Senior Policy Counsel, where I would have the honor of working with lawmakers, other advocates, former juvenile lifers, family members of people serving sentences, and victims of youth violence to abolish life-without-parole sentences for children. Much of my job would involve helping people envision a justice system that affirms that no child should ever be condemned to die in prison.

Changed people can help change people.

In May of 2019, I was cleaning out a decade's worth of clutter from my desk at the Board of Professional Responsibility, excited to begin the next chapter at the CFSY. I found hundreds of letters from people in prison with whom I had exchanged correspondence. They were like markers along the journey, tokens that signified I needed to continue trusting the current. As I prepared to start my new job working to ensure that no child is ever consigned to a future without hope and that all kids are deemed deserving of our care and attention, one letter stood out. It was postmarked June 1, 2009, almost exactly one decade earlier. It was the first letter Cyntoia ever sent me. Her words from ten years ago were prescient, and once again, I was stopped in my tracks.

> Dear Preston,
>
> It was so good to hear from you. ... Right now you may be uncertain on what exactly you will do, but I am certain it will come to you ... just imagine what you wish you could have done for me before I got into this mess. Imagine what you might have said, what you might have tried, and apply it to the group you would be aiming to help. All of the youth you encounter may not respond, but if just ONE can be saved, trust me your efforts will be well worth it.

Lady Justice In All Her Glory

In the days of the Wild West, Samuel Colt developed an efficient killing machine, a revolver ironically dubbed "The Peacemaker." This moniker fits right in with the myth of redemptive violence, that responding to violence with more violence will beget peace.

We assume that we can punish our way to healing and wholeness, and we act surprised when our rates of recidivism remain high. For an experience of true justice, we need a new way of seeing, a new set of questions, a new paradigm.

Eric Alexander, my friend and now colleague at the CFSY, had his own childhood experiences with the injustice of a criminal legal system that seeks only to punish. When he was seventeen years old, he tagged along with a friend who was planning to shoplift a case of beer from a convenience store. He waited outside while his friend entered the store. He didn't know his friend had brought a gun. As he stood watch, he was startled when he heard a gunshot, and when he rushed into the store, he found the store clerk lying in a pool of blood. Eric froze. When the police arrived, he was still staring in disbelief at the clerk, who had died.

Eric pled guilty to murder and received two twenty-five-year sentences to avoid a life without parole sentence.

Too many children in our country have faced similar scenarios. They are with the wrong people in the wrong place at the wrong time, and in a split-second, something tragic happens that alters the future forever.

Yet they are still children.

When I was about twelve years old, I shoplifted some baseball cards from Target while my Mom was getting things in another part of the store. I knew it was wrong. I don't know why I did it.

As we left, we were stopped by store security. Mom was simultaneously horrified and furious. After I admitted what I did, the security officer let us go without pressing criminal charges. I think he sensed what I was in for when I got home.

The fact is I was also a white, middle-class kid with my mom. I wonder how different things might have been if I had been Black, by myself, or with a group of older kids. What if Target had called the police? What if I had been prosecuted in juvenile court? What if, based on the conviction, I had been kicked out of the school I attended? My privilege prevented me from dealing with any consequences, save those my parents imposed.

I've made plenty of bad decisions since then. I abused alcohol in college and drove while under the influence. I smoked marijuana, which was and continues to be illegal in Tennessee. Lots of these bad decisions were the product of peer pressure, and a few times I've been swept into situations beyond my control.

However, I've never, ever been deemed unworthy of a second chance for actions I committed as a teenager.

A justice system that knows only how to heap more trauma onto an already traumatized child must be dismantled. The question is not whether the criminal legal system is effectively meeting its goals, but the legitimacy of the goal of endless punishment.

There is a better way.

I think again of how Cornel West put the matter, "Justice is what love looks like in public."

Given our tendency to think of justice and punishment as synonyms, we often set love and justice as opposites that are in tension with each other. I have heard preachers and professors of religion who are certain that God's love and justice are competing aspects of the divine personality. I wonder, however, whether such a superficial and unsatisfactory view is the product of not having thought deeply about either one.

My friends in prison have taught me that justice and love are not opposing forces or in any way at odds with each other. They are intimately connected, two sides of the same coin.

When Dr. King, standing on the steps of the Lincoln Memorial before more than 200,000 people who had gathered for the March on Washington for Jobs and Freedom, echoed the prophet's demand to see "justice roll ... down like waters," he was not speaking of a force antagonistic to love. He knew, long before President Obama affirmed, that justice is about recognizing ourselves in each other. Justice is about loving our neighbor as ourselves. Justice is about expanding the perimeter of our concern until no one stands outside of it.

It is injustice that is the opposite of love. Injustice is what allows us to not regard one another as neighbors. Injustice permits me to pretend that the indignities and pain suffered by others does not affect me. Injustice is what causes us to think of some people as irredeemable and therefore disposable.

"The first duty of society is justice," which is to say that our first duty is to love one another. When something goes wrong, when relationship is broken by violence, our concern for the healing and wellness of both parties compels us to do whatever we can to try to make things right.

To paraphrase the psalmist, justice and mercy kiss (Psalm 85:10). What is required of us is simply to act in the interest of true justice, to embrace mercy and compassion, and to always remain humble and teachable (Micah 6:8).

An Education Behind Bars

In May 2019, with three months to go before her release, Cyntoia completed her coursework and earned a bachelor's degree. She graduated with a perfect 4.0 grade point average.

When I first taught in the LIFE program in 2007, my perspectives about people who were incarcerated and their potential to make dramatic positive change immediately began to shift. I no longer saw people who were in prison simply in the context of one bad action. Week after week, as we sat in a circle sharing our thoughts and experiences, their stories deeply impacted me. These were profoundly gifted, kind, generous, good people who, like all of us, had made bad decisions. But theirs had carried terrible consequences. Even so, their mistakes were not the product of a depraved heart and mind, but of a perfect storm of bad circumstances, typically including prior victimization, mental health issues, poverty, substance abuse and addiction, and lack of meaningful educational and employment opportunities.

My heart softened as I came to realize the overwhelming majority of these people, whom I came to regard as friends, had not only created victims but were victims themselves.

Fortunately, the LIFE Program is only one example of programs in Tennessee and across the nation that are making college education available to people who are caged. Hopefully we are learning, slowly but surely, important lessons from the disaster that has been the era of mass incarceration—most importantly, that we must not foreclose on hope for anyone.

Relationship Is Essential

Relationship is essential. We were created for it. As Naomi Tutu, like her father, teaches, the South African concept of *ubuntu* recognizes that we cannot be human without relationship. Lately, when I read the words attributed to God in the first chapter of the Bible, "Let us make humans in our own image, in our likeness," what I hear is that the very nature of God is relationship. I don't think salvation can be had apart from it.

Proximity to others is therefore crucial. Richard Goode knew this when he invited me to teach the inaugural course in the LIFE Program. Janet Wolf knew this when she put me in proximity to Ndume Olatushani and the other men on death row.

The story of my conversion from a prosecutor to an ally of people who are incarcerated is a testament to the impact of proximity. When we engage with those who are different from us, it can make a profound difference in how we view important issues, the larger world, and even ourselves.

This is the invitation: To go to the dark places, the poor places, the despised and hurting places, to discover our inherent oneness as children and image-bearers of God. When we do, we do so not to save poor lost and misguided souls. Instead, we go to encounter the divine. We go more to listen than to talk, more to learn than to teach. Through those we encounter, we experience transformation and salvation from a way of thinking that defines all our existence in terms of us v. them.

Fear, however, remains a powerful obstacle. It clouds our vision and paralyzes us.

Politicians and the media exploit our fears to garner votes and ratings. We're made to be fearful and suspicious of immigrants and refugees. We're afraid of criminals. We're afraid of transgender people using our bathrooms. We're afraid of Muslims. We are frozen in our little bubbles of ignorance and fear, and we recoil at the thought of actually being friends and standing in solidarity with people who live in prisons, in poverty, or in fear of deportation.

I think of those traditional Lipscomb students on their first night of class in the prison way back in 2007. They were so afraid of being taken hostage, and one never even made it to the classroom. He was so intimidated by the outside of the prison that he did a U-turn and headed back to campus.

Yet we need not be hostages of our fear.

Buddhist teacher Thich Nhat Hanh said, "Though we all have fear and the seeds of anger within us, we must learn not to water those seeds and instead nourish our positive qualities—those of compassion, understanding, and lovingkindness." He reminds us that the opposite of fear is not bravery, but love. As John, one of Jesus' closest friends wrote, "There is no fear in love. But perfect love drives out fear, because fear has to do with punishment. The one who fears is not made perfect in love." (I John 4:18 NIV)

That Easter Sunday in 2016 when my friend Rahim Buford accompanied me to a rural prison where he had been caged for eight long years, he relied on love to drive out his fear. Of course, he never really wanted to lay eyes on that razor wire again or be patted down by a guard. He'd been out of prison for less than a year, and he was understandably apprehensive. However, Rahim knew how important it is to go to places that may intimidate you.

Like Mary Magdalene, who had to go to the tomb to encounter the risen Jesus, Rahim had to go back to that prison, to that place of suffering and death, to experience the resurrection power of Easter. He's lectured at many universities and churches, but on this Easter evening, he had to return to that dark prison to find an old enemy and serve as a minister of reconciliation. Rahim bids you and I to follow his gospel example.

In the end, we cannot escape each other.

We must never underestimate the power of compassion working through proximity. Simply listening to others' stories and recognizing our common humanity can alter the course of our lives. Once we are willing to leave our familiar surroundings, confront our fears, and experience solidarity with people who may not look like us or come from similar backgrounds, we never know what resurrection we may witness.

As Cyntoia and I discovered, proximity has the power to change an adversary into an ally.

A Vision of Shalom

In all of this, the goal is reconciliation. It is our common vocation. We are all called to be, in our own particular way and context, ambassadors of reconciliation.

Reconciled communities are what ubuntu and shalom are all about. Too often, our institutions—courts, companies, corporations, universities, and even churches—frustrate, rather than nurture, authentic expressions and experiences of community.

Reflecting on the fallenness of institutions, Dr. Richard Goode wrote,

Public or private, for-profit or non-profit, sacred or
secular; whether the institution is the United States of
America, the Republic of Iraq, the New York Yankees,
Lipscomb University, the Crips, the Bloods, or the mafia,
the ethic is the same. Win.

Fail to advance the institutional mission, fail to enhance
the institution's position, exhaust one's utility, or
embarrass the institution, and one is a "liability"—best
dismissed before damaging "the brand."[1]

I am reminded here of Lipscomb University firing my friend when
a mob of parents determined their little white children should never
have to learn about the history of racism in which they were, at that
very moment, participating . I think too about how quick Lipscomb
was to cut ties with me as soon as I spoke out publicly against the
firing of the brilliant Black dean of intercultural development. I also
felt the familiar institutional backlash when two Tennessee Supreme
Court justices asked my boss why she was employing someone mixed
up in the Cyntoia Brown story that was on the national news.

Institutions are, to use biblical language, our "principalities and
powers."

Not so with community.

Again, Richard Goode offers a helpful word: "So, how is a
community different from an institution? First and foremost, a
community always values the worth of an individual."[2]

Now I am thinking of the shepherd who left ninety-nine sheep to
find one who was lost and struggling. It is a mindset utterly foreign
to institutional life. As Professor Amy Jill Levine has noted, the
shepherd only knew the sheep was lost because he counted them
all. Communities are particularly concerned with anyone who is
made to feel like they don't count, and then give them special honor.

"Communities take risks on individuals, while institutions risk
individuals. ... [C]ommunities trust love. ... They can forgive rather

---

[1] Richard C. Goode, "From Institution to Community," in *And the
Criminals with Him: Essays in Honor of Will D. Campbell and All the
Reconciled*, eds. Will D. Campbell and Richard C. Goode (Eugene, OR:
Cascade Books, 2012), 8.

[2] Goode, "From Institution to Community," 10.

than punish, include those discarded by society, eradiate lines of distinction, and listen rather than announce."[3]

Reconciled communities extend compassion to those who commit offenses and ask better questions that facilitate healing and accountability. When we work toward transformation instead of dehumanization and belonging instead of exclusion, we find that even people who have acted violently have great potential to do good.

Relationship and community, not rules and procedure, are at the heart of what it means to do restorative justice.

Putting It All Together

My job leading the legislative advocacy work for the Campaign for the Fair Sentencing of Youth provides me with endless opportunities to encourage policy makers to rethink their definitions of justice, relationship, and community. In asking them to support sentencing reforms that leave room for the hope of redemption and a second chance, I'm essentially inviting them to recognize themselves in the "other," to stop the demonization, and to expand the sphere of their compassion and concern.

In November 2019, I was working with lawmakers in Ohio to draft and pass legislation to end life without parole for children. Knowing firsthand the power of proximity to change hearts and minds, I invited Republican Senator Peggy Lehner to travel south to spend time with a remarkable group of people who, before changes in the law like the one we were working on in Ohio, had been condemned as children to life in prison without parole. Senator Lehner, CFSY staff, and members of the Incarcerated Children's Advocacy Network met in Montgomery, Alabama—one of the most important locations for the Civil Rights Movement—to expand our sense of community, kinship, and justice.

Together we toured the EJI Legacy Museum and National Memorial for Peace and Justice and learned that, nationwide, well over 60 percent of the children who have been sentenced to die in prison are Black. Our shameful history of racism—too often ignored, denied, or even celebrated with memorials to Confederate traitors— has found a home in a vengeful system that claims to do justice.

---

[3] Goode, "From Institution to Community," 11.

As we walked together from the Memorial back to our hotel, processing what we had just witnessed, Senator Lehner was resolute: "Preston, we have to get this bill passed."

For people like Senator Lehner and me, proximity and education are critical in elevating our moral consciousness and inspiring us to action.

Of course, we don't have to do it all. We can't immediately dismantle the behemoth that is the prison-industrial complex, free all of America's 2 million captives, or eradicate systemic, institutional, and individual racism once and for all. As Mother Teresa famously said, "I alone cannot change the world, but I can cast a stone across the waters to create many ripples."

Senator Lehner was committed to making ripples that would eventually form a current that would lead to change. She put forward a bill to eliminate life without parole and create a review process so that no child is ever thrown away again in Ohio. She convinced several of her colleagues to serve as cosponsors of the legislation. Together, we assembled a chorus of diverse voices—faith leaders, business owners, Cleveland Browns football players, and family members of people serving—to testify at committee hearings.

One of the most impactful witnesses to testify in support of the bill was Rukiye Abdul-Mutakallim. In 2015, her thirty-nine-year-old son was murdered as he walked home with food for their family. His assailants, the youngest of whom was fourteen, took the food, his cell phone, and $40. Yet Rukiye recognized that we should never foreclose upon hope for a child.

"I saw those boys in court. When I saw them, I thought I was going to see men," Rukiye told the committee members. "They were babies, and I knew I had to look deeper, so I did, and that's why I'm here."[4]

Rukiye testified in favor of our bill because, despite the suffering the loss of her child had brought her, she wanted Ohio to stop "burying children alive in prison. ... If we are throwing our babies away, we have no future."[5]

---

[4] Jessie Balmert, "Victim's Mother Backs Bill to Bar Life Without Parole for Juveniles," *The Columbus Dispatch*, February 20, 2020, https://www.dispatch.com/story/news/crime/2020/02/20/victim-8217-s-mother-backs/1671790007/.

[5] Evan Millward, "Mother of Murder Victim Advocated for New Parole Changes," WCPO, January 11, 2021, https://www.wcpo.com/news/local-news/mother-of-murder-victim-advocated-new-for-parole-changes.

Based on the efforts of Senator Lehner, Ms. Rukiye, and many, many others, Ohio abolished life without the possibility of parole in January of 2021. At the time of this writing, approximately thirty people are now home who previously had no hope of ever living outside prison walls.

Growing the Circle of Compassion

Following the victory in Ohio, the CFSY immediately pivoted to Maryland to support the Juvenile Restoration Act. We found bipartisan bill sponsors, Democratic Delegate Jazz Lewis and Republican Senator Chris West. About the legislation, Senator West said, "People can change. Redemption is possible. When that happens, as a society we should rejoice. We should be willing to give such a person a second chance."

As in Ohio, we were grateful to have support from former juvenile lifers, business leaders, faith communities, and people who had suffered youth violence. One of the most poignant moments in the campaign occurred while Paul LaRuffa was testifying before a legislative committee.

In September of 2002, Paul, who owned a restaurant, was leaving for the night when seventeen-year-old Lee Boyd Malvo approached the driver's side window of his car and shot him five times. Malvo would go on to assist forty-one-year-old John Allen Muhammad in the notorious D.C. sniper attacks that left seventeen people dead and ten more wounded over a horrifying ten-month period. For his part in the crimes, Malvo was given multiple consecutive life without parole sentences.

Paul testified that at the time of sentencing, he was greatly relieved that Malvo received a sentence that left no room for a chance of release. As the years went on, however, he experienced physical, mental, emotional, and spiritual healing, and his thoughts and feelings began to change. Paul eventually met with members of the Incarcerated Children's Advocacy Network, most notably Eddie Ellis, and saw the power of the hope of redemption. Accordingly, even though it would have meant Lee Malvo being parole eligible, Paul stood in support of the Juvenile Restoration Act.

One of the committee members, incredulous, asked Paul, "Are you telling this committee that you think Lee Malvo should be allowed to come home?"

"I don't know Lee Malvo," Paul answered. "I don't know what he needs. But I don't like the idea of you throwing a seventeen-year-old kid away and telling him he has no hope."

Like me and Senator Peggy Lehner, Paul LaRuffa had a life-changing experience with formerly incarcerated people, and as a result of that proximity, had in mind a circle of compassion, and he saw the circumference of the circle expand until no one stood outside of it, including the young person who shot him five times.

Maryland passed the Juvenile Restoration Act in 2021.

The Arc of the Moral Universe Bends Toward True Justice

In 2023, Illinois, New Mexico, and Minnesota all passed laws abolishing life without the possibility of parole for children.

In Illinois, Senator Don DeWitte, speaking to his colleagues in support of the legislation, said, "I consider myself a law-and-order Republican. But I do also believe in rehabilitation. If you believe that these convicted young people can prove that they can become contributing members of our society ... vote that people can redeem themselves."

Sister Helen Prejean, writing in support of the legislation in New Mexico, stated, "When a child causes harm, we must join with our communities in mourning alongside those harmed. But we must not forget that within a hurt child is an invitation for redemption. The ultimate practice of justice is to heal those who cause harm, not to harm them further."

In Minnesota, Republican Representative Patricia Mueller said, "We have to find that balance between holding people accountable and allowing them to be new, to be redeemed."

As I listened to all these statements, I was reminded of my many friends who put flesh on these words. We need communities of reconciliation that are willing to take chances on individuals for true justice to be done.

Felicia Ybanez, a member of the original cohort of inside students in the LIFE Program, who was recently released after serving over twenty-seven years for a crime she committed when she was seventeen, wrote, "It takes one person to speak out, but it takes a community to surge towards what is right in order to get the attention of the masses."

This is the work.

For too long we have blindly assumed that justice is vengeance. We have elevated process over right outcome. We have ignored the racism inherent in our systems and institutions. We have tried to punish our way out of every conceivable social issue. And countless lives, families, and communities have suffered.

However, we have glimpsed something better. We recognize that the current has brought us to this point for a reason. In light of all these stories, facts, and statistics, we must respond.

It is nothing less than conversion to which I was and am still being called. Although the prospect of conversion can feel scary, like a loss, even a little like dying, I pray that my own conversion story shows how much more we stand to gain when we allow the wind to blow where it will. As we are converted to broader and deeper and richer levels of compassion, connectedness, and community, our work for shalom is grounded always in hope.

I leave you with the words of retired Episcopal bishop and Choctaw citizen Steven Charleston:

> Hope makes room for love in the world. We can all share it, we can all believe in it, even if we are radically different in every other way. We no longer need to fear our differences because we have common ground. We can hope together—therefore, hope liberates us. It frees us from our fear of the other. It opens our eyes to see love all around us. It unites us and breaks our isolation. When we decide to embrace hope—when we choose to make that our goal and our message—we release a flow of energy that cannot be overcome. Hope is a light that darkness can never contain.[6]

---

[6] Steven Charleston, *Ladder to the Light: An Indigenous Elder's Meditations on Hope and Courage* (Minneapolis: Broadleaf Books, 2021), 67–68.

Afterword

By Janet Wolf

It is likely that our theological problem in the church is that our gospel is a story believed, shaped and transmitted by the dispossessed; and we are now a church of possession for whom the rhetoric of the dispossessed is offensive.
—Walter Brueggemann[1]

I will not tire of declaring that if we really want an effective end to violence we must remove the violence that lies at the root of all violence: structural violence, social injustice, exclusion of citizens from the management of the country, repression. All this is what constitutes the primal cause, from which the rest flow naturally.
—Archbishop Oscar Romero, El Salvador, September 23, 1979[2]

This is the crime of which I accuse my country and my countrymen and for which neither I nor time nor history will ever forgive them, that they have destroyed and are destroying hundreds of thousands of lives and do not know it and do not want to know it.
—James Baldwin, *The Fire Next Time*[3]

I have been going into prisons since 1975 and I still get it wrong. I remember sitting in one of our circles inside a maximum-security

---

[1] Walter Brueggemann, *Through the Eyes of a Woman: Bible Studies and the Experience of Women*, ed. Wendy Robins, (Geneva: World Council of Churches Publications, 1995), 29.

[2] Oscar Romero, *The Violence of Love* (Maryknoll, NY: Orbis Books, 2004), 166.

[3] James Baldwin, *The Fire Next Time* (New York: Dell, 1967), 15.

prison. One of the inside facilitators asked each person to say his or her name and one thing they were thankful for that day. When it came to Frederick, a newer member who had recently been moved from death row into the less restrictive "low side" of the prison, he simply said, "grass."

I felt my irritation rise. *Really? We just spent two hours in this rich, thick discussion and you're going to offer thanks for grass, for dope, for marijuana?* But I didn't say that aloud, I simply said, "Would you like to say more?"

And Frederick responded, "Yeah. I'm thankful for grass. On death row, you get an hour a day in the outside cage if you are lucky. Concrete floor, wire on the sides and top. And every time I got to go in there, I'd stretch my fingers out through that wire trying to touch the grass. You can't—it's just out of reach. But I don't know nobody who don't try."

Two weeks later, one of the members in our circle on death row was moved to the low side. On his way to his new unit, he fell into the grass and rolled around, stuffing grass into his mouth and pockets, laughing and laughing. The officers let him, knowing what I would never have known without proximity, ongoing partnership with those who are caged. After all those years of concrete and steel, the gift of touching something soft, green, alive ... grass.

As Preston—a friend, collaborator, and coconspirator writes—the power of social location to narrow and limit our worldview and our theology cannot be underestimated or ignored. Where we stand, who we listen to, whose stories we value, whose voices we dismiss—all of this shapes the way we understand the world and the Bible. For those of us immersed in the dominant culture of the United States, especially those of us who are white and economically secure, it can be difficult to hear stories that challenge our interpretation of the world around us. And yet, this is precisely what the gospels demand.

In his book *Jesus and the Disinherited*, Howard Thurman—pastor, prophet, mentor with Dr. Martin Luther King, Jr.—argues that there are communities and nations of people who are forced by economic, political, social, and religious systems and structures to live with their backs against a wall, with no way out. Here, he argues, is precisely where Jesus is born—into an impoverished, militarily occupied, oppressed, and battered community, a people with their backs against a wall. There, among those with their backs to the wall, is where much of the Hebrew Bible, the prophets, the gospels, and the early church abide. And yet, Thurman writes, "It cannot be denied that too often the weight of the Christian movement has been on the side of the strong and the powerful and against the weak and oppressed—this, despite the gospel."[4]

Vincent Harding, historian, architect of Dr. King's April 4, 1967, "Breaking the Silence" speech, wrote a foreword to Thurman's book, declaring:

> [Those] who stand with their backs against the wall ... the poor, the disinherited, the dispossessed ... are rarely within hearing or seeing distance of the company of Jesus' proclaimed followers ... those wall-bruised people find no space for their presence in the places where the official followers are comfortably at worship.[5]

Preston Shipp challenges us to respond to the gospel call to do theology from the margins; to listen to, learn from, be identified with, and stand by the side of those individuals and communities who are occupied, possessed, inhabited by the forces of death.

What does it mean for those claiming faith in Jesus—this one who was arrested and convicted on trumped-up charges, who was criminalized and caged, beaten and battered, executed in a state sanctioned murder—to be so stunningly silent about and complicit with mass criminalization, mass incarceration, and the death penalty?

Preston reminds us that the charge from Jesus is larger than visiting, identifying with, or sitting beside those in prison, although surely that is where we must start. In 1972, Will Campbell and James Holloway reflected on Luke 4, writing:

> In Jesus God proclaims freedom for those in prison. The prisoners are to be turned loose. Literally ... not reform. Not rehabilitation. Not parole ... Liberation. ... What Jesus is talking about is unlocking the doors, dismissing

---

[4] Howard Thurman, *Jesus and the Disinherited* (Boston: Beacon Press, 1976), 31.
[5] Vincent Harding, "Foreword" in *Jesus and the Disinherited* by Howard Thurman (Boston: Beacon Press, 1996).

the Warden and all his staff, recycling the steel bars into plowshares, and turning the prisoners loose.[6]

Charity is dangerous because it makes us feel good while masking our complicity with systems that cause the problems in the first place. Justice demands partnership with those who are oppressed—it requires ministry *with*, not ministry *to* or *for*; this authentic, mutual partnership becomes the priority that redefines everything else, not one more program. Justice means showing up in the prisons and jails, not with answers but with questions, hungry to learn gospel good news from folks for whom breaking chains and opening prison doors is urgent; showing up with a willingness to challenge and transform a system that incarcerates a higher percentage of its citizens than any country in the world.

Preston's stories of "ongoing conversion," of struggle and transformation through persistent practices of proximity and partnership, challenge us to live into and out of God's vision of shalom, of justice that liberates and heals, that reconciles and restores. Learning from, being challenged and changed by, being held accountable and being held, and being accompanied by a community of those who have been or are now caged is life-*altering* and life-*altaring*. As Preston says, "I have learned more from people who either are or have been in prison about the nature of God, about the gospel of joy, peace, justice, forgiveness, reconciliation, redemption."

As Vincent Harding writes, "There are new worlds to build, new companions at the wall, new ways to begin. ... Shall we gather at the wall?"[7]

---

[6] Will D. Campbell and James Y. Holloway, "The Good News from God in Jesus Is Freedom to the Prisoners," *Katallagete* (Winter–Spring 1972); in *And the Criminals with Him: Essays in Honor of Will D. Campbell and All the Reconciled*, eds. Will D. Campbell and Richard C. Goode (Eugene, OR: Wipf and Stock, 2012), 17.

[7] Vincent Harding, "Foreword."

Acknowledgments

Any time I'm invited to share my story, I feel humbled and grateful. My dear friend and mentor, Janet Wolf, was the first person who encouraged me to do so publicly at the Children's Defense Fund conference in Cincinnati in 2012. It was there that I first considered writing a book. To this day, Janet is the most empowering individual I have ever met. Her wise encouragement and guidance, along with her willingness to put me in challenging situations, have been invaluable. I am so grateful to her for planting the seeds of this project over a decade ago and for contributing her gracious afterword.

As soon as I determined to write a book, I knew I wanted my friend David Dark to provide the foreword. So often his insight has helped me better understand and articulate my own thoughts and experiences concerning faith and vocation. I think of him as a kindred spirit, as he too has been profoundly impacted by our friends behind prison walls.

Thank you to my co-writer, Eric Wilson, for preparing the first draft of this book. Putting pen to paper has been daunting to me for years, and he did the hard work for me!

I am deeply indebted to my good friend David Woodard for his commitment to bringing the project to fruition. After reading about my relationship with Cyntoia in the *Nashville Scene* in 2011, he was convinced that a book was in my future. Through his position at Chalice Press, he and Chalice President Brad Lyons made that vision a reality. I cannot thank David enough for believing in me and my story and walking with me through every stage of the writing, editing, and publishing process. This telling of my story would not have been possible without him. Moreover, for over two decades, David has been a steadfast, trusted companion and invaluable conversation partner as we have both attempted to unlearn what we were taught in almost identical circles about the meaning of God, faith, and all the rest, and lean into something more life-giving. I am so very glad we are friends.

Jeff McInturff is another friend who has been with me all along this journey. Fifteen or so annual pilgrimages to the Abbey of Gethsemani in Kentucky, hundreds of Friday mornings reading from the *Tao Te Cheng* and reciting the Lord's Prayer, and countless smokes in the Waffle House parking lot have left an indelible mark on my spirit. Thanks be to God.

Apart from the vision of Dr. Richard Goode that culminated in the LIFE Program, and his gracious invitation to have me lead the Judicial Process discussions, I may never have started to remove the retributive blinders that kept me so invested in the myth of redemptive violence and a system of institutionalized vengeance.

When I think of all of my friends who are or have been caged by America's system of mass retribution, knowing as they all do of my former complicity in that system, I am filled with wonder, humility, and gratitude at the grace they have shown me. People like Cyntoia Brown, Ndume Olatushani, Sarah Bryant, Rahim Buford, Ashlee Sellars, Fred Sledge, Shayne Lovera, Jerry Cammuse, Felicia Ybanez, Barbi Brown, Jacob Davis, Dean Mullins, all of the amazing students in the LIFE Program and the members of the Lifer's Club at the Turney Center have always made me feel accepted, welcomed, and valued. They have been for me ministers of reconciliation in the truest sense of the phrase, and they are among the finest people I have ever known.

I owe specific thanks to Eric Alexander. After hearing my story of being converted from a tough-on-crime prosecutor to an advocate for restorative justice and criminal justice reform, he believed that I could help other people change their minds as well. Fortunately, Jody Kent Lavy agreed with him, and they gave me the opportunity to join the Campaign for the Fair Sentencing of Youth, which felt like coming home. It is a joy and honor to work alongside Eric and all the other outstanding people at the CFSY.

I am so grateful to my parents, Mike and Julia, for modeling for me and my sister Emily a Christian faith that manifests itself in concern for people who are incarcerated. I am confident that had they not, I, like the overwhelming majority of Christians, would have never set foot inside a prison, despite Jesus' clear commandment that we do so. Their example set me on this journey, and I am thankful for what they passed down to me and my family, and to Emily, her husband Mikeal, and their sweet boys, Henry and James. Thanks also to my in-laws, Dan and Sherrie Herring, who have always supported my trips to prisons, even when they have pulled me away from family gatherings.

I cannot thank my children—Lila Joy, Ruby Faith, and Levi— enough for the love and support they have given me over the years. I started visiting the Turney Center Prison in 2002, and Lila was born in 2004. Ruby was born in January of 2007, at the very beginning of my first semester teaching in the LIFE Program at the Tennessee Prison for Women. Levi was born in April of 2009, at the end of my second time teaching at the prison. There has never been a time when they have not known me to be invested in visiting people in prison. Every fourth Sunday of the month, they know that I will be leaving at about 3:00 in the afternoon to make the trip to the Turney Center. At least four times that has meant cutting short our family Christmas and Easter celebrations. During the semesters when I've taught college classes, I'm away every Wednesday night of the semester. This has been normal for them their whole lives.

Now that I lead the policy work for the CFSY, I keep a pretty demanding travel schedule, especially when the legislatures are in session. I often have to fly to state capitols to meet with lawmakers, advocates, and family members of people serving extreme prison sentences, testify at committee hearings, conduct trainings for lawyers and parole board members, and attend conferences. The kids always tell me they miss me, but they have never once complained. They have seemed to always understand, from the time they were babies, the responsibility that we have to invest in work that matters by serving others, and they did that by sacrificing time with me.

Hebrews 13:3 states, "Continue to remember those in prison as if you were together with them in prison, and those who are mistreated as if you yourselves were suffering." Lila, Ruby, and Levi have abided by this teaching since before they could read. In fact, when Lila was six and Ruby was four, they went with Sherisse and me to a Christmas party at the Tennessee Prison for Women. On the way home, little Lila remarked, "They don't seem like prisoners." Thirteen years later, this past Christmas Eve, Lila, now nineteen, went with me to the Turney Center Prison. The work I do is very much their work as well. Lila, Ruby, and Levi, I love you with all of my heart and am so very thankful to be your dad.

More than anyone else, I owe my deepest thanks and gratitude to my wife, Sherisse. She has been steadfast and unwavering in her love and support. As we sought to navigate the current together, she has been a constant source of encouragement. She has always been confident that the current was leading us precisely where we needed to go, and she has always had the courage to do what it required of us. Had she not been by my side, I likely would not have had the patience to wait for the current or the faith to trust it. Those are her gifts, and this story would not have happened apart from them.

Every trip to the prison, every LIFE class, every conference or invitation to speak meant that Sherisse was home by herself with three kids, which was no small feat when they were all five years old or younger! But she has done far more than hold down the fort while I've been away. She has gone to the prison with me and cultivated her own relationships by exchanging recipes with women in the LIFE Program. She has prepared meals and welcomed people into our home after their release, just as my parents did when I was young. And when one of the girls from the LIFE Program had her first baby, Sherisse assembled a literal truckload of baby clothes and toys for me to deliver. I simply could not ask for a better partner in this work, and it would have been impossible without her.

Sherisse got far more than she bargained for when she said yes to my proposal over Baskin Robbins ice cream 25 years ago. At every turn, when it felt as though the religion I had grown up with was a harmful straitjacket, when my chosen career was at odds with my desire to do justice, and when friends and family wondered why I had gone off the deep end, her love for, commitment to, and faith in me remained solid as a rock. She has been an invaluable sounding board as I tried to make sense of everything I was learning.

Sherisse, none of this would have been possible without you, so to you I dedicate this book. From the bottom of my heart, thank you.